THE VANITY OF POWER

CONTRIBUTIONS IN AMERICAN HISTORY

SERIES EDITOR

STANLEY I. KUTLER

Department of History

University of Wisconsin

THE VANITY OF POWER

American Isolationism and the First World War 1914–1917

John Milton Cooper, Jr.

CONTRIBUTIONS IN AMERICAN HISTORY
Number Three

GP

Greenwood Publishing Corporation
WESTPORT, CONNECTICUT

Library of Congress Catalog Card Number: 79-95505
SBN: 8371-2342-9

Greenwood Publishing Corporation
51 Riverside Avenue, Westport, Conn.
Greenwood Publishers Ltd.
42 Hanway Street, London, W1, England

Printed in the United States of America

FOR JUDY

. . . we are in danger of sacrificing our ancient policy of aggrandizement in the arts of peace, a policy which our splendid isolation makes possible—we are in danger of surrendering that for the aggrandizement of military prowess. It is the vanity of power gaining mastery over the pride of a higher, better, and more humane enlightenment.

Senator Porter J. McCumber
of North Dakota, March 17, 1916

Contents

Acknowledgments

For permission to quote from manuscript collections, I wish to thank the Bancroft Library, University of California, Berkeley, for the Hiram Johnson, Chester Rowell, and John D. Works Papers; Columbia University Library for the Randolph Bourne Papers; Houghton Library, Harvard University, for the Walter Hines Page Papers; and Massachusetts Historical Society for the Henry Cabot Lodge Papers.

For permission to quote from published works, may I thank *The Atlantic Monthly* for "Trans-National America," by Randolph Bourne, copyright 1915, The Atlantic Monthly Company; Constable & Company Limited for *The Letters and Friendships of Sir Cecil Spring-Rice,* edited by Stephen Gwynn; E. P. Dutton & Company for *Cobb of "The World,"* edited by John L. Heaton, copyright 1924, E. P. Dutton & Company; Harper & Row, Publishers for *The Public Papers of Woodrow Wilson,* edited by Ray Stannard Baker and William E. Dodd; Alfred A. Knopf for *Not So Wild a Dream,* by Eric Sevareid, copyright 1946; Little, Brown & Company for *U.S. Foreign Policy,* by Walter Lippmann; and *The New York Times* for "Preserve U.S. from Europeanism," by Samuel P. Orth, copyright 1915, The New York Times Company.

A number of people who have contributed to my work on this book deserve far more thanks than the bare mention I can give here. The Faculty Appointments Committee of Wellesley College and Miss Ruth M. Adams, president, supplied several grants that defrayed costs for some final research and preparation of the manuscript. Librarians and manuscript curators across the country facilitated my work in their collections in countless thoughtful ways. Miss Marion Kanaly, reference librarian of Wellesley College, was tireless and highly resourceful in locating and borrowing materials. Arthur S. Link and William E. Leuchtenburg shared with me their knowledge of sources for the period under study. Henry Graff, Sigmund Diamond, and Walter Metzger read an earlier version of this work and made valuable suggestions regarding its organization and conceptualization. Richard Hofstadter guided my efforts from the beginning with his customary keen insight, wise criticism, and insistence upon intellectual independence. Edward V. Gulick gave me the benefits of his knowledge of diplomatic history and fine sense of style. The dedication is to my wife, to whom I owe my greatest debts.

Introduction

"ISOLATIONISM" is a term that historians have inherited rather than invented. As recurrent charges of "isolationism" have shown in recent years, the word remains loaded with emotional connotations that present barriers to any analysis. Yet "isolationism" refers to an important phenomenon in twentieth-century American history, which requires study on a level more elevated than the uses of the term in political debate. This book examines the emergence of isolationism as a distinct political position in the United States during the months leading to American intervention in the First World War. Two considerations have dictated the perspective on isolationism as a political position and the selection of the period between the outbreak of the World War in 1914 and American entry into the conflict in 1917. One is a definition of isolationism. The other is attention to certain intellectual issues in the emergence of the position.

Because of its origins as an epithet in public debate, the term "isolationism" can be used with so little precision that the only proper definition must be cumbersomely inclusive.

Isolationism is an attitude, policy, doctrine, or position opposed to the commitment of American force outside the Western Hemisphere, except in the rarest and briefest instances. The essence of isolationism is refusal to commit force beyond hemispheric bounds, or absolute avoidance of overseas military alliances. Some isolationists have favored nonforceful commitments elsewhere in the world; some have supported military alliances in the Americas; others have accepted neither. But rejection of forceful commitments beyond the hemisphere is the point on which all have agreed. It affords, therefore, the only valid distinction between who was and who was not an isolationist.

The perspective on isolationism as a political position serves to overcome the major difficulty in interpretation caused by the inclusiveness of the term. Most scholars who have previously studied isolationism have followed either a behavioral or a rhetorical approach, and following only one of these approaches has prevented them from seeing isolationism as a whole. Because the term properly describes only men's actions within limited situations, the bulk of interpreters have understandably sought to correlate some manifestation of isolationist behavior, most often Congressional voting, with such factors as geographical, ethnic, and partisan influences, usually from the Middle West. On the other hand, a few scholars have attempted to explain that behavior by concentrating on what isolationists, particularly intellectuals and politicians, have said and thought.[1] The perspective of a political position shows that those approaches have emphasized complementary dimensions of isolationism, which must be viewed together for a full understanding. Like any political position, isolationism existed on several levels. Each level had characteristic expressions, normally emotion and self-interest among the populace, in contrast to intellectual formulations of policy and doctrine among the leaders. Bringing those levels together was what formed a political position.

Besides being a neglected phase in the history of isolationism, the period from 1914 to 1917 witnessed the formation of a distinct political position. Isolationist policies, interests, sentiments, and doctrines all existed before then, but a clear-cut position did not emerge before the First World War because circumstances up to that time had never required the fusion of those elements.[2] The isolationist position then emerged in response to the specific historical circumstances surrounding American entry into the World War. The physical threat of embroilment in the conflict interacted with the intellectual challenges of internationalist ideas to bring about the conjunction of popular noninterventionist sentiment with carefully through-out policies and doctrinal statements of opposition to overseas involvement. Exactly how those sentiments and ideas came together needs to be understood, since the manner in which the isolationist position was formed fixed its essential features.

Certain intellectual issues played an important though little noticed part in the emergence of isolationism as a political position. American opinion on foreign policy during the First World War and for a long time afterward can be compared to a circle split along both its vertical and horizontal axes. One division lay between isolationism and internationalism, over the question of overseas commitments. The other division separated idealists from ultranationalists. Idealists believed that the purpose of American foreign policy was to promote peace, freedom, and justice in the world; ultranationalists held that power, prestige, and security were the only legitimate ends for foreign policy. The two divisions overlapped, with isolationists and internationalists falling into both the idealist and ultranationalist camps.

Of the two, the division between idealism and ultranationalism cut deeper intellectually. Idealistic isolationists and internationalists disagreed only over means. Isolationists called for assiduous nonparticipation in international politics outside the hemisphere for the sake of reforming those politics through righteous example. Internationalists advocated forceful involvement in international politics outside the hemisphere for the sake of reforming those politics through active intervention. Both arguments drew upon the traditional belief that America was the world's exemplar of freedom and virtue and therefore had a mission to spread its values throughout the whole world. Similarly, ultranationalists disagreed simply over methods of serving national self-interest. Isolationists among them demanded unfettered pursuit of power and security, whereas internationalists held that those ends required at least limited overseas commitments.

Idealism and ultranationalism have hardly formed mutually exclusive categories, since both morality and security have concerned virtually every American statesman. Yet the divergence of the fundamental values behind these positions needs to be stressed, because of its effect not only on the emergence of isolationism but also on all alignments of opinion during and after the First World War. It should be noted that idealists in fact played a much larger part than ultranationalists in the formation of the isolationist position. Not only did idealism account for more of the leaders and followers, but it also furnished the basis for the most penetrating isolationist arguments. For those reasons, idealism receives the greater share of attention in this study.

In the two and a half years preceding American intervention in the war, the division over commitments outside the hemisphere gradually came to supersede the divergence between idealism and ultranationalism. Many Americans, especially idealists, found themselves torn in their desires as they chose between isolationism and internationalism. The greatest number of public figures hesitated to espouse either isolationism or internationalism until 1917, when intervention forced them to take a stand. Some, idealists and ultranationalists alike, switched sides between isolationism and internationalism. As a result, the two opposing positions marshaled diverse, sometimes ill-defined, coalitions when the question of overseas involvement finally became paramount. This book examines how one of these coalitions formed the isolationist position.

NOTES

1. For a critical discussion of interpretations of isolationism, see Bibliographical Essay, pp. 241–257.
2. In this regard it is interesting to note when the word "isolationism" was first used. Although the root word "isolation" had been in use since 1862, and "isolationist" since 1899, "isolationism" does not appear to have been used until 1922. See Mitford M. Mathews, ed., *A Dictionary of Americanisms on Historical Principles* (Chicago: University of Chicago Press, 1951), 1:891.

1

Prelude to an Isolationist Position

Isolationism emerged as a distinct political position during the First World War because long-established ideas became fused with immediate popular interests. The ideas, which dated back to Colonial times, were those of a special American mission toward the world and of isolation from political commitments outside the Western Hemisphere. The popular interests sprang from several sources. Ethnic ties with the Central Powers contributed to potential opposition to overseas involvement, especially when linked with impartiality toward the belligerent nations felt in the Middle West and West. Equally important were political attitudes, notably among agrarian-based reformers, toward the relation of foreign to domestic affairs. The threat of involvement in the World War posed by German submarine attacks early in 1915 created the situation in which these ideas and interests could be drawn together. The previous history of ideas of mission and isolation and the ethnic, sectional, and political attitudes manifested in the opening months of the World War provided, therefore, the prelude to the emergence of an isolationist position.

Mission and Isolation

Dreams of a pure new society arising in America sprang up soon after Columbus's discovery. Implicit in the name "the New World" was the vision of a veritable state of nature, which beckoned reenactment of the social compact on a wiser basis and could not fail to teach great lessons to those who stayed behind. It would be nothing less than a fresh start for Western man.[1] For the Puritans who settled New England in the seventeenth century, establishing a world-redeeming community was more than a dream. They had a covenant with the Lord, declared John Winthrop, to remain "better preserved from the Common corrupcions of this evill world to serve the Lord," so that He would "make of us a prayse and glory, . . . for wee must Consider that wee must be as a Citty upon a Hill, the eies of all people are uppon us. . . ." But if they failed to keep the covenant, Winthrop warned, "wee shall be made a story and a by-word through the world, wee shall open the mouthes of enemies to speak evil of the ways of god [*sic*]." [2] For the Puritans the establishment of New England was analogous to their individual conduct as Christians. In each sphere they sought both their own salvation and the conversion of the world, and thereby risked not only being damned but also bringing calumny on the ways of righteousness.

The Puritans first implanted the conviction of special mission in America. Although their specific religious intentions proved ephemeral, their central belief that a community in America must live like the individual Christian became the enduring essence of the idea of mission. The Puritans' experience with the idea also revealed the opposing uses to which it could be put. Their original vision contemplated building a model for the reformation of the English church and society. Later, however, when their example went unheeded, they justified their community as a unique possession which the Old World could not share.[3] These expressions showed that the idea of mission had both an activist and a defensive potential. In that way, the Puritan experience prefigured the time when American idealism would furnish transcendent justifications for both internationalist and isolationist arguments.

Ideas of isolation from overseas commitments came to America during the eighteenth century as an extension of English debates over foreign policy. Isolation, which had been advocated as an expedient of national reserve for England in the seventeenth century, was presented after 1715 as a positive policy of England's turning its back on European connections in order to pursue more important interests, particularly commercial ones, overseas. Such arguments elicited a warm response from the American colonists, for whom policies of isolation corresponded with a growing estimate of their own importance to the empire. Benjamin Franklin, for example, argued in the 1760s that "the Foundations of the future Grandeur and Stability of the British Empire lie in America." He also spoke scornfully of "European quarrels" and "continental connexions." [4] But the farthest-reaching application of isolation to the American colonies was not a rationale for their living within the Empire. Rather, isolation became an argument for separating from Britain and becoming an independent nation. Thomas Paine had absorbed arguments for England's separation from the Continent before coming to America, and in his famous pamphlet *Common Sense* he pushed those arguments to the logical culmination of demanding America's comparable separation from England.[5]

In *Common Sense* Paine wedded isolation to the idea of mission. "The cause of America," he avowed, "is in large measure the cause of all mankind." In America's geographical position, "the distance at which the Almighty hath placed . . . America," and in the date of its discovery, just before the Reformation, Paine perceived signs of divine plan: "As if the Almighty graciously meant to open a sanctuary to the persecuted in future years, when home should afford neither friendship nor safety." [6] Others likewise justified independence by uniting isolation with the notion of a separate American destiny in contrast to Europe. By the 1770s, Franklin had discarded his imperial vision and decried the disparity between "the extreme corruption prevalent among all orders of men in this old, rotten state, and the glorious public virtue so predominant in our rising country." [7]

Once independence was declared, the combination of mission and isolation formed the foreign policy of the new nation. The Continental Congress agreed in the debates of 1776, as John Adams said, that America must "avoid all obligations and temptations to take part in future European wars; that the business of America with Europe was commerce, not politics or war. . . ." [8] Those principles had to be laid aside during the Revolution in favor of a traditional alliance, but they constituted the nation's basic diplomatic outlook, which Americans longed to pursue as soon as independence was won.[9]

Although the idea of mission promulgated during the era of the Revolution was not specifically Christian, it clearly sprang from the earlier Puritan conception. In 1783 the Reverend Ezra Stiles, president of Yale College, called the United States "GOD'S American Israel," where "a DEMOCRATICAL polity for millions" was being "carried to the highest perfection" and would "illumine the world with TRUTH and LIBERTY." Individual and national behavior continued to be viewed as analogous. "I know but one code of morality for man whether acting singly or collectively," wrote Thomas Jefferson in 1789.[10] The Revolutionary idea of mission also revealed the opposing potentialities of American idealism. On the one hand, world-reforming intentions were apparent in remarks like Stiles's, while a defensive thrust could be detected in the desire to sever ties with corrupt Europe in order, as Paine put it, to "prepare in time an asylum for mankind." [11] These expressions again portended uses of the idea of mission to justify both internationalism and isolationism.

But isolation could be used in the pursuit of ends other than an idealistic mission. Alexander Hamilton revealed those ends in *The Federalist* in 1787, when he admonished his country "to awake from the deceitful dream of a golden age" and seek power, as all nations must. Hamilton argued that the division of the world into spheres "each having a distinct set of interests" invited the United States, by cutting all overseas ties, "to aim at an ascendant in the system of American affairs." [12] This brief for isolation as a way of seeking self-interested goals foreshadowed the formulation of ultranationalist isolationism.

But clear-cut idealistic or ultranationalist arguments did not develop immediately after the Revolution. Rather, events at the end of the eighteenth century fostered the growth of a consensus behind isolation as the basic foreign policy of the United States. Fervent ideological attachments of Federalists for England and Republicans for France, in the wake of the French Revolution, proved disillusioning, especially after Europe became a cockpit of conflicting despotisms with Bonaparte's advent. Moreover, every threat to national security and growth emanated from Britain, Spain, and France. As a result, all shades of American opinion supported separation from outside ties. The consensus arose from the absence of intellectual challenge, not from a lack of physical involvement. The United States was almost continuously ensnarled in international conflicts from 1793 until 1815, but those involvements only strengthened the conviction that America's true concerns, measured by either idealistic or self-interested standards, were best served by isolation.

After 1815 European statesmen gradually turned their attentions from the Western Hemisphere. This shift of international competition allowed Americans to direct their attentions almost exclusively inward and treat foreign affairs with complacent disregard. The century after 1815 became the heyday of what C. Vann Woodward has termed "free security," when the United States was able to gratify its desires and maintain its security without serious opposition, while at the same time continuing to affirm the American idea of mission.[13] Only rarely would citizens' unconcern for world affairs be shaken, but in these exceptional moments there were a few further indications of how internationalist and isolationist positions might evolve.

The consensus behind isolation received its first jolt during the absolutist counterattack by the Holy Alliance following the Congress of Vienna. Many Americans perceived a threat to their own country in the assaults on liberty and republicanism. In January, 1816, Henry Clay warned that "European potentates" were carrying "their ideas of legitimate government . . . to an extent destructive of every principle of liberty. . . . Do we know . . . whether we shall escape their influence?" Clay responded by partially reasserting the activist side of the idea of mission. He advocated making common cause with the Latin American republics against attempts to restore colonial rule, and declared that he "considered the release of any part of America from the dominions of the Old World, as adding to the general security of the new." Republican sympathies ignored geographical restrictions, however, when many Americans joined in the outpouring of romantic philhellenism that greeted the Greek revolution in 1821.[14] This revival of the activist aspect of the idea of mission foreshadowed idealistic internationalism in the expression of desires for the United States to intervene abroad in order to promote its values.

Those who upheld isolation appealed to both ideals and self-interest. One newspaper dismissed the notion of pan-American solidarity as "Quixotic," suggesting that Americans "attend exclusively to our own concerns before we go 'colonelling' in pursuit of independence for South American provinces." [15] On the idealistic side, John Quincy Adams spurned "the doctrine that it is the duty of America to take an *active* part in the future political reformation of Europe." Adams held that there was an "inevitable tendency of a direct interference in foreign wars, even wars for freedom, to change the very foundations of our own government from *liberty* to *power*." America must be, instead, "the well-wisher to the freedom and independence of all" but "the champion and vindicator only of her own. She will recommend the general cause by the countenance of her voice and the benignant sympathy of her example. But any further action would embroil the nation in all the wars of interest and intrigue, of individual avarice, envy, and ambition which assume the colors and usurp the standard of freedom."[16] This assertion that America could promote freedom in the world only by spurning power politics in order to provide an unblemished example was a lucid statement of the essence of idealistic isolationism.

But these isolationist and potentially internationalist arguments did not begin a line of development toward political positions. A relapse into inattention followed these responses to autocratic reaction. That was true not only in the 1820s but also after comparable outbursts at suppression of the Revolutions of 1848. The arguments at the end of the 1840s partially reflected concurrent debates over territorial expansion at the end of the Mexican War. After 1848, activist expressions of the idea of mission again pointed toward idealistic internationalism. Stephen A. Douglas asserted in 1851 that a "struggle between liberal and absolute principles" was raging, and Americans must be "ready to do whatever our duty may require when a case shall arise." Significantly, Douglas also affirmed the "Manifest Destiny" of the United States to extend its sway over most of North America. A Democratic party faction called "Young America" similarly advocated assertive national expansion together with intervention abroad on behalf of republican ideals. The time had come, declared one of its spokesmen, for "the abandonment now of our impolitic, unwise, and unjust system of neutrality." The United States must "interpose both *her moral and physical power*" to promote liberty, either alone or with "the occasional cooperation of other countries."[17]

Likewise, defenders of isolation presented self-interested and idealistic arguments. One Southern Senator contended that the United States should manage its "own concerns at home, without traveling beyond the Atlantic to interfere with concerns of other nations." Charles Sumner, on the other hand, admonished Americans to "offer sympathy and God speed to all, in every land who struggle for Human Rights," but to reject "any idea of armed intervention in European affairs. Such a system would open phials of perplexities and ills which I trust our country will never be called to affront." [18] Most of the men who criticized the idea of intervention abroad also opposed territorial expansion.

A reversion to unconcern for world affairs followed those expressions, too. Most nineteenth-century Americans, as Cushing Strout has observed, happily resolved any troublesome thoughts about ways of pursuing the nation's special destiny by believing that their ideals applied universally but had been realized only in their own country. "Here then is *our* mission," declared a Cincinnati newspaper in 1852, to make America perfect at home in order to "reflect back on Europe and on every land and every clime . . . and in due time break the chains, as sure as there is a future and a just God, to whom we can pray." [19] Such attitudes continued to prevail even after the brief imperialistic venture at the end of the nineteenth century. Arguments over isolation and the idea of mission figured once again in public debate.

Imperialists employed an activist conception of missionary idealism. Senator Albert Beveridge, for example, averred that God "has marked the American people as His chosen nation to finally lead in the regeneration of the world. This is the divine mission of America. . . ." [20] Not that idealism was the sole appeal of the imperialists. There was a strong ultranationalist strain, too. Beveridge held out the promise of great commercial profits, while others delighted at the increase in the nation's power. But a conjunction between activist idealism and self-interested nationalism was not new. Young America's earlier combination of expansion with the idea of mission had typified many nineteenth-century arguments for territorial aggrandizement.[21] Yet if imperialists were not unalloyed idealists, they did espouse the activist side of mission, and, interestingly, their expressions of American destiny were the most overtly religious of any since the Revolution.

Anti-imperialists were not pure idealists, either. Their arguments included observations on the costliness of ruling the Philippine Islands and often betrayed a racist animus against their inhabitants. But their dominant theme was a defensive idealism. William Jennings Bryan asserted that America, by renouncing colonial expansion and remaining "true to its principles in the hour of trial will do more to extend the area of self-government and civilization than could be done by all the wars of conquest that we could wage in a generation." Carl Schurz warned that "our great mission to further the progress of civilization by enhancing the prestige of democratic institutions" was about to be "seduced by false ambitions and running headlong after riches and luxury and military glory . . . down the fatal slope into vice, corruption, decay and disgrace." [22]

But both these constructions of the idea of mission bore only a loose relation to isolation. Although a few imperialists advocated abandoning isolation, most stood with Senator Henry Cabot Lodge in believing that traditional American policies had "no bearing on the extension of the United States." [23] Likewise, whereas Bryan denounced imperialism as "a long step . . . toward those entanglements against which Washington and Jefferson warned their constituents," he, Schurz, and other anti-imperialists also favored guaranteeing the independence, territorial integrity, and security of the Philippines. The Democratic platform of 1900, on which Bryan ran, called for an American protectorate over the islands and maintenance of a naval base there.[24] Imperialist and anti-imperialist contentions foreshadowed clear-cut internationalist and isolationist positions less clearly than earlier arguments.

The debate over empire also failed to dispel public unconcern with foreign affairs. Anti-imperialism aroused little excitement as an issue in the 1900 campaign, and imperialism fared little better. As Richard W. Leopold has pointed out, the United States acquired no other important possessions, declined to set up a central agency for administering its colonies, and failed to expand or reorganize its armed forces sufficiently to defend them.[25] During the first decade of the twentieth century President Theodore Roosevelt's actions in mediating the Russo-Japanese war and sending a delegate to the Algeciras conference attracted no more than fleeting interest. Walter Lippmann, then one of the country's brightest young political thinkers, could not "remember taking any interest whatsoever in foreign affairs until after the outbreak of the first World War. . . . In spite of college and much reading about public affairs, I remained quite innocent of any understanding of the revolutionary consequences of the Spanish-American War." [26]

As a consequence of this overriding disregard for foreign affairs, established views appeared to offer reliable guides for policy even down into the decade before the First World War. Secretary of State William H. Seward wrote in the 1860s that the policy of isolation had "become a traditional one, which could not be abandoned without the most urgent occasion, amounting to a manifest necessity." President Grover Cleveland in 1885 called isolation "the policy of independence, favored by our position and defended by our known love of justice and our power." [27] Even after the acquisition of the Philippines, all official statements upheld isolation as stoutly as ever. In 1906 and 1908 the Senate affixed reservations to the Algeciras and Hague conventions insisting that agreeing to them was "without purpose to depart from the traditional American foreign policy." Speaking for the Roosevelt Administration on the Algeciras conference, Senator Lodge asserted that "in entangling alliances, of course, no man wants to engage this country; we have no concern with the wars of Europe. . . ." [28]

The traditional consensus containing the ideas of mission and isolation evidently remained intact as the century after 1815 neared an end. In 1913 the new Secretary of State was William Jennings Bryan, who had broadened his anti-imperialism since 1900 into a pacific Christian idealism. "Service is the measure of greatness," Bryan never tired of declaring, and he believed that America would bring peace and freedom to the world "when our aim is to do something for each other." Woodrow Wilson, the President who appointed Bryan, announced in May, 1914, ". . . in the confidence and definiteness of our own purpose we need not and we should not form alliances with any nation in the world. Those who are right, those who study their consciences in determining their policies, those who hold their honor higher than their advantage, do not need alliances." [29] Wilson's statement came less than three months before the beginning of the First World War.

Initial Reactions to the World War

The outbreak of the World War in August, 1914, provoked comparisons with a natural catastrophe or a supernatural occurrence. A North Carolina Congressman and a Nebraska Senator independently called it "lightning out of a clear sky," while Theodore Roosevelt found it "on a giant scale like the disaster to the *Titanic*." Preferring Biblical terminology, *Collier's* declared, "If this be not Armageddon, we shall never suffer the final death grip of nations." [30] Yet Americans also felt fortunately removed from the war. "Again and ever I thank heaven for the Atlantic Ocean," wrote the American ambassador in London.[31] Others believed that their country's remoteness from the conflict owed more to American virtue and wisdom. The *New York Times* contrasted its outbreak with the opening of the Panama Canal by observing, "The European ideal bears its full fruit of ruin and savagery just at the moment when the American ideal lays before the world a great work of peace, goodwill, and fair play." *The World's Work* commented, "Our policy of friendship to all and entangling alliances with none was made for us by wise men a hundred years ago who had before them Europe in torment even as we have now . . . may we in wisdom and humility learn as much from it as did they!" [32] In short, the World War seemed to provide spectacular confirmation of traditional beliefs in the moral separation between America and Europe and ample justification for continued isolation.

The official posture of the United States toward the war faithfully reflected the public reaction. On August 19, President Wilson declared that "it is entirely within our own choice what its [the war's] effects on us will be." The nation's sole concern should be "performance of our duty as the one great nation at peace, the one nation holding itself ready to play a part of impartial mediation and speak counsels of peace." Americans must remain, therefore, "impartial in thought as well as in action" and thus be "fit and free to do what is honest and disinterested and truly serviceable for the peace of the world." [33]

At the other end of Pennsylvania Avenue, Congressmen and Senators echoed those sentiments. In typical remarks, Illinois' flowery Democratic Senator James Hamilton Lewis invited Americans to contrast the European carnage "to your own Nation, her industries active and prosperous, . . . her Nation [*sic*] at peace with the world, teaching liberty to mankind, furnishing an example of freedom to the enlightenment of earth and the salvation of man." [34]

The opening months of the war offered only three important exceptions to the prevailing feelings of detachment and superiority. The first exception was the expression of sympathies for one side or the other, which arose in spite of Wilson's admonition. The broadest survey of sympathies for the belligerents was a nationwide canvass of newspaper editors by the *Literary Digest* in November, 1914. Only one-third of the respondents expressed preferences for either side; the rest declared themselves impartial. Opinion showed wide sectional variation. Impartiality came closest to being balanced with approval for one side in the South, where 49 percent of the editors expressed no sympathies and 46 percent favored the Allies. Sentiments in the Northeast registered 60 percent impartial and 39 percent pro-Allied. In neither of those sections was there any appreciable sympathy for the Central Powers.

What approval there was from the other side, observed the

Literary Digest, corresponded closely to the concentrations of German-Americans. Ethnic loyalties may have accounted for much of the sectional variation. The greatest concentrations of German-Americans lived in the Middle West, although pro-German sentiment among the editors registered slightly lower there, at 7 percent, than it did in the Far West, where 8 percent favored the Central Powers. Pro-Allied sentiments were also lower in those sections than in the South or Northeast, 9 percent in the Middle West and 22 percent in the West. Impartiality was considerably higher, too, 84 percent in the Middle West and 70 percent in the West. Interestingly, traditional Irish-American Anglophobia evoked no comment.[35]

This survey was hardly a comprehensive or penetrating assessment of public opinion. But it was the most complete sample taken, and certain inferences can be drawn from it. Evidently, the great majority of the American people had no predilection for either side. Indifference may have contributed to that impartiality, and the higher incidence of impartiality in the Middle West may have stemmed from that region's insularity. Yet it seems curious that the South, which could be called the most "insular" section of the country in that it was the most rural, poorest, and least educated, was lowest in impartiality. Middle Western feelings of impartiality are probably better interpreted as a by-product of the presence of pro-German sentiment. Since sympathy for the Central Powers sprang almost entirely from German-Americans' ties of blood and kinship, their neighbors' impartiality may have reflected a desire not to offend them, or, at the same time, a revulsion from the kind of passionate attachment that those ethnic loyalties engendered.[36] Such an interpretation of Middle Western sentiment gains further weight from the substantially lower incidence of pro-Allied feeling there than in other parts of the country.

Except for ethnically based pro-German sentiments, however, sympathies for the belligerents did not contradict the prevailing mood of remoteness from the World War. The *Literary Digest* considered sympathy for both sides "that of the distant observer," while Mark Sullivan compared it to the cheering of baseball fans sitting in the bleachers.[37] Pro-Allied feelings, which ran five times greater than pro-German sentiment on the national average, appear to have been singularly detached. The perceptive British Ambassador in Washington, Sir Cecil Spring Rice, repeatedly noted that "a very little" could dispel Americans' pro-Allied sentiments. It was "useless and misleading to depend on these people for help or for practical sympathy," argued Spring Rice, because they regarded "the war either as a bore, or as an immensely interesting spectacle provided for their entertainment, of which they were commencing to be rather tired." [38] Ironically, sympathy for the Allies probably increased feelings of detachment. The incidents which prompted that sympathy, like the German invasion of Belgium, the Chancellor's remark about a "scrap of paper," and the destruction of the library at Louvain and the cathedral at Rheims, all reinforced the notion of a moral contrast between Europe and America.[39]

The second major exception to the mood of detachment from the World War was the controversy over the nation's military preparedness. A drive for greater preparedness began on October 15, 1914, when Representative Augustus Peabody Gardner, Republican of Massachusetts, charged that the nation's defenses were woefully weak and outmoded. The outbreak of the war in Europe, which Gardner had just returned from witnessing, had buttressed his belief "that bullets cannot be stopped by bombast nor powder vanquished by platitudes." Americans "must remember that since the beginning of time victorious nations have proved headstrong and high-handed. We must begin at once to reorganize our military strength if we expect to be able to resist high-handedness when the day of necessity comes." [40] The President made light of these charges and Gardner's demand for a Congressional investigation. He brushed them aside smilingly to reporters as "good mental exercise" but the kind of talk he had been hearing since he was a boy of ten. Although several Republican and Progressive papers supported Gardner, Wilson's dismissal appeared to quell criticism.[41]

Actually, the proponents of increased preparedness, who also included Roosevelt, Lodge, and former Secretary of War Henry L. Stimson, were preparing to attack in earnest when Congress reconvened in December, 1914. A well-informed magazine and a leading newspaper predicted that their efforts might reunite Republicans and Progressives over the preparedness issue.[42] The prospect of a major partisan assault evidently worried Wilson enough to make him reply seriously to critics in his address to Congress on December 8. Looking Gardner straight in the eye, he defended the Administration's program of moderate increases in the army and navy and declared that anything more would signify "that we had been thrown off our balance by a war with which we have nothing to do, whose causes can not touch us, whose very existence affords us opportunities of friendship and disinterested service which should make us ashamed of any thought of hostility or fearful preparation for trouble." [43]

The outcome of the confrontation over preparedness confirmed the prevailing popular mood. Instead of the predicted attack on the Administration, politicians of all factions and parties rushed to emulate Wilson's ridicule for the notion that the United States might become ensnared in the ramifications of the World War. During brief Congressional debates over Gardner's resolution for an investigation, Representative Martin Dies, Democrat of Texas, told his Massachusetts colleague to soothe himself by reading Washington's Farewell Address and by remembering, "Separated from all the warring nations of the earth by broad oceans . . . it would seem that God had planted this great people here to work out a shining example of liberty." Only a few challenged the mood of detachment. Senator Lodge, Gardner's father-in-law, warned, "The ocean barrier which defended us in 1776 and 1812 no longer exists. Steam and electricity have destroyed it." [44]

The dominant Congressional belief in American remoteness from the war was even more strikingly revealed when antipreparedness forces in the House nearly succeeded in slashing the Navy Department's moderate program for battleship construction. On February 5, 1915, an amendment to the naval appropriation bill to cut the number of new battleships from two to one failed by only sixteen votes. Who supported the amendment was almost as embarrassing to the Administration as the narrow margin of defeat. Of the 155 Representatives voting or announced in favor, 139 were members of Wilson's own party, including both the retiring Majority Leader, Oscar Underwood of Alabama, and his successor, Claude Kitchin of North Carolina, as well as several important committee chairmen.[45]

That vote supplied another illustration of the way in which the outbreak of the war had left the consensus behind isolation intact. The large number of Democrats who favored cutting naval preparedness were displaying established tendencies to give less support than Republicans to a larger navy. The sectional composition of the vote for the amendment included ninety-four Representatives from the South and forty-eight from the Middle West. That distribution conformed to previous dispositions of those two "interior" sections to provide more resistance to enlarging the navy than the East or West Coasts.[46] Public opposition to greater preparedness followed similar sectional lines. In January, 1915, the *Literary Digest* found 39 percent of the editors it polled opposed to increases in the army and 28 percent against enlargement of the navy; Gulf Coast and Middle Western states provided most of the opposition. Straw votes in a number of cities in the Middle West showed about 60 percent of the people against increased preparedness.[47]

In addition to highlighting the lack of change in attitudes toward foreign affairs, the vote on the battleship amendment disclosed a significant political outlook. The bulk of the Congressmen favoring the measure were Southern and Middle Western Democrats usually identified with the party's agrarian progressive wing. The remarks that some of them made in the debates on the naval appropriation bill expressed a well-worn antimilitarist persuasion of that faction. Dies asked, in chiding Gardner, "Can you point to a nation of militarism that maintained the liberty of the people?" Representative Cyrus Cline of Indiana agreed that the influences of militarism "are always political; because it seeks always to belittle and secretly subvert the civil authority." Rather, insisted Cline, "Our protection lies in our system of government, in the dissemination of power, in our democracy." [48]

Those statements expressed arguments which had been offered since the 1890s, first by Populists and later by Bryan and his associates among the Democrats. As early as 1892,

Tom Watson, the Georgia Populist leader, had asserted that geographical isolation meant that "the enemies we have to dread in the future are not Great Britain, not France . . . not Mexico, but our own people. . . . I mean bad laws here at home; . . . class legislation . . . overgrown and insolent corporations . . . the greed of monopolies here at home." Bryan had warned in 1899, "Militarism is the very antithesis of Democracy"; and the Democratic platform of 1900 had denounced militarism as "the strong arm which has ever been fatal to free institutions. It is what millions of our citizens have fled from in Europe." [49] Although foreign policy had failed to become a major concern during the years that followed, Bryan had continued to denounce imperialism and militarism. A number of Democratic Congressmen had similarly denounced preparedness as a distraction from pressing internal concerns and a symptom of "that old spirit of conquest and war that has dominated every monarchy." [50]

The antimilitarism of the agrarian Democrats was a logical extension of their domestic beliefs. They derived their assumptions of antipathy between democracy and a professional military class, the ideological contrast between America and Europe, and secure geographical isolation all from a near-religious devotion to Thomas Jefferson. The Populists and Bryanite Democrats were, as Merrill Peterson has called them, "code-Jeffersonians." [51] The intellectual basis of their politics was an effort to maintain and restore the idealized vision of rural and small-town society which they found justified in their reading of the Virginian. A Jeffersonian fundamentalist view of preparedness and foreign relations also suited their own political predilections. It allowed them to believe, as their statements indicated, in the primacy of domestic affairs. They were convinced that achievement of their reform programs would play a vital part in the fulfillment of America's mission in the world. Foreign affairs remained an occasionally troublesome distraction at best. Some Bryanite Democrats like Representative Clyde Tavenner of Illinois had come to believe that diplomacy furnished the hunting ground of the "war trust" which stirred up international strife for profit.[52]

This view of preparedness and foreign policy was not completely confined to Democrats. Fifteen Republicans, all but two of whom were Middle Westerners, also voted for the amendment to cut the number of new battleships.[53] Several of these Republicans can be identified as progressives, including two from Wisconsin who were followers of Senator Robert M. La Follette. La Follette himself had earlier warned against a "world-wide organization . . . stimulating and fomenting discord in order that it may make profit out of the furnishing of the munitions of war. . . ." Representative Silas Barton of Nebraska, a Republican progressive who voted for the amendment, had previously scorned "the siren songs of the interests who sell guns." [54] During the debates of January, 1915, another progressive Republican supporter of the amendment, Representative James Manahan of Minnesota, contended that greater preparedness would invite war: "Look at Europe. . . . Shall we, as a Nation, yield to that same base avarice that has wrecked the civilization of Europe and brought hopeless woe upon her helpless millions?" [55]

Though few, these espousals of the agrarian viewpoint were significant because progressive Republicans, unlike their Democratic counterparts, had often in the past supported imperialism and big armed forces, particularly during the Roosevelt years. Under succeeding Presidents, however, several leading progressive Republicans had changed their views. In addition to La Follette, Senators George W. Norris of Nebraska,

John D. Works of California, and, sometimes, William E. Borah of Idaho had attacked various manifestations of imperialism.[56] The support for the battleship amendment offered further evidence of a drift among Republican progressives away from approval for assertive diplomacy and big armaments. More important, the vote on the amendment and the remarks made in the accompanying debate had revealed an outlook on foreign affairs that could contribute to an isolationist political position.

The third exception to the mood of detachment was the effort to prohibit the shipment of munitions to the nations at war. Idealistic and ingenuous in appearance, the embargo scheme had in fact originated with German-American organizations. It would have aided the Central Powers by preventing arms from reaching the Allies, whose supremacy on the seas made them the only side receiving munitions from the United States. In the fall of 1914 the National German-American Alliance had commenced a massive public campaign to halt the arms trade, financed in part by the German ambassador. When Congress convened in December, a flood of pro-embargo letters, telegrams, and petitions, including one with two million signatures, descended upon Senators and Representatives. Embargo resolutions were introduced at the opening of the session in the House by Richard Bartholdt, Republican of Missouri, and Henry Vollmer, Democrat of Iowa, both German-Americans, and in the Senate by Gilbert M. Hitchcock, a Nebraska Democrat close to his state's German community.[57]

The advocates of the arms embargo supported the plan with idealistic appeals. Congressman Vollmer asserted that his resolution embodied "America's highest moral obligation . . . to observe absolute, genuine, and not merely sham neutrality. . . ." It would keep the United States from standing "as the arch hypocrite among the nations of the earth, praying for peace . . . and furnishing the instruments of murder to one side only of a contest in which we pretend that all the contestants are our friends. . . ." Several German-American spokesmen also used arguments reminiscent of some agrarian progressives' charges when they warned that a "conspiracy" by the "Money Trust" lay behind loans to Britain.[58] Yet embargo advocates could not completely deny its unneutral effects. Congressman Bartholdt admitted that "withholding from the belligerent nations the sinews of war" would gain the friendship of the Central Powers, which would "come in mighty handy" in the future.[59]

The pro-German thrust of the arms embargo repelled most recognized peace advocates and international idealists, in spite of the humanitarian appeals.[60] Bryan's reaction illustrated the suspicions that greeted the scheme. Although the Secretary of State had earlier taken the same humanitarian line in urging a ban on loans to belligerents, he declared that "the *purpose* of the [Bartholdt] resolution is plainly to assist one party at the expense of the other." Bryan led Administration opposition to efforts to stop the arms trade, and, with the cooperation of Lodge and the Republican leadership on Capitol Hill, he helped to keep the embargo resolutions safely buried in committee.[61]

Surprisingly, however, the arms embargo attracted broad public and Congressional support. The *Literary Digest* polled editors in February, 1915, on whether they favored halting munitions shipments. Among the respondents, 38 percent wanted some kind of embargo, while 55 percent opposed such schemes and 7 percent were undecided. The embargo appeared to be most popular in the Middle West. Opinion was also generally divided between urban and rural areas. In towns of less than 10,000, 49 percent of the editors favored ending the arms trade, as against 34 percent in cities over 10,000.[62] Congressional support for the scheme surfaced on February 18, 1915, when thirty-seven Senators opposed tabling an amendment to the ship purchase bill which would have prohibited arms exports to belligerents. Fifteen votes were cast by Senators from Middle Western states with large German communities, including both members from Illinois, Iowa, Michigan, Nebraska, and North Dakota. Eleven Senators who opposed tabling were from the Far West, and seven were from the South.[63] Support for the arms embargo was clearly too extensive to be accounted for entirely by pro-German ethnic loyalties.

One explanation for the plan's appeal was that its "catchy reasonableness," as the *New Republic* put it, suited the feelings of detachment and moral superiority toward the World War.[64] Middle Western and, to a lesser degree perhaps, Far Western support for the embargo apparently stemmed from a combination of German-American sympathies and a high degree of impartiality among the rest of the population. Senatorial approval for the arms embargo also reflected the agrarian progressive viewpoint on foreign affairs. At least eleven of the fifteen Democrats who voted against tabling the amendment belonged to that wing of the party, including Thomas Hardwick of Georgia, Robert Owen of Oklahoma, Morris Sheppard of Texas, and James K. Vardaman of Mississippi. Significantly, too, almost none of those Democratic Senators represented a state with a sizable German-American element. Evidence of the agrarian Democratic outlook could also be detected in the remarks of Senator Charles S. Thomas of Colorado, who did not vote against tabling but did support the embargo in principle. Thomas denounced the "world-wide aggregation of capital behind the manufacture and sale of war equipment." [65]

Connections between such views of foreign affairs and support for the arms embargo were clearer among Republicans. Thirteen of the twenty-one Republican Senators who voted against tabling the amendment were Middle Western or Western progressives, including La Follette, Norris, Works, Borah, and Albert Cummins of Iowa. Works and La Follette, the leading proponents of the embargo, explicitly connected it with idealistic conceptions of America's role in the world, as well as distrust of big business. "We are claiming to be in favor of universal peace," asserted Works. "We are not acting up to our pretensions. If the business men of this country are not patriotic enough and humanitarian enough . . . the Government should prevent the sale and furnishing of these materials of war to the belligerents." La Follette agreed that the munitions trade had "but one purpose, and that is to sacrifice human life for private gain." He also called for nationalizing the manufacture of munitions as a step toward world disarmament and, as such, "a worthy example for all the world." [66]

The arms embargo debates supplied several portents of support for an isolationist position. The Senators who favored the scheme by applying an agrarian progressive viewpoint to America's relation to the World War again showed that their outlook on foreign affairs was close to idealistic isolationism. Arguments for the embargo also disclosed that appeals to missionary idealism could be used in conjunction with pro-German ethnic loyalties. This is not to say that there is any evidence that these Senators were pro-German. Nor do they appear to have been imitating the German-American leaders who masked unneutral intentions with idealistic phrases. But the arms embargo was politically useful for someone like La Follette, for instance. His organization in Wisconsin had suffered reverses in the 1914 elections, and he seemed to be eager to appease the state's powerful German element.[67] The embargo offered a way for La Follette to satisfy a significant bloc of voters while remaining in perfect accord with his own foreign policy views. Since many Republican progressives had substantial German-American constituencies, such a conjunction of motives could, particularly in the event of tension between the United States and the Central Powers, furnish powerful pressures toward support for isolationism.

But the major revelation of these early months of the war was that few Americans felt the least worry over any prospect of involvement in the conflict. Each of these exceptions simply underscored the feelings of remoteness, which appeared to be undiminished at the beginning of 1915. By January, newspaper coverage of the war had shrunk to a few front-page columns in the New York dailies and passing references in many papers in the interior of the country. In April, a leading New York Socialist affirmed that "conditions in the United States" revealed "a complete absence of all factors that naturally make for war, and a combination of conditions calculated to insure lasting peace." Also in April, a journalist close to President Wilson wrote, "The world looks to us for the highest ideals of government and international amity," thus making the United States "a balancing-force, ever working for the advancement of civilization and the cause of humanity. . . ."[68] Plainly, the initial impact of the World War on the United States had reinforced the traditional consensus behind isolation.

The Threat of Intervention

Recognition of the dangers of embroilment in the war grew slowly for some Americans. In spite of his public pronouncements, Wilson started worrying about diplomatic difficulties as soon as the war broke out. His advisor, Colonel Edward House, along with Roosevelt and Lodge, became convinced fairly early that the United States had a critical interest in the outcome of the conflict. After German submarines began sinking merchant vessels early in 1915, statements like the *Wall Street Journal*'s quip that "Sherman omitted to go on record about neutrality" indicated that at least some of the feeling of remoteness from the war had been dispelled.[69] But for most Americans, the first realization that they might become involved apparently came when the *Lusitania* was sunk by a German submarine on May 7, 1915, with a loss of 1,198 lives, including 124 of their countrymen. So shocking was the sinking of the *Lusitania* that many people could remember years later, Mark Sullivan discovered, the exact details of what they had felt and done when they had first heard the news and for the rest of the day.[70]

Americans were reacting not only to the enormity of the disaster but also to the sudden recognition of possible ensnarement in the World War. Although nearly every editor and public figure denounced the sinking as a crime or an outrage, almost no one cried for war. One observer found the public "in a graver mood than I have known in my lifetime, or than anybody has known it since the spring of 1861." Ray Stannard Baker and William Allen White, progressive journalists, discovered "everywhere a feeling of great sobriety" and a conviction "that it would be just [as] sensible to declare war on a madman just out of bedlam, as to go shoot up the Kaiser in his present state of international paranoia." Only six out of the 1,000 editors who telegraphed their opinions to New York newspapers suggested intervention.[71]

Popular awareness of the danger of involvement created one condition that might foster the emergence of an isolationist political position. Heated resistance to involvement arose from an expected quarter. The German-language press was nearly unanimous in deploring any thoughts of war with the Fatherland. Referring to reports of munitions in the *Lusitania*'s cargo, *New Yorker Herold* charged that "the steamer might be considered not a passenger-ship but an army-supply ship." The New York *Volkszeitung* held, in contrast, that the sinking "can not be excused" but preferred over war "other methods of punishing Germany for her wanton slaughter." Similarly, German-American spokesmen and politicians with large German constituencies eschewed all notions of intervention. George Sylvester Viereck, editor of *Fatherland,* urged that the "Government . . . warn Americans that their lives are in constant danger aboard any British merchantmen." Governor E. L. Philipp of Wisconsin declared, "Our country can settle no question of human liberty, nor will we gain any desirable end by participating in the European War." [72]

Those utterances betokened beginnings of an isolationist political position. Viereck's call for government warning against travel on belligerent ships foreshadowed a program for maintaining neutrality. Philipp's ready contrast between America and Europe presaged idealistic arguments linking mission and isolation. Although their positions were tainted with overtones of unneutrality, as in the case of the arms embargo, opposition to involvement emanated from broader sources than the German-American community.

Resistance sprang from roughly the same groups which had supported the embargo and attacked large-scale preparedness. Among the progressive Republicans, Works called the United States "morally responsible" for the sinking of the *Lusitania* because it had permitted the arms trade to continue. La Follette stated simply, ". . . I am opposed to war." [73] Democrats apparently provided the greatest opposition. Senator William J. Stone of Missouri, chairman of the Foreign Relations Committee, observed that "a British ship, flying the British flag" had been sunk after "official warning by the German Government." Privately, top Democratic Congressional leaders warned Bryan and, through him, Wilson that they and their colleagues had not been able to reach "the conclusion that war should result from any questions growing out of the destruction of the *Lusitania* and the incidental loss of American lives." [74]

Other aspects of an emergent isolationist position had begun to be developed within the Wilson Administration even before the sinking of the *Lusitania*. Wilson himself broached the question of reconciling America's ideals with the World War in a manner that appeared to be isolationist, but actually reflected internationalist tendencies. The first submarine incidents involving American citizens caused him "the greatest anxiety" and led him to attempt to prepare the public for the dangers of involvement.

In two speeches in April, 1915, Wilson stressed that "the supreme test" of a nation was "the power to resist excitement, to think calmly." America required self-mastery so that it would not do "exactly the way every other nation does" and thereby forget "what she was born for," which was to serve "the cause of righteousness as ministered to by those who hold their minds quiet and judge according to principle." Wilson declared that "our whole duty, for the present at any rate, is summed up in this motto, 'America First.' Let us think of America before we think of Europe, in order that we may be fit to be Europe's friend when the day of tested friendship comes." America must remain neutral "because there is something so much greater to do than fight. . . ." The United States must be like "the self-mastered man . . . who, you know, has at bottom a much more fundamental and terrible courage than the irritable, fighting man." [75]

Those remarks stated the problem of maintaining the nation's mission in the face of embroilment in world politics. In using the motto "America First," Wilson was invoking the conviction that the nation's uniquely moral character demanded avoidance of the base passions which beset other countries. He likewise reasserted the classic analogy between individual and national behavior by drawing upon his own model of personal conduct. These public exhortations for national self-control contained the same concept and sometimes even the same phrases that Wilson had used in private confessions of his need for self-possession in order to overcome despondency after his wife's death, which coincided with the beginning of the World War.[76] Wilson again drew an analogy between personal and national conduct just after the sinking of the *Lusitania*. America, he reiterated, must offer a "special example" of peace "because peace is the healing and elevating influence of the world and strife is not. There is such a thing as a man being too proud to fight. There is such a thing as a nation being so right that it does not need to convince others by force that it is right." [77]

Besides coining what would later become isolationist watchwords, Wilson anticipated the basic argument of idealistic isolationists. He pictured America as a nation apart, whose chief concern was to resist entanglement in the evils of power politics in order to provide a righteous example. Actually, Wilson was expressing part of the idealistic internationalist position that he would develop during the next two years. As early as August, 1914, he had said privately that there must be "an association of nations, all bound together for the protection of the integrity of each, so that any one breaking this bond will bring upon herself war; that is to say, punishment, automatically." [78] Wilson's remarks disclosed the premises that idealistic internationalists would share with their isolationist counterparts.

A number of Americans had been discussing internationalist proposals during the early months of the war. Its outbreak had impelled Ray Stannard Baker, for example, to perceive the need for "an international police force." On Capitol Hill, La Follette and Democrats like Senators John F. Shafroth of Colorado and Francis J. Newlands of Nevada and Congressman Walter Hensley of Missouri had all discussed similar ideas in the months that followed. The most important source of internationalist thinking during this period, however, was a group of public figures, mostly conservative Republicans, headed by ex-President William Howard Taft, who met in New York to explore plans for an international organization empowered to prevent war. Taft presented their program in several speeches in the spring of 1915, and a convention was scheduled to meet in Philadelphia in June to set up an organization which would promote their plans.[79]

These internationalist proposals presented the intellectual challenge against which isolationist doctrines would be formulated as a response. At the same time, steps toward isolationism had started also within the Wilson Administration, with Secretary of State Bryan. As a near-pacifist and champion of international concord, Bryan had been stunned by the outbreak of the war. It had come just as he had completed the thirty conciliation or "cooling off" treaties through which he hoped that the United States would begin a definitive movement toward world peace.[80] Bryan quickly became convinced that "as the leading exponent of Christianity and as the foremost advocate of worldwide peace" the United States must persuade the belligerents "to lay down their arms and begin the work of reconstructing a permanent peace on the basis of justice and friendship." During the early months of the war he had grown obsessed with mediation, which he had repeatedly urged upon an unwilling Wilson.[81]

The first submarine incidents in March, 1915, alerted Bryan to the danger of American embroilment in the war. Like Wilson, he staked out his response in April, before the sinking of the *Lusitania.* Concerned fundamentally with "the almost unanimous desire of our country . . . that we shall not become involved in this war," Bryan wished to reply to Germany "without increasing the tension already sufficient to cause anxiety." His answer to the immediate problem of Americans traveling on belligerent vessels was to deny "the right of a citizen to involve his country in war when by exercising ordinary care he could have avoided danger." The Secretary's major suggestion, however, was that the United States "make, not a secret, but a public appeal for the acceptance of mediation. . . . As the well-wisher of all we should act; as the leader in the peace propaganda we should act; as the greatest christian [*sic*] nation we should act. . . ." America must realize that it is "better to try to bring peace for the benefit of the whole world than to risk the provoking of war on account of one man." [82]

Bryan was on the way to becoming a self-conscious isolationist. His approach to individuals' responsibilities in submarine incidents verged on the demand that the government warn them not to travel on belligerent vessels—a demand that others had already raised.[83] Bryan himself would soon call for such warnings, together with a variety of policies designed to keep the nation from being drawn into the war. Furthermore, he implied that the goal of those policies was more than simply preserving neutrality in the present crisis. His ultimate reliance on mediation sprang from the conviction that the United States had much more to lose through intervention than just its own interests or its citizens' lives and property. Bryan had drawn upon the notion of moral contrast between America and the rest of the world for the purpose of showing that the nation's mission would be betrayed through entanglement in such awful affairs. This portended an idealistic isolationist argument.

Bryan's position also contained deeply personal elements which would play a critical role in his conduct during the *Lusitania* crisis. Bryan resembled Wilson again in casting the United States in a part in international affairs patterned after his own self-image. Whereas Wilson stressed self-discipline to control passions and maintain ideals, Bryan reached both for devices to insure the avoidance of evil conduct and for opportunities to persuade others to desist from such conduct. The picture of Bryan which emerges is the familiar one of the Great Commoner, who, as Lawrence W. Levine has shown, sought in all his varied activities, political, religious, social, and international, to find ways to save men from a clearly prescribed catalogue of sins.[84] It is also the picture of the Boy

Orator of the Platte. Inasmuch as Bryan's whole career as a political leader had sprung from his gifts as a speaker, his thought consequently revolved around an unshakable belief in the efficacy of talk in human affairs.

The desire to insure that the United States would not be drawn into the war governed Bryan's initial response to the sinking of the *Lusitania*. Wilson decided to pursue a two-pronged policy of trying "to carry out the double wish of our people, to maintain a firm front . . . and yet do nothing that might by any possibility involve us in the war." The United States demanded in a diplomatic protest that Germany disavow the sinking and guarantee that no similar acts would occur in the future, but, significantly, no specific threats were made nor was a deadline set for compliance. Joining in the protest "with a heavy heart," Bryan tried to assure a peaceful outcome by supplementing it with several expedients. Those included warning citizens not to travel on belligerent vessels, refusing to allow ships with cargoes of munitions to carry passengers, balancing the *Lusitania* protest with a remonstrance against Allied restrictions on American shipping, and, most important to Bryan, communicating to Germany some intimation that the United States expected a peaceful solution to the crisis. In the last connection, he noted that although the Germans had not signed one of his conciliation treaties, they had endorsed their essential principle of a year's delay before resorting to arms. He saw, therefore, "no reason why this policy should not control as between the United States and Germany." The two nations should act like individuals who "postpone the settlement of disputes until such differences can be considered calmly and on their merits." [85]

Those expedients represented a step further toward articulation of an idealistic isolationist position. The next step in that direction came after Wilson declined to adopt the expedients. Bryan's heated reaction showed how deeply his personal feelings had become involved. Losing his normal placidity and good humor, he exploded angrily at reporters and Cabinet colleagues. "Mary," he complained privately to his wife, "what does the President mean! *Why* can't he see that by keeping the way open for mediation and arbitration, he has an opportunity to do the greatest work man can do!" [86] That remark revealed Bryan's need to assure righteousness for America.

Bryan's decision to resign from his post as Secretary of State rather than agree to sign a second note of protest to Germany in June, 1915, stemmed most immediately from his conviction that he could work wonders through talking. As a private citizen, he told Wilson in his letter of resignation, he could seek peace, "the end which you have in view by means which you do not feel at liberty to use." He explained to his Cabinet colleagues on the day he resigned, "I believe that I can do more on the outside than I can do on the inside. I can work to control popular opinion. . . ." [87] Few men except Bryan could have pictured themselves as being more effective in keeping the nation at peace on the stump than at the head of the State Department. Wilson, Josephus Daniels, and Franklin D. Roosevelt each believed that by resigning Bryan threw away his greatest opportunity to keep the nation out of war. It is interesting that Bryan kept his intentions secret from Daniels, his closest friend in the Cabinet, for fear of being dissuaded. This suggests that he knew that his action could be interpreted as a blow to peace and he did not want to be reminded of it.[88]

Basically, Bryan appears to have resigned more from personal preference than from devotion to principle. Earlier in

1915, before the submarine incidents, he had remarked to Wilson, "To have been associated with you in the trying times through which we have passed is compensation for the trials and restraints incident to a Cabinet position." Two days after his resignation a reporter found him "a different man today from the Mr. Bryan of day before yesterday. His shoulders are squared, the joy of battle shines in his eyes, the irritation has disappeared and he seems happy." Evidently he was, since he told an audience two weeks later, "Now, I am free to speak. . . . Now, my friends, I can speak to you extemporaneously, as I have been speaking for twenty-five years." The relief and joy Bryan felt over having relinquished the only major office he ever held made his resignation seem less a sacrifice, as most historians have viewed it, and more an act of escape and reversion to type. In leaving the State Department, Bryan was abandoning what less than a year earlier he had called "the greatest school" he had ever attended, in order to return to the more congenial environment of the hustings.[89]

Bryan's resignation hastened his progress toward formulating an isolationist argument. During his final confrontation with Wilson over the second protest to Germany, Bryan dwelled even more insistently on the "thirty treaties" and warned, "This may be our last chance to speak for peace. . . ." Then, in his letter of resignation, he observed that although he and Wilson were both "desirous of a peaceful solution . . . we find ourselves differing irreconcilably as to the methods which should be employed." Immediately after resigning Bryan stated those differences publicly, declaring, "I believe that this nation should frankly tell Germany that we are willing to apply in this case the principle which we are bound to in disputes between the United States and the thirty countries with which we have made treaties providing for the investigation of disputes of every character and nature." [90] Bryan was drawing a contrast between his thinking and Wilson's through which he would be led to the point of divergence between isolationist and internationalist idealism.

He moved closer to that point in his next statement to the press, on June 11, 1915, two days after his resignation. His difference with the President, asserted Bryan, was "between systems." Of the two "pre-eminent and antagonistic" methods in international relations, "force and persuasion," Wilson's policies represented force, "the old system" of which "war is the chief cornerstone" and the European conflict its "ripened fruit." His own position epitomized persuasion, "the new system" which would be "established through the uplifting power of example." Knowing what force had done "in the old world," Americans must not let it "cross the Atlantic" but must keep themselves pure so that they might "lead the world out of the black night of war into the light of that day when 'swords shall be beaten into plowshares.' " [91] Bryan had nearly reached the point at which isolationist and internationalist idealists parted company. That was over the question of whether America's mission should be carried out by grasping and redirecting the forceful instruments of world politics or by spurning those instruments for the sake of showing the world how to live without them. Bryan needed only to draw a more explicit connection between mission and isolation and he would have formulated a clear-cut idealistic isolationist argument.

A powerful stimulus toward drawing that connection was supplied when the convention called by Taft's group met in Philadelphia on June 17. It established the League to Enforce Peace, the first major internationalist organization in the United States. Taft, who was chairman of the convention and would soon be president of the organization, declared, "We have got to depart from the traditional policy of this country." The departure was required not only because America must "assume certain obligations in the interest of the world and in the interest of mankind" but also because the World War threatened that "we are likely to be drawn in ourselves." [92] Coming from a leading public figure with the backing of a well-publicized organization, this presentation of the intellectual challenge of an internationalist argument had an excellent chance of evoking an equally well-defined defense of isolation.

NOTES

1. For the impact of the discovery of America on the European consciousness, see Gilbert Chinard, "The American Dream," in Robert Spiller et al., eds., *Literary History of the United States* (New York: Macmillan Co., 1948), 1:192–194. The best discussion of the idea of mission in its historical evolution is Cushing Strout, *The American Image of the Old World* (New York: Harper & Row, 1963). See also Edward McNall Burns, *The American Idea of Mission: Concepts of National Purpose and Destiny* (New Brunswick, N. J.: Rutgers University Press, 1957).

2. Sermon aboard the *Arabella*, 1630, in Perry Miller and Thomas Johnson, eds., *The Puritans* (New York: American Book Co., 1938), pp. 197–99. The casual Puritan usage of the letters "u" and "v" has been standardized here according to present practice.

3. See Perry Miller, *The New England Mind: From Colony to Province* (Cambridge, Mass.: Harvard University Press, 1953), pp. 119–125, 157–160.

4. Franklin to Lord Kames, January 3, 1760, in Leonard W. Labaree, ed., *The Papers of Benjamin Franklin* (New Haven, Conn.: Yale University Press, 1966), 9:7. On the English debate and American reactions, see Felix Gilbert, *To the Farewell Address: Ideas of Early American Foreign Policy* (Princeton, N. J.: Princeton University Press, 1961), esp. pp. 34–35.

5. See Gilbert, *To the Farewell Address*, pp. 41–42.

6. Philip Foner, ed., *The Complete Writings of Thomas Paine* (New York: Citadel Press, 1945), 1:3, 21.

7. Franklin to Joseph Galloway, February 25, 1775, in John Bigelow, ed., *The Works of Benjamin Franklin* (New York: G. P. Putnam's Sons, 1904), 6:431.

8. Adams to Robert Livingston, February 5, 1783, in Charles Francis Adams, ed., *The Works of John Adams* (Boston: Little, Brown & Co., 1853), 8:35.

9. Gilbert, *To the Farewell Address,* pp. 54, 84–85.

10. Ezra Stiles, *The United States Elevated to Honor and Glory: A Sermon Preached . . . at Hartford, at the Anniversary Election, May 8th, MDCCLXXXIII* (Worcester, Mass.: Isaiah Thomas, 1785), pp. 9, 26, 89; Jefferson to James Madison, August 28, 1789, in Julian P. Boyd, ed., *The Papers of Thomas Jefferson* (Princeton, N. J.: Princeton University Press, 1958), 15:367.

11. Foner, ed., *Complete Writings of Paine,* 1:31.

12. Benjamin F. Wright, ed., *The Federalist* (Cambridge, Mass.: Harvard University Press, 1961), 6:113, 11:141.

13. C. Vann Woodward, "The Age of Reinterpretation," *American Historical Review* 66 (October, 1960): 2–9.

14. U.S. Congress, *Annals of Congress,* 14th Congress, 1st Session, January 20, 1816, p. 723; Jan. 29, 1816, p. 790; Adams to John Quincy Adams, January 5, 1818, quoted in Samuel Flagg Bemis, *John Quincy Adams and the Foundations of American Foreign Policy* (New York: Alfred A. Knopf, 1949), p. 342, n. 4. On the philhellenic outburst, see Edward Mead Earle, "American Interest in the Greek Cause, 1821–1827," *American Historical Review* 33 (October, 1927): 41–63.

15. *Washington National Gazette,* February 10, 1821, quoted in Arthur P. Whitaker, *The United States and the Independence of Latin America, 1800–1830* (Baltimore: Johns Hopkins Press, 1941), p. 334.

16. Adams to Robert Walsh, July 10, 1821, in Worthington C. Ford, ed., *Writings of John Quincy Adams* (New York: Macmillan Co., 1917), 7:117; Adams to Edward Everett, January 31, 1822, ibid., p. 201; Adams, *An Address Delivered at the Request of the Committee on Arrangements for Celebrating the Anniversary of Independence at the City of Washington on the Fourth of July, 1821* (n.p., 1821), pp. 32–34.

17. U.S. Congress, *Congressional Globe,* 32nd Congress, 1st Session, December 11, 1851, pp. 70–71 (hereafter cited as *Globe*); speech of Senator Isaac Walker (D-Wis.), ibid., December 16, 1851, p. 105. On the faction, see Merle Curti, "Young America," *American Historical Review* 32 (October, 1926): 34–55.

18. Jeremiah Clemens (Ala.), *Globe,* 32nd Cong., 1st sess., December 10, 1851, p. 53; Sumner, ibid., December 10, 1851, p. 51.

19. Strout, *American Image of the Old World,* pp. 60–61; *Cincinnati Weekly Gazette,* January 29, 1852, quoted in Norman Graebner, ed., *Ideas and Diplomacy: Readings in the Intellectual Tradition of American Foreign Policy* (New York: Oxford University Press, 1964), pp. 289–290.

20. U.S. Congress, *Congressional Record,* 56th Cong., 1st sess., January 9, 1900, p. 711 (hereafter cited as *Record*).

21. See Albert K. Weinberg, *Manifest Destiny: A Study of Nationalist Expansion in American History* (Baltimore: Johns Hopkins Press, 1935).

22. Bryan speech of February 22, 1899, in William Jennings Bryan et al., *Republic or Empire? The Philippine Question* (Chicago: Independence Co., 1899), p. 37; Schurz article of September, 1898, in Frederic Bancroft, ed., *Speeches, Correspondence, and Political Papers of Carl Schurz* (New York: G. P. Putnam's Sons, 1913), 5:510 (hereafter cited as *Schurz Speeches*).

23. Henry Cabot Lodge, "Our Blundering Foreign Policy," *Forum* 19 (March, 1895):16.

24. *Republic or Empire?*, p. 64; Schurz to George F. Hoar, October 26, 1898 in Bancroft, ed., *Schurz Speeches,* 5:528; Schurz to C. F. Adams, January 16, 1899, ibid., 6:38; Kirk H. Porter and Donald B. Johnson, eds., *National Party Platforms, 1840–1956* (Urbana, Ill.: University of Illinois Press, 1956), pp. 112–113 (hereafter cited as *National Party Platforms*).

25. Richard W. Leopold, "The Emergence of America as a World Power: Some Second Thoughts," in John Braeman et al., eds., *Change and Continuity in Twentieth Century America* (Columbus, Ohio: Ohio State University Press, 1964), pp. 13–16. On the election, see Thomas A. Bailey, "Was the Presidential Election of 1900 a Mandate on Imperialism?", *Mississippi Valley Historical Review* 24 (June, 1937): 43–52.

26. Walter Lippmann, *U. S. Foreign Policy: Shield of the Republic* (Boston: Little, Brown & Co., 1943), p. x.

27. Seward to William Dayton, May 11, 1863, in John Bassett Moore, ed., *A Digest of International Law* (Washington: Government Printing Office, 1906) 6:23; James D. Richardson, ed., *A Compilation of the Messages and Papers of the Presidents, 1789–1897* (Washington: Government Printing Office, 1898), 8:301.

28. William Malloy, ed., *Treaties, Conventions, International Acts, Protocols, and Agreements between the United States of America and Other Powers, 1776–1909* (Washington: Government Printing Office, 1910), 2:2183, 2247; *Record,* 59th Cong., 1st sess., January 24, 1906, p. 1470.

29. William Jennings Bryan, *The Prince of Peace* (Independence, Mo.: Zion Publishing Co., 1925), p. 51; Wilson speech of May 16, 1914, in Ray Stannard Baker and William E. Dodd, eds., *The Public Papers of Woodrow Wilson* (New York: Harper & Bros., 1926), 4:109 (hereafter cited as *Wilson Public Papers*).

30. Robert N. Page to Walter Hines Page, November 12, 1914, Walter Hines Page Papers, Houghton Library, Harvard University, English Period, Folder 999 (hereafter cited as W. H. Page Papers); Gilbert M. Hitchcock address of February 22, 1922, Gilbert M. Hitchcock Papers, Library of Congress (hereafter cited as Hitchcock Papers); *New York Times,* September 27, 1914; *Colliers,* 52 (August 22, 1914): 14. See also George Harvey, "Europe at Armageddon," *North American Review* 200 (Sep-

tember 2, 1914): 321–332; William Howard Taft to Hamilton Holt, August 2, 1914, William Howard Taft Papers, Library of Congress, Box 285, General Correspondence (hereafter cited as Taft Papers).

31. Walter Hines Page to Woodrow Wilson, July 29, 1914, Woodrow Wilson Papers, Library of Congress, Series II, Box 103 (hereafter cited as Wilson Papers).

32. *New York Times,* August 16, 1914; *World's Work* 18 (October, 1914): 483. Cf. *New York Evening Post,* July 30, 1914; *New York World,* August 29, 1914; *Current Opinion* 57 (September, 1914): 153; *Literary Digest* 49 (August 15, 1914): 260.

33. *Wilson Public Papers,* 3: 157–159. Privately, Wilson seems to have been less sure of America's detachment. In August he told his brother-in-law that he feared that "something will happen on the high seas that will make it impossible for us to stay out of the war." (Ray Stannard Baker interview with Stockton Axson, February 8, 10, 11, 1925, Ray Stannard Baker Papers, Library of Congress, Series I, Box 19 (hereafter cited as R. S. Baker Papers, LC). Also, on September 30, he told Colonel Edward House that he dreaded an historical repetition: "Madison and I are the only Princeton men that have become President. The circumstances of the war of 1812 and now run parallel" Diary of Edward M. House, September 30, 1914, Yale University Library, 5:187 (hereafter cited as House Diary). Yet two days earlier House had found Wilson "singularly lacking in appreciation of the importance of this European crisis" (ibid., September 28, 1914, 5:182).

34. *Record,* 63rd Cong., 2nd sess. October 14, 1914, p. 16580. It would be wrong to infer that the war was widely discussed in Congress, since these remarks were among the few instances of notice being taken in either House.

35. *Literary Digest* 49 (November 14, 1914): 939–941, 974–978. For the percentages of German- and Scandinavian-born in Middle Western states see Table 3 in the Appendix.

36. Sympathy for the Central Powers was rare outside the German-American community and some (but not all) traditionally Anglophobic Irish-American circles. The only prominent Americans not of such backgrounds who sympathized with the Central Powers early in the war were the political scientist John W. Burgess, a Germanophile since his graduate student days in Berlin; Beveridge, who admired German militarism and governmental efficiency, distrusted the Allies because of Russian encroachments in the Far East, and hoped that the United States would replace a defeated Britain as the world's leading seapower; and retired Rear Admiral French E. Chadwick, who apparently shared similar views on the navy. See John W. Burgess, *America's Relation to the Great War* (Chicago: A. C. McClurg & Co., 1916), pp. 165–178, 179; Mark Sullivan to Beveridge, October 24, 1914, Albert J. Beveridge Papers, Library of Congress, Box 201 (hereafter cited as Beveridge Papers); House to Wilson, March 8, 1915, Wilson Papers, Series II, Box 117; Chadwick to Wilson, September 12, 1914,

ibid., Box 106; Josephus Daniels, *The Wilson Era: Years of Peace, 1910–1917* (Chapel Hill, N. C.: University of North Carolina Press, 1944), pp. 574–575 (hereafter cited as Daniels, *Wilson Era*).

37. *Literary Digest* 49 (November 14, 1914): 939; Mark Sullivan, *Our Times* (New York: Charles Scribner's Sons, 1926), 5:59.

38. Sir Cecil Spring Rice to Lord Newton, October 21, 1914 and Spring Rice to Sir Edward Grey, April 16, 1915, in Stephen Gwyn, ed., *The Letters and Friendships of Sir Cecil Spring Rice* (London: Constable & Co., 1929), 2:239, 262 (hereafter cited as Gwyn, ed., *Spring Rice Letters*). Cf. Spring Rice to Sir Valentine Chirol, November 13, 27, 1914, ibid., pp. 243, 249.

39. The once popular notion that British propaganda played a large part in creating this sentiment is demolished by Arthur Link in *Wilson* (Princeton, N. J.: Princeton University Press, 1960), 3:40–43.

40. *New York Times,* October 16, 1914.

41. Ibid., October 20, 1914; *Literary Digest* 49 (October 31, 1914): 835–836.

42. See Augustus P. Gardner to Henry L. Stimson, October 23, 1914 and Stimson to Gardner, October 26, 1914, Henry L. Stimson Papers, Yale University Library, Box 117 (hereafter cited as Stimson Papers); Stimson to S. Stanwood Menken, November 9, 1914 and Gardner to Stimson, November 27, 1917, ibid., Box 118; *New York Times,* November 15, 22, December 2, 1914; Theodore Roosevelt to Hiram Johnson, November 16, 1914, Hiram Johnson Papers, Bancroft Library, University of California, Berkeley, Part II, Box 28 (hereafter cited as Johnson Papers); Henry Cabot Lodge to Roosevelt, December 11, 1914, Theodore Roosevelt Papers, Library of Congress, Box 278 (hereafter cited as Roosevelt Papers); *The New Republic* 1 (December 5, 1914): 3; *New York Evening Post,* December 7, 1914.

43. *Wilson Public Papers,* 3:226; Gus J. Karger to Taft, July 27, 1915, Taft Papers, Box 316 (Gen. Corr.).

44. *Record,* 63rd Cong., 3rd sess., December 10, 1914, p. 105; ibid., January 15, 1915, p. 1610. See also *The Nation* 99 (December 10, 1914): 679; *The Commoner* 14 (December, 1914): 2; *The New York Times,* December 5, 8, 10, 1914. Gardner's resolution was bottled up in the House Rules Committee, where the Democratic chairman and majority refused to report it out. *New York Times,* December 9, 1914.

45. *Record,* 63rd Cong., 3rd sess., February 5, 1915, p. 3152. For a statistical description of this vote, see Table 4 in the Appendix.

46. See Harold and Margaret Sprout, *The Rise of American Naval Power, 1776–1918* (Princeton, N. J.: Princeton University Press, 1946), pp. 294–295, 313–314.

47. *Literary Digest* 50 (January 23, 1915): 137–138, 162–169.

48. *Record,* 63rd Cong., 3rd sess., December 10, 1915, p. 105; ibid., January 29, 1915, pp. 2721–2724. Cf. the remarks of Kenneth McKellar (D-Tenn.), ibid., January 21, 1915, p. 2048; William S. Howard (D-Ga.),

ibid., January 21, 1915, pp. 2070–2071; and William S. Cullop (D-Ind.), ibid., February 2, 1915, pp. 2893–2894.

49. *Record,* 52nd Cong., 1st sess., April 16, 1892, pp. 3360–3361; *Republic or Empire?,* p. 49; *National Party Platforms,* p. 113. Cf. the Populist platform of 1900, ibid., p. 117.

50. The quotation is from a speech by Representative Gilbert M. Hitchcock (D-Nebr.), *Record,* 58th Cong., 2nd sess., February 20, 1904, p. 2152. Cf. addresses by Thomas W. Hardwick (D-Ga.), ibid., February 20, 1904, p. 2157, and William W. Kitchin (D-N. C.), ibid., February 22, 1904, p. 2231.

51. See Merrill D. Peterson, *The Jefferson Image in the American Mind* (New York: Oxford University Press, 1960), pp. 255, 259–260. In fact, the Democratic platform of 1900 quoted Jefferson's dictum against entangling alliances and approved "this wholesome doctrine" as opposed to "the Republican departure which has involved us in so-called world politics. . . ." *National Party Platforms,* p. 115.

52. *Record,* 63rd Cong., 3rd sess., *Appendix,* February 15, 1915, p. 418. Cf. remarks of Representatives E. W. Saunders (D-Va.) and Samuel A. Witherspoon (D-Miss.), ibid., 2nd. sess., April 24, 1914, pp. 7216–7221; ibid., April 25, 1914, p. 7278.

53. As did one Progressive, Clyde Kelly (Pa.).

54. *Record,* 63rd Cong., 2nd sess. May 29, 1914, p. 9459; ibid., April 21, 1914, p. 7020. An article by Tavenner denouncing the "war trust" appeared in *La Follette's Weekly* 6 (August 1, 1914): 4.

55. *Record,* 63rd Cong., 3rd sess., January 29, 1915, p. 2734.

56. On Norris, see Richard Lowitt, *George W. Norris: The Making of a Progressive, 1861–1912* (Syracuse, N. Y.: Syracuse University Press, 1963), p. 154, and *Record,* 63rd Cong., 2nd sess., May 1, 1914, pp. 7539–7542. On Works, see ibid., 62nd Cong., 2nd sess., February 8, 1912, pp. 1834–1836; and on Borah, ibid., 61st Cong., 1st sess., June 15, 1909, p. 3237. On progressive support for imperialistic policies, see William E. Leuchtenburg, "Progressivism and Imperialism: The Progressive Movement and American Foreign Policy, 1898–1916," *Mississippi Valley Historical Review* 39 (December, 1952): 483–504. Although Leuchtenburg is on sound ground regarding early progressive *Republican* support for imperialism and the intimate relation between reform and aggressive foreign policies in the thinking of Roosevelt and Beveridge, his general contentions about connections between progressivism and imperialism are open to serious question. Two articles which differ by implication regarding individual progressives are Padraic C. Kennedy, "La Follette's Foreign Policy: From Imperialism to Anti-imperialism," *Wisconsin Magazine of History* 46 (Summer, 1963): 287–293, and John Milton Cooper, Jr., "William E. Borah, Political Thespian," *Pacific Northwest Quarterly* 46 (October, 1965): 145–153. A statistical study which shows a different picture of progressive foreign policy views is Howard W. Allen, "Republican Reformers and Foreign Policy, 1913–1917," *Mid-America* 44 (October, 1962): 222–229. For

a general reassessment of the problem, see Cooper, "Progressivism and American Foreign Policy: A Reconsideration," ibid., 51 (October, 1969): 260–277.

57. See Clifton J. Child, "German-American Attempts to Prevent the Exportation of Munitions of War, 1914–1915," *Mississippi Valley Historical Review* 25 (December, 1938): 351–368; Link, *Wilson,* 3: 164; *Record,* 63rd Cong., 3rd sess., December 7, 1914, pp. 6, 12. A copy of Hitchcock's resolution is in the Hitchcock Papers. For a sample of letters, telegrams, and petitions containing predominantly German names, see William E. Borah Papers, Library of Congress, Box 172 (hereafter cited as Borah Papers).

58. *Record,* 63rd Cong., 3rd sess., December 16, 1914, p. 268; statements quoted in Child, "German-American Attempts to Prevent Exportation of Munitions," *Mississippi Valley Historical Review* 25 (December, 1938): 364, 366.

59. *Record,* 63rd Cong., 3rd sess., December 16, 1914, p. 268. Cf. Bartholdt's comment in his autobiography, *From Steerage to Congress: Reminiscences and Reflections* (Philadelphia: Dorrance & Co., 1930), pp. 366–367.

60. See, e. g., David Starr Jordan, *The Days of a Man: Being Memories of a Naturalist, Teacher and Minor Prophet of Democracy* (Yonkers, N. Y.: World Book Co., 1922), 2:652; *The Public* 18 (January 15, 1915): 51. An exception, favoring the embargo, was *Survey* 33 (January 2, 1915): 387.

61. Bryan to Wilson, January 6, 1915, and Wilson to Bryan, January 7, 1915, William Jennings Bryan Papers, National Archives (hereafter cited as Bryan Papers, National Archives). See also Bryan to William J. Stone, *Papers Relating to the Foreign Relations of the United States, 1914: Supplement, the World War* (Washington: Government Printing Office, 1928) pp. vii–xiv; Lodge to Roosevelt, March 8, 1915, Henry Cabot Lodge Papers, Massachusetts Historical Society, Roosevelt-Lodge Correspondence (hereafter cited as Lodge Papers, Roosevelt-Lodge Corresp.). Bryan's suspicions of the arms embargo may have stemmed in part from his long-standing feud with the German-American Alliance over temperance and with Senator Hitchcock, a wet, who was his chief rival among Nebraska Democrats. See Bryan to Wilson, January 14, 1915, Bryan Papers, National Archives.

62. *Literary Digest* 50 (February 6, 1915): 225–226.

63. *Record,* 63rd Cong., 3rd sess., February 18, 1915, p. 4016. The actual vote was 51 to 36 in favor of tabling the amendment. Senator James A. Martine (D-N. J.) announced that he had voted incorrectly.

64. *New Republic* 1 (January 9, 1915): 3.

65. *Record,* 63rd Cong., 3rd sess., February 12, 1915, p. 3633.

66. Ibid., December 14, 1914, p. 202; ibid., February 12, 1915, p. 3633; *La Follette's Magazine* 7 (February, 1915): 2. Cf. Representative Manahan's speech, *Record,* 63rd Cong., 3rd sess., January 29, 1915, p. 2734.

67. See La Follette to Herman Ekern, November 16, 1914, Herman

Ekern Papers, State Historical Society of Wisconsin, Box 16 (hereafter cited as Ekern Papers); Mrs. La Follette's column in *La Follette's Weekly* 6 (October 17, 1914): 6; Paul O. Husting to Wilson, January 5, 1915, Wilson Papers, Series II, Box 113.

68. See, e. g., *New York Times, New York World, New York Evening Post, New York American* January–February, 1915; Cedric C. Cummins, *Indiana Public Opinion and the World War, 1914–1917* (Indianapolis: Indiana Historical Bureau, 1945), p. 103; Morris Hillquit speech of April 2, 1915 in Augustus P. Gardner and Morris Hillquit, *Must We Arm: A Debate . . . Held in Carnegie Hall, New York, April 12, 1915, under the Auspices of the Rand School of Social Science* (New York: Rand School of Social Science, 1916), p. 27; David Lawrence, "Our Foreign Policy and the War," *North American Review* 201 (April, 1915): 553.

69. Wilson to Mary A. Hulbert, August 2, 1914, Wilson Papers, Wilson-Mary A. Hulbert Correspondence (hereafter cited as Wilson-Hulbert Corresp.) ; R. S. Baker interview with Stockton Axson, February 8, 10, 11, 1925, R. S. Baker Papers, LC, Series I, Box 19; House to Wilson, August 22, 1914, Wilson Papers, Series II, Box 105; Roosevelt to Hugo Munsterberg, November 2, 1914, Roosevelt Papers, Letterbook 92; Lodge to Roosevelt, December 7, 1914, ibid., Box 278; Lodge to Roosevelt, January 15, 1915, ibid., Box 281; *The Wall Street Journal* quoted in *Literary Digest* 50 (April 3, 1915): 740.

70. Sullivan, *Our Times,* 5:120, n. 5.

71. E. A. Alderman to W. H. Page, May 12, 1915, W. H. Page Papers, English Period, Folder 20; journal entry, May 19, 1915, Notebook 5, R. S. Baker Papers, LC, Series II, Box 122; William Allen White to Chester Rowell, August 25, 1915, Chester Rowell Papers, Bancroft Library, University of California, Berkeley, Box 26; David Lawrence, *The True Story of Woodrow Wilson* (New York: George H. Doran Co., 1925), pp. 197–198. Even the German Ambassador reportedly condemned the sinking in private. See Oswald Garrison Villard to Sir Valentine Chirol, July 19, 1925, Oswald Garrison Villard Papers, Houghton Library, Harvard University, File 229.

72. *Literary Digest* 50 (May 15, 22, 1915): 1134, 1200; *New York Times,* June 1, 1915.

73. Works to Frederick Dixon, May 18, 1915, John D. Works Papers, Bancroft Library, University of California, Berkeley, Box 1 (hereafter cited as Works Papers, Berkeley); *New York Times,* May 12, 1915. Cf. Works's statement, ibid., June 1, 1915.

74. *New York Times,* May 9, 1915; Bryan to Wilson, June 4, 1915, Bryan Papers, National Archives; Thomas S. Martin and Hal D. Flood to Bryan, June 5, 1915, William Jennings Bryan Papers, Library of Congress, Box 30 (hereafter cited as Bryan Papers, LC). Cf. statements of Senators Vardaman (D-Miss.) and Hoke Smith (D-Ga.), *New York Times,* May 10, 1915.

75. Wilson to Bryan, April 6, 1915, Bryan Papers, National Archives;

addresses of April 19, 20, 1915, *Wilson Public Papers,* 3:299–300, 302–306. Actually, Wilson had foreseen that a situation like this might arise when the German submarine decree was first published. See Wilson to Mary A. Hulbert, February 14, March 7, 1915, Wilson-Hulbert Corresp.

76. See esp. Wilson to Mary Hulbert, September 6, 1914, Wilson-Hulbert Corresp.; entry of November 14, 1914, *House Diary,* 5:227. Link has noted that Kipling's lines, "If you can keep your head when all about you/ Are losing theirs and blaming it on you," were among Wilson's favorites (Link, *Wilson,* 3:380).

77. Speech of May 10, 1915, *Wilson Public Papers,* 3:321.

78. R. S. Baker interview with Stockton Axson, February 8, 10, 11, 1925, R. S. Baker Papers, LC, Series I, Box 19.

79. Journal entry, August 2, 1914, Notebook 3, R. S. Baker Papers, LC, Series II, Box 122; *La Follette's Weekly* 7 (January, 1915): 15; *Record,* 63rd Cong., 3rd sess., January 12, 1915, p. 1484; ibid., February 3, 1915, p. 2941; ibid. February 12, 1915, p. 3631; ibid. February 27, 1915, p. 4837; Taft to Mabel T. Boardman, April 12, 1915, Taft Papers, Series VIII, Letterbook 30; *New York Times,* May 14, 1915.

80. Bryan to Wilson, September 19, 1914, Wilson Papers, Series II, Box 107; Spring Rice to Sir Edward Grey, August 25, 1914, in Gwyn, ed., *Spring Rice Letters,* 2:220; *Commoner* 14 (October, 1914): 3. The unhappy coincidence was not lost on newspaper wits. See *Literary Digest* 49 (August 8, September 26, 1914): 222, 564.

81. Bryan to Wilson, December 1, 1914, Bryan Papers, National Archives. Other mediation suggestions are in Bryan to Wilson, October 7, December 17, 1914, February 24, 1915, ibid.

82. Bryan to Wilson, April 2, 7, 1915, Bryan Papers, National Archives; Bryan to Wilson, April 23, 1915, Bryan Papers, LC, Box 30.

83. Senator Wesley Jones (R-Wash.), for example, had suggested it shortly after the original German submarine decree was published. *Record,* 63rd Cong., 3rd sess., February 26, 1915, p. 4705.

84. Lawrence W. Levine, *Defender of the Faith: William Jennings Bryan: The Last Decade, 1915–1925* (New York: Oxford University Press, 1965), esp. p. 54.

85. Wilson to Bryan, June 7, 1915, Bryan Papers, National Archives; *Papers Relating to the Foreign Relations of the United States, 1915: Supplement, the World War* (Washington: Government Printing Office, 1928), pp. 393–396; Bryan to Wilson, May 9, 1915 and May 12, 1915 (two letters), Wilson Papers, Series II, Box 120; Bryan to Wilson, May 13, 14, 1915, Bryan Papers, National Archives.

86. Wilson to Bryan, May 13, 1915 (two letters) and May 14, 1915, Bryan Papers, LC, Box 30; Lindley M. Garrison to R. S. Baker, November 12, 1928, Ray Stannard Baker Papers, Princeton University Library, Box 1 (hereafter cited as R. S. Baker Papers, Princeton); Wilson to House, May 18, 1915, Edward M. House Papers, Yale University Library (hereafter cited as House Papers); Wilson to Bryan, May 20, 1915, Bryan

Papers, National Archives; Oswald Garrison Villard to Wilson, June 7, 1915, Wilson Papers, Series II, Box 121; David F. Houston, *Eight Years with Wilson's Cabinet: 1913 to 1920* (Garden City, N. Y.: Doubleday, Page & Co., 1926), 1:132–138; William Jennings Bryan and Mary Baird Bryan, *The Memoirs of William Jennings Bryan* (Philadelphia: John C. Winston Co., 1925), pp. 420–421 (hereafter cited as *Bryan Memoirs*).

87. Bryan to Wilson, June 9, 1915, Wilson Papers, Series II, Box 121; Houston, *Eight Years with Wilson's Cabinet,* 1:146.

88. E. David Cronon, ed., *The Cabinet Diaries of Josephus Daniels, 1913–1921* (Lincoln, Neb.: University of Nebraska Press, 1963), p. 472 (hereafter cited as Cronon, *Daniels Cabinet Diaries*); Daniels to R. S. Baker, August 8, 1936, R. S. Baker Papers, Princeton, Box 1; Franklin D. Roosevelt to Daniels, October 3, 1934, quoted in Frank Freidel, *Franklin D. Roosevelt: The Apprenticeship* (Boston: Little, Brown & Co., 1952), p. 250; Katherine E. Brand interview with Daniels, August 8, 1936, R. S. Baker Papers, LC, Series I, Box 28.

89. Bryan to Wilson, March 19, 1915, Wilson Papers, Series II, Box 118; Gus J. Karger to Taft, June 10, 1915, Taft Papers, Box 311 (Gen. Corr.); speech of June 24, 1915, *Commoner* 15 (July, 1915): 9–10; entry for August 30, 1914, House Diary, 5:151. Cf. comments of Bryan's daughter, Grace Bryan Hargreaves, in her manuscript biography of her father, Bryan Papers, LC, Box 65.

90. Bryan to Wilson, June 3, 1915, Bryan Papers, National Archives; Bryan to Wilson, June 5, 9, 1915, Wilson Papers, Series II, Box 121; *Commoner* 15 (June, 1915): 2.

91. *Commoner* 15 (June, 1915): 3.

92. *League to Enforce Peace: American Branch: Conference Held in the City of Philadelphia, Bunker Hill Day (June 17th), 1915* (New York: League to Enforce Peace, 1916), p. 18 (hereafter cited as *League to Enforce Peace*).

2

Formulation of Isolationist Doctrines

BY the middle of 1915 the stage was set for the emergence of an isolationist position. The threat of entering the World War had evoked popular resistance, causing a number of politicians to espouse anti-interventionist policies; but the organization of the internationalists into the League to Enforce Peace demanded still stronger isolationist opposition. A major step toward the formation of a cohesive political position was taken when four men independently formulated isolationist doctrines in direct response to internationalist proposals. Bryan became the opposition's first spokesman when he distilled his earlier views into a clear statement of idealistic isolationism. His idealism contrasted vividly with the ultranationalist remarks being uttered at the same time. The other important formulators of isolationist doctrines were three intellectuals, the scholars Samuel P. Orth and Ellery Stowell, and the writer Randolph Bourne. Like Bryan, they presented idealistic arguments. By putting forward their doctrines before the question of overseas involvement burgeoned into a major political issue, these spokesmen illuminated the purely intellectual bases of idealistic isolationism.

Bryan versus the Ultranationalists

Bryan arrived at his isolationist stand fairly quickly, but not before some faltering in his thinking. After drawing the distinction between force and persuasion, he merely repeated previous arguments in his next few statements to the press. Agitation by Roosevelt and Gardner for a tough line toward Germany even made him emphasize his and Wilson's common idealism. "Happy for our nation," he asserted, "that we have in the White House at this time a president who believes in setting the old world a good example, instead of . . . a president inflamed by the false philosophy which has plunged Europe into the abyss of war!" [1] Bryan's difficulty was that he did not yet have a statement of idealistic internationalism against which to define his position. His problem was—to use a fitting religious analogy—like that of the fundamentalist, who distinguishes his position in response, not to the heathen, but to fellow Christians who are theological liberals.[2] What Bryan required in order to formulate an isolationist argument was not Roosevelt's and Gardner's militant nationalism but a program based upon idealistic premises.

The founding of the League to Enforce Peace came as a godsend to Bryan. Responding to the League's proposals two days later, on June 19, 1915, in a speech at Carnegie Hall in New York, Bryan put forward a doctrine of idealistic isolationism. Taft's organization, he charged, was not the peace group it appeared, but one whose "intent and effect are to aid rather than obstruct the Roosevelt propaganda" for large-scale preparedness and belligerency. Its program was "a policy of 'fighting the devil with fire' " by forming "an international police force, which will COMPEL peace, and COMPEL IT BY THE USE OF FORCE." That would mean repudiating both Washington's rule against alliances and the Monroe Doctrine, for the sake of making "ourselves partners with other nations in the waging of war."

Above all, Bryan demanded rejection of the League's program because "we have sought to aid the world by example." Joining with other nations in an agreement "by the terms of which we let them declare war for us and bind ourselves to furnish our quota of men and money . . . would not be an ascent to a higher plane; it would in itself be a descent and would impair our influence and jeopardize our moral prestige." Rather than follow such a course, which really contemplated "military glory" and "empire," Americans must "remain true to the ideals of the fathers and . . . be content with the glory that can be achieved by a republic. . . ." Inasmuch as America's "mission is to implant hope in the breast of humanity and substitute higher ideals for the ideals which have led nations into armed conflicts," the program of the League to Enforce Peace must be rejected in order to continue "to rely upon the uplifting power of that which is good and pure and noble. 'I, if I be lifted up from earth will draw all men unto me.' . . . It is infidelity to the spirit of our religion to cast aside this most potent of all regenerating influences, in the individual, in society, and in the state." [3]

Two characteristics were especially striking in this statement of idealistic isolationism. On the one hand, Bryan was obviously responding to the internationalists. Without their challenge he could not have reached this position as clearly or as rapidly as he did. On the other hand, Bryan was behaving just as he had before leaving the Cabinet. He was still casting the United States in a role fashioned after his own political character. His main concern, as ever, was to avoid sin. The references to "our religion" and the invocation of Jesus' words from the Gospel of St. John showed that Bryan's isolationism was of a piece with the rest of his political and social thinking. It all derived from his Protestant fundamentalism, in which the overpowering concern was assurance of salvation.[4]

Stress on oratory was another way in which Bryan's self-image entered into his formulation of an idealistic isolationist doctrine. His condemnation of the League to Enforce Peace as an unwitting tool of Rooseveltian militarism and "empire" followed logically from the earlier distinction between force and persuasion. That dismissal of internationalist proposals allowed Bryan to define non-forceful policies for the United States in world affairs in a way that permitted the nation to do little besides talk. An almost exclusively oratorical stance, in turn, meshed neatly with the moral perfectionism of his particular brand of fundamentalist Christianity. Virtually any use of power in international relations, no matter how idealistic in purpose, was scorned as a ruse for committing the sin of imperialism. In short, America would act like Bryan the fundamentalist by avoiding sin and like Bryan the evangelist by preaching to the unredeemed.

Idealistic isolationism formed a natural culmination to the Great Commoner's earlier views on international politics. It was pacific but not really pacifist. Bryan had never been a thoroughgoing pacifist. He had served as an Army officer during the Spanish-American War, although he never saw combat and his notions of a soldier's function bordered on the fanciful. He had frequently admitted that under some circumstances wars might be justified.[5] Fittingly, Bryan's favorite religious writer on international affairs was his friend, the Reverend Charles E. Jefferson, who had recently argued, "The enemy to be faced and conquered is not war, but militarism. Militarism is not war, but it is something out of which war comes." America, in Jefferson's view, could avoid militarism and still maintain "an army and a navy for police purposes," which were "both honorable and Christian." [6]

The difference between Bryan's position and pacifism was that his chief concern was not war and peace, but assuring righteousness, particularly for the United States. That difference reflected a little noticed but powerful strain of egocentric nationalism which had long figured in Bryan's views on international affairs. He appealed to national egoism in condemning the League to Enforce Peace's proposal to let other nations declare war for America or demand troops and funds under international agreements.[7] But the deeper nationalistic element in Bryan's thinking was faith in the traditional notion of moral contrast between America and Europe. That notion was implicit when he condemned internationalism as a descent from the nation's already exalted level of moral prestige. The difference between idealistic isolationists like Bryan and ultranationalist isolationists would not be greater or lesser national feeling. Rather, the difference was concentration on self-righteousness instead of self-interest.

Bryan seems to have realized that he had achieved an intellectual breakthrough in his speech of June 19. He soon further denounced the League to Enforce Peace in an editorial in his magazine, *The Commoner*. There, he went on to repudiate the League for advocating "entrance into the politics of Europe," which were permeated with the "false philosophy" of reliance upon force. "This is not the doctrine that prevails in the New World and our country cannot afford to tie itself to the nations that believe in this doctrine. . . ." St. Paul's counsel, " 'Be ye not unequally yoked together' is an admonition that may well be heeded in international affairs." By adhering "to the ideals of the past and to the traditions of our nation" and seeking "to make the world better through the influence of high example . . . we LEAD the world and should be satisfied with our primacy. . . . We could at best be a poor second if we so changed our national policy as to become a part of the European police force." [8]

Plain as egocentric nationalism might be in Bryan's isolationism, however, the essential element was clearly idealism. For Bryan, the path to national greatness lay through adherence to religious and political ideals. Closing *The Commoner* editorial condemning the League to Enforce Peace, he warned that abandonment of traditional isolation would signify that Americans "are tired of being good and hunger for the excitement of the camp and the man hunt." [9]

Nothing corroborated the essential idealism of Bryan's isolationism better than the contrast between it and ultranationalist arguments. Consider, for example, the remark made by Senator Boies Penrose, Pennsylvania's Old Guard Republican boss, on June 22, 1915, three days after Bryan's first presentation of his idealistic isolationist position. Penrose condemned the League's program as "fantastic and nonsensical," and he contended that the United States could maintain peace with honor only by building a large navy and instituting universal military training.[10]

Penrose's criticism was neither the first nor the most important ultranationalist attack upon idealistic internationalism. Six months earlier, in January, 1915, Congressman Gardner had assailed the ideas of an international peace-keeping organization when such proposals had first been discussed. The concepts, Gardner had charged, were just "a new dream" added onto the efforts of peace advocates "to persuade the world that a flexible spine is a better defense than a mighty biceps. . . ." An international tribunal empowered to enforce its decisions would be particularly pernicious because it might require Americans to surrender their rights in such matters as excluding Oriental and restricting European immigration. Worse, such a tribunal in the past could easily have decided against the United States over the annexation of Texas or in favor of the Confederacy in the secession crisis. The United States must continue, Gardner had concluded, to exercise sovereign judgment, backed by sufficient force of arms. Then America would not "be at the mercy of any nation's friendliness" but could regard even the most powerful country "the way one strong man ought to feel toward another strong man." [11]

Gardner's remarks foreshadowed Theodore Roosevelt's attack on the League to Enforce Peace in August, 1915. Roosevelt fulminated against "the infinite folly, the discreditable folly" of the League because it sought world peace before the United States had acquired "a military force sufficient to entitle us to speak with the voice of authority in international matters. Let us not live in the realm of childish make-believe. Let us not make new and large promises in a spirit of grandiloquent and elocutionary disregard of facts unless and until we are willing by deeds to make good on the promises we have already made. . . ." [12]

This was hardly an outright rejection of internationalism. Roosevelt had long favored various kinds of overseas ties. He also believed, as he explained a few months later, that eventually "something can be accomplished along the lines of the

League to Enforce Peace." But progress in that direction could never begin "until there is [*sic*] force and serious purpose behind it . . . until this country keeps its plighted faith and quits entering into utterly silly peace and arbitration treaties . . . and, above all, until it prepares itself and its armed strength back of its purpose to do right." [13]

The difference between Roosevelt's and Gardner's criticisms of the League to Enforce Peace illustrated how ultranationalists could also be split between internationalists and isolationists. Others went further than Roosevelt in favoring far-reaching international commitments. In June, 1915, Lodge, who was the ex-President's closest friend and Gardner's father-in-law, originated the phrase that would one day become the hallmark of internationalism. He called for the development of a "united nations" to maintain peace and order in the world.[14] Even some of the League's founders held views that were close to Roosevelt's and Gardner's. Their original plans contemplated what Taft called "a league of the great powers of Europe with the United States." Taft lent apparent weight to Bryan's charge that the League was unwittingly imperialistic. He asserted in his address to the Philadelphia convention, ". . . we don't propose to have the constitution of our court complicated by a demand for equal representation of the many smaller nations." In the same speech he also affirmed, "We are not peace-at-any-price men, because we do not think we have reached the time when a plan based upon the complete abolition of war is practicable." [15]

The different attitudes toward the proposals of the League to Enforce Peace illuminated the divergence between idealism and ultranationalism. The basis of this divergence was subtler than it might at first appear. Roosevelt, as Robert Osgood has pointed out, could be as much of an idealist, by his own combative, muscular canons, as Wilson or Bryan.[16] Likewise, Wilson's and Bryan's statements showed that they were as thoroughgoing nationalists, albeit in a moralistic way, as Roosevelt and Gardner. The basic divergence between idealism and ultranationalism lay in attitudes toward the current system of power politics in international affairs. Among the ultranationalists, even Taft assumed the basic soundness of the system. He differed with Roosevelt and Gardner simply over timing and methods in rationalizing the system, in order to decrease conflict. Wilson and Bryan clung to the traditional tenet of American idealism that power politics, inasmuch as they were dominated by Europeans, were corrupt and unjust. Their differences were over methods of replacing that system.

This divergence between idealists and ultranationalists stemmed from underlying philosophies of personal conduct and images of man. Roosevelt and Gardner employed a kind of Darwinian model of self-reliance and physical strength, with overtones of a concern for virility.[17] Wilson and Bryan used a Protestant Christian model of self-restraint and moral strength, with allusions to the problems of sin and salvation. Ultimately, the roots of the divergence might well be traced to differing psychological attitudes toward power. These affirmations and distrust of power owed a great deal to differences in personal background. Both Roosevelt and Gardner, for example, held elevated social positions and had pivotal military experiences in early manhood. Other factors may have played a broader role in shaping political outlooks. The competing intellectual heritages of Hamiltonianism and Jeffersonianism almost certainly exercised formative influences. Perhaps most important of all may have been the respective positions of men and parties in and out of power during America's brief imperial heyday at the turn of the century.[18]

At the middle of 1915, the divergence between idealism and ultranationalism was more important and more recognizable than the division between isolationism and internationalism. Bryan emphasized his closeness to Wilson in his letter of resignation and in his reply to Roosevelt's call for increased preparedness. Similarly, Roosevelt sniffed that the only difference between Wilson and Bryan "was merely one as to the proper point of dilution of tepid milk and water." [19] Even Taft, who took practically the same stand as the President on diplomatic matters, wrote in August, "Wilson is being forced up against facts, and facts which brook no settlement by mere words. This is always an embarrassment for phrasemakers." [20] The sharpness of the division between idealists and ultranationalists would last until internationalist programs became a major political issue at the beginning of 1917. The contrast would remain so vivid in no small part because during those months the two leading critics of the League to Enforce Peace were Roosevelt and Bryan—the Rough Rider versus the Prince of Peace.

Three Isolationist Intellectuals

Three succeeding formulations of isolationist doctrines showed that Bryan's position represented a wider response to overseas involvement than merely his individual views. Two weeks after his first statement of an isolationist position, another man independently made a similar presentation. It came in an article in the *New York Times'* Sunday magazine section of July 4, 1915, entitled "Preserve U. S. from Europeanism," by Samuel P. Orth, professor of government at Cornell University. Orth's premises were that "the spirit of Europe is very different from the spirit of America" and that Europe would cease "to be a bully" only when "she is either dead or democratized." Orth believed that democracy might grow in time through the efforts of the European labor parties and liberals to whom "the American Union is an example of democratic federation, often cited, frequently praised. . . ." But he warned, "International peace will rest only upon international democracy."

Until Europe became democratized, Americans must reject all proposals for "a world balance of power, . . . which is merely a soft synonym for world bullying. . . ." It was the nation's "perfectly plain" duty to avoid all entanglements in "the hypocrisies and delusions of Europe's secret intrigues" and resist "the glitter of 'world influence.' " Furthermore, the United States must work toward creating a new spirit of co-operation in the Western Hemisphere, both "in formulating an all-American neutral zone" and in building a genuine community of nations "dedicated to the American ideal." Pan-Americanism and resistance to "the voices of sirens" from Europe, concluded Orth, furnished the right way to answer the fundamental question of the World War: "whether America shall proceed to develop her ideals of humanity and democracy in her own way as she has heretofore attempted, or whether she is to be driven into a world swirl of empires and thereby lose herself in the destructive orgies of international ambitions and hatreds." [21]

In most respects, Orth's isolationist argument resembled Bryan's. Although Orth did not respond to specific internationalist proposals, he repudiated collective security when he scorned the idea of a "world balance of power." Perhaps after the establishment of worldwide democracy the United States could join in an international peace-keeping organization.

But by then, presumably, all forceful arrangements would have become unnecessary. Orth went beyond Bryan in his pan-Americanism, although the Commoner had similarly alluded to the different spirit of the New World. Idealistic isolationists would differ over how much of the Western Hemisphere was encompassed within the ideological separation from Europe, but they agreed that American ideals were unequivocally opposed to the power politics of the Old World and demanded resolute aloofness from them.

The similarity of these two presentations illustrated how isolationist idealism could be intellectually attractive to someone with a background unlike Bryan's. The son of a Congregational minister, Orth was born in Michigan in 1873. He first became interested in politics and government while a student at Oberlin College. After brief graduate study in law and political science at the University of Michigan, he taught in Ohio for five years and earned his doctorate at Columbia University in 1903. Before joining the Cornell faculty in 1912, Orth practiced law in Cleveland, where he held the post of Assistant United States Attorney for three years during Roosevelt's second term. He also served as president of the Cleveland school board and lectured at Oberlin and at Western Reserve University.[22]

Politically, Orth started out as a Republican of moderately progressive views. In his doctoral dissertation on state government in Ohio, he sharply criticized official "inertia" and "unwillingness to depart from precedent" in dealing with burgeoning economic and social problems. Government, he wrote in 1904, "must march *pari passu* with progress," adapting itself to the new America in which "society is urban and wealth corporate." He remained a staunch Republican, tracing his party's origins back to Hamiltonian nationalism as opposed to Democratic sectionalism.[23] A real turning point in Orth's thought came in 1911 and 1912, when he traveled for several months in Europe to study socialism at first hand. Although he persisted in objecting to what he called socialism's "hordeist" philosophy, Orth drew upon his European experience to become an advanced progressive. He advocated a new "Social Democracy" which would strike "a balance between individual duty and collective energy" and thus "use the gifts of all for the benefit of all." [24]

Exposure to European thought and conditions also put Orth on the path which eventually led him to isolationism. He could not help observing a basic contrast between Europe and America, "owing to our isolation both geographical and historical. We are practically as far separated from feudalism and monarchy as the Aztecs. And the oceans have secured us that isolation which to-day is essential to our national individuality." Orth did not mean, however, that the United States was exempt from the ills of Europe, even though "we have no burdensome militarism, no hereditary tinsel. . . ." Unless Americans immediately addressed themselves to the problems of industrialism and enacted far-reaching reforms, they would inexorably continue "becoming Europeanized. Proletarian and bourgeois, lower class and middle class, capitalist class and working class, are the unwelcome words in our new political vocabulary. We are fostering a European 'remedy'—Socialism—class cleavage." [25]

Sensitivity to the ideological contrast between Europe and America formed the backdrop to Orth's isolationist conclusions. He came to view the World War as "the most colossal recrudescence of the imperial instinct of modern times," for which Germany deserved special blame. Although his mother had come from Germany, Orth condemned that country's "feudal-ocracy" in 1913, and during the war he singled out its "imperialistic idea of centralized, mechanical force" as the most important reason for the conflict.[26] Then, when the danger of involvement arose and others began to advocate joining with European nations in the enforcement of peace, Orth formulated his isolationist argument in response. He arrived at an isolationist position by combining his view of the war with his belief that reform was necessary to save America from degenerating to European conditions. Many Americans held similar opinions of the war, and other progressives had also appealed to the idea of mission as a justification for reform. Orth's espousal of an idealistic isolationist doctrine illustrated, therefore, intellectual affinities which could become important in the support for a political position.[27]

Orth himself did not become a prominent isolationist spokesman. His only other comment on foreign policy during the World War appeared after American intervention, in an article attacking "the fatal delusion that there is a distinction between the ambitions of the Kaiser and of his people." He also revealed an animus against Germany, together with undiminished progressivism and Republicanism, in the small volumes of American social history that he was writing at the same time.[28] Orth nevertheless remained faithful to his isolationist convictions. In 1921 he wrote an article in which he applauded the rejection of American membership in the League of Nations. The organization was "a European League, founded on European precedents, imbued with the European spirit of intrigue and counter-alliance, and intended to do the work of Europe's great powers screened behind the opulence and naïveté of America. . . ." Orth hailed the decision to uphold the traditional policy of "friendliness and alertness towards all, hatred and jealousy towards none," because Americans could pursue "any plan of international disarmament and international comity which appears to them to be free from greater dangers than those that are being avoided." That was Orth's last published work. Less than a year after its appearance, while on sabbatical leave from Cornell, he died in France.[29]

At the same time that Bryan and Orth were formulating their arguments, another scholar was gradually moving toward a similar idealistic isolationist doctrine. He was Ellery C. Stowell, assistant professor of international relations at Columbia University. As early as November, 1914, Stowell privately perceived "the greatest danger" in the idea of an international organization. Such a body might become, he feared, an instrument of the strongest powers "to attempt to enforce an interpretation conforming to their selfish interests," thereby "laying the foundation for a world struggle many times greater than that which we are now witnessing." During the following year, Stowell grew increasingly suspicious of "the interesting but chimerical project for world organization, such for example as the League for Judicial Settlement of International Differences." The idea could perhaps help "urge the nations along the right path; but a hastily or unwisely organized world state or police force would be like a skyscraper built on a weak foundation. It would be sure to come down and we should be fortunate if it did not involve many lives and much property in its fall." [30]

Stowell's disaffection from internationalist ideas mounted during 1916. In an article in the *Columbia University Quarterly* in June he compared "the schemers after a world state" to "the religious zealots of the Middle Ages who were so absorbed in preparation for the life hereafter that they gave no heed to the pressing needs of the world in which they lived." What particularly bothered him, he explained a few months later, was that an international organization "gives great advantage to the status quo" and would inevitably drive dissatisfied nations to resort to force.[31]

Elaborating upon that objection brought him to present his isolationist argument in an article, "A League of Nations," in the December 7, 1916, issue of the *Nation.* The plan of the League to Enforce Peace could mean only two things, Stowell insisted. If it were a cover for joining the Allies, then it would simply be a euphemism "glossing over our departure from the traditional policy of the United States of holding aloof from entangling alliances." If, however, a truly universal organization were contemplated, including the Central Powers, it would suffer from "the same disrupting political currents which are an inevitable feature of the international situation." Consequently, the League, like the Holy Alliance a century before, "would burst asunder after a few years, or would become a political machine for coercing the minority."

Instead of "advocating an impossibility," Americans should devote their attention to "needs more pressing for the advancement of civilization." They should work for "the widest possible voluntary adoption of international arbitration and mediation or conciliation," encourage public understanding of international law, and "above all" try to secure "the widest extension of publicity for governmental acts. Here is a programme certain to bring forth fruitful results. The panacea of the world state, on the contrary, is doomed to bitter disappointment." [32]

This isolationist argument differed from Bryan's and Orth's in being less explicitly nationalistic. Rather than picturing America as the righteous nation in a sinful world, Stowell offered a generalized view of international politics. Idealism was the essence of his position. He objected to internationalist programs on the grounds that they would merely institutionalize, and thus strengthen, the existing system of power politics. Replacing the system required men and nations to refrain from its practices and pursue more wholesome forms of conduct. This was another way of stating the basic question of method over which idealistic isolationists differed with their internationalist counterparts.

Stowell's previous career and earlier views on international relations further highlighted the idealism of his isolationist argument. Born in Massachusetts in 1875, Stowell was graduated from Harvard College, where he was only an average student. After working for two years in business, he took a trip around the world for the purpose of self-discovery. The journey introduced him to both his vocation and his convictions about the nature of world politics. Deciding to become a specialist in international law and relations, Stowell studied at the Universities of Berlin and Paris, receiving his doctorate from the latter in 1909. He also served in minor capacities with the American delegations to the second Hague Conference in 1908 and the London Naval Conference in 1909. Upon his return to the United States, Stowell began his academic career, teaching diplomacy and international law, first at George Washington University and later at the University of Pennsylvania, before going to Columbia in 1913.[33]

Like most members of his pioneering generation of American students of international relations, Stowell entered the field at least partly from a desire to reform world affairs. His disturbing firsthand observation of German militarism in 1903 was apparently the critical experience which, as he later explained, impelled him "to make the institution of war my study." Stowell conceived his function to be like scholarly study of the Bible, "to apply the higher criticism of science to the religion of peace." [34] The true path to peace, he declared in 1910, consisted basically of "engendering among the nations a feeling of responsibility to a common law." Its end would be reached, he further stated in 1915, when "the individuals composing the state will prevent their government from overriding the international or humanitarian ideal even for the preservation of the nation's life." These convictions made Stowell quell strong pro-Allied sympathies after the outbreak of the World War and conclude that the duty of the United States was "to write her name in history as the humanizer of war and the safeguarder of the rights of neutrals." [35]

Stowell's subsequent career and views revealed how an idealist could convert from isolationism to internationalism. After American intervention in the war, his isolationist position underwent steady erosion. Stowell's ardent support for the war as secretary of the Patriotic Service League precipitated his resignation from Columbia in 1918, in a dispute with President Nicholas Murray Butler over the right of faculty members to participate in outside public activities.[36] He then went to Washington, where he practiced international law and taught for a number of years at American University. Throughout this period, Stowell was becoming an internationalist. During the controversy of 1919 and 1920 over joining the League of Nations, he was apparently willing to accept American membership in the belief that the international organization would soon collapse of its own weight. In 1921, however, he viewed the failure to join the League as "a defect" in his countrymen's willingness to uphold and abide by international law. Ten years later he hailed the League's establishment "as the most significant event in all political history." After the 1920s, Stowell seldom spoke out on foreign policy. He eventually retired to San Francisco, where he died in 1958.[37]

The most interesting presentation of an isolationist argument came from Randolph Bourne, the hunchbacked young political and cultural radical of Greenwich Village, devotee of the "experimental life." Bourne put forward his isolationist doctrine in "Doubts about Enforcing Peace," a six-page typewritten "communication" apparently intended for some journal but never published. The date of this manuscript cannot be established exactly, but it contains allusions to remarks made by Wilson in the 1916 Presidential campaign. Contextual and circumstantial evidence also suggest that Bourne intended the paper to be a response to a *New Republic* editorial of December 9, 1916, which approved the extensive support in the United States for internationalism.[38]

Bourne found the spokesmen of the League to Enforce Peace "more realistic than the professional pacifists," but he warned that their program might bring "tremendous possibilities of peril to this country. . . ." As an "alliance of all against each," the international organization proposed by the League could plunge the United States into "wars in which we perhaps had no concern whatever. . . ." Moreover, no matter which nations were included, either the Allies alone or together with a "sobered Germany," such a league "would be little more than a mutual guarantee of the status quo. . . . Would not such a league contain the seeds of new wars? And would not such a war be like the present war, the fruit of a European system in which the United States has historically no part?" The League's plan would, in short, make American "participation in a war to enforce order in the European system be a mere Quixotic free gift of her armed power."

A safer and wiser course for the United States, contended Bourne, was to form a non-forceful "League of Neutrals." That would "prove a more powerful deterrent of a general war within the European system than a League of Nations organized on a plan which practically ensures that every war within the system would be a world-war. . . ." Establishing "international justice" should be "the issue upon which all our attention should be focused," especially on removing "the concrete injuries of the European system," like unfair boundaries which caused "irredentism" and the "imperialistic lust" of the great powers. The United States faced a momentous choice, Bourne concluded. "We can either prematurely join a League which would be a continuance of the European system. This would mean our immediate militarization and indefinite postponement of democratic reconstruction. It would mean for us a process of Japanization, in order to bring ourselves into the current of the Western world. Or we can maintain our strictly defensive armament, throw in our lot with the neutrals outside the European system, and labor to make neutrality and non-military coercion the curber and delimiter of war." [39]

This essay made the same points as the preceding idealistic isolationist arguments, but in a singularly arresting fashion. In responding to internationalist proposals, Bourne based his position on the broader philosophy of idealistic nationalism which he had been evolving for several years. Bourne's radical politics, as Christopher Lasch has pointed out, were intensely personal; they were a direct extension of his own struggles to overcome physical handicaps and the cultural and emotional barrenness of his small-town, middle-class background.[40] Nationalism played an important part in his conception of politics as a "means to life." Although Bourne was shaken by the World War, which threatened that European civilization was

appreciated their recognition that the war drew upon deep-seated human emotions that no institutional devices could easily or perhaps should entirely suppress. Yet far from agreeing with the ultranationalists, Bourne was convinced that the United States must not laud or indulge such feelings. Those emotions contained an unalterable potential for brutality, which must be directed into truly civilized channels. The description of that process as part of being "too proud to fight" was ironic. Whereas Wilson's phrase and his internationalist thinking rested upon the Christian idea of self-repression, Bourne's isolationist argument was part of his national analogue of Nietzsche's concept of self-overcoming.

This isolationist doctrine assumed a central place in Bourne's corrosive criticisms of American participation in the World War during 1917. He attacked the League to Enforce Peace again in May for advocating "international order founded on universal militarism." World politics could be reformed, he reiterated, only through such measures of "international justice" as the elimination of unfair boundaries, trade rivalries, and imperialism. Those concrete achievements "must precede the mischievous intellectualisms of a League to Enforce Peace." What was particularly pernicious in its ideas, he added in June, was that they contained "no provision for dynamic national growth or international economic justice" and thus were "reactionary" schemes which sought "to petrify and federate the nations as political and economic units." [45]

For Bourne, American belligerency verified his objections to internationalist ideas. Abroad, he asserted in July, 1917, the United States had become "a rudderless nation, to be exploited as the Allies wish, politically and materially, and towed to their aggrandizement. . . ." At home, he declared not long afterward, democracy was reeling before the onslaught of the "ideal of the State," which was "the organization of the herd offensively or defensively against another herd similarly organized." America had fallen victim to international "power politics," which consisted of nothing more than the relations between "what States infallibly and calamitously are, huge aggregations of human and industrial forces that may be hurled against each other in war." [46] After 1917, Bourne seems to have turned much of his attention away from political criticism. The shift of concern did not result from persecution, as some stories have maintained, but apparently came because he was always more deeply interested in personal and cultural matters. Women and literature formed the subjects of most of Bourne's remaining writings before his death in December, 1918.[47]

The Outlines of Idealistic Isolationism

The arguments of these three men, together with Bryan's statements, disclosed the main intellectual features of idealistic isolationism. On an obvious level, they showed that isolationist arguments could represent a legitimate intellectual position. This is an aspect of isolationism that most interpreters have slighted. Isolationist arguments have usually been explained either as rationalizations for mass emotions or as facile statements of goals tacked onto immediate policies.[48] These original presentations demonstrated that idealistic isolationist arguments could stand by themselves as interpretations of America's character and international conduct. Of these early proponents of isolationism, only Bryan was a professional politician who sought to express popular opinions, and only he had been in close touch with current diplomatic problems. The rest were removed from present controversies and were taking a long view of the situation of the United States in world affairs. Their arguments showed that isolationism would emerge in much the same manner as many political positions. It was not simply a welling up of popular desires. The isolationist position was formed as the result of mass interests being combined with independently formulated doctrines.

The identity and background of the three intellectuals certainly suggest that there was more to isolationism than popular prejudice or simple xenophobia. Orth and Stowell were widely respected scholars. Bourne possessed one of the most gifted and original, if also sometimes unfocused, minds in America. Significantly, too, all four, including Bryan, had traveled widely in Europe or in other parts of the world. Their isolationist arguments expressed respectable, even occasionally insightful ideas. Stowell and Bourne, for example, made an astute observation when they contended that an international peace-keeping organization could become the instrument of dominant, satiated powers for securing their own positions against aspirations of have-not nations. In the 1930s, the British writer E. H. Carr would use a similar point—that law and organization tend to favor nations which have already arrived—in a searching critique of internationalist ideas.[49]

Bryan alone of these men could be accused fairly of softheadedness or catering to public prejudices. Yet even he touched upon an important concept. His distinction between force and persuasion foreshadowed an argument that would be advanced for the outlawry of war during the 1920s. John Dewey then took the position that international peace could never be achieved through institutional improvements in a system based upon an ultimate resort to force; rather, reform of international affairs would have to come through the promulgation of noncoercive methods.[50] These early statements of idealistic isolationism would have distinguished intellectual progeny.

The idealism of the doctrines was indisputable. Not that idealistic isolationists were impervious to prudence or national self-interest. Even in these first formulations one could detect traces of what later became the "save America first" psychology. Regarding the European war, Bryan declared in October, 1915, that if the United States could "not yet stay the hand of blood over there, we should at least cultivate here the spirit of peace. . . ." [51] On philosophical grounds isolationist idealism contained plenty of room for accommodating national interest. The union between mission and isolation required only negative restraints on American conduct, for the sake of setting a good example. Since no positive actions were called for on behalf of international betterment, the United States could avoid actions which might be costly or dangerous.

But the ways in which these proponents advanced their arguments left no doubt of their own highmindedness. Bryan advocated various conciliation devices and tireless preaching. Orth championed pan-Americanism. Stowell presented a program for the voluntary extension of international law. Bourne favored a League of Neutrals. The necessity of the intellectual challenge of internationalism was also apparent. Interestingly, Orth and Bourne implied that their disagreements with internationalist idealism were not immutable. They held that joining an international organization would be fatal to American values only under existing conditions. Presumably, after basic international injustices had been rectified, the United States could participate in a peace-keeping league. Such an organization, however, would hardly be necessary then, since the sources of conflict among nations would have been removed. Of the other two exponents of isolationist doctrines, Stowell later became an internationalist, while Bryan eventually renounced his isolationism to take up a half-hearted advocacy of an internationalist program.[52]

Finally, these statements of the idealistic isolationist position disclosed an important source from which support would be drawn for a political position. All four men came from the liberal or progressive side of the political spectrum. Bryan was in many ways the living link between Populism and progressivism. Orth was an advanced progressive. Bourne was a philosophical radical who espoused, by turns, highly personalized forms of progressivism, socialism, and quasi-anarchism. Even Stowell, who took little interest in domestic politics, joined the Progressive party. Also, while teaching at Pennsylvania, he had participated in a reform group opposed to the Philadelphia machine which formed Penrose's power base.[53] Their coming from the progressive side of politics indicated a potential source of support for an isolationist position. It bore out the indications that had been implicit earlier in the antimilitarism of the agrarian-based progressives in Congress: that the special affinity of reformers for the idea of mission could furnish an important impetus toward idealistic isolationism.

There was nothing inexorable, however, about that affinity. The idea of mission was so well-established that it could be espoused with equal sincerity by men of almost any political persuasion. During the controversy over acquiring the Philippines at the turn of the century imperialists and anti-imperialists alike had appealed to America's mission, with men of the left and right aligned on both sides. The anti-imperialists, whose arguments had occasionally foreshadowed those of the isolationists, had included some socialists and progressives, but the most prominent of them had generally been redoubtable conservatives. Similarly, in the 1930s, both liberals and conservatives supported isolationism in much the same fashion.[54]

Philosophically, the isolationist position was unmistakably conservative. Its stated aim was the preservation of traditional ways and values against change. Veneration of the past was a principal appeal used in its favor. As a matter of fact, the isolationist doctrines were formulated exactly according to the pattern in which political theorists have contended that full-fledged conservative ideologies are formed—as defenses against the physical threat of upheaval, combined with the intellectual challenge of opposing liberal or radical ideologies.[55]

It may seem anomalous, then, that these original formulators of isolationist doctrines were all progressives. Actually, the ideology of American progressivism contained conservative elements which could easily become attuned to arguments in defense of isolation.[56] Also, Bourne's remark about the "postponement of democratic reconstruction" disclosed the situational conservatism that had begun to grip many progressives and even a number of radicals and socialists. The elections of 1914 had thrown the forces of reform in the United States clearly on the defensive, and many of their spokesmen had started to feel uneasy about preserving gains which they had already made.[57] In view of the earlier agrarian arguments that preparedness and foreign adventure distracted from pressing domestic needs, it would not be hard for progressives, in their conservative mood, to distrust international embroilments. Combined with their genuine humanitarianism and the revulsion toward the World War that they shared with most Americans, the progressives' distrust could easily impel them toward isolationist views. Thus, the first formulations of isolationist doctrines pointed toward an important source of support for a political position.

NOTES

1. *Commoner* 15 (July, 1915): 7.

2. Bryan later wrote to Daniels, "My difference with the Pres[ident] is more religious than political. His course seems to me a repudiation of all that is essential in the Christian religion as applied to international affairs." Bryan to Daniels, February 22, 1916, Josephus Daniels Papers, Library of Congress, Box 37 (hereafter cited as Daniels Papers).

3. *Commoner* 15 (July, 1915): 9.

4. John 12: 32. As might be expected, the words have a meaning in context which is rather different from Bryan's use of them. On the religious basis of Bryan's political and social thought, see Levine, *Defender of the Faith,* pp. 248–251, 274; Paul W. Glad, *The Trumpet Soundeth: William Jennings Bryan and His Democracy, 1896–1912* (Lincoln, Neb.: University of Nebraska Press, 1960), pp. 1–20, 27–29; Willard H. Smith, "William Jennings Bryan and the Social Gospel," *Journal of American History* 53 (June, 1966): 41–60.

5. See *The Public* 17 (November, 1915): 1092; Paxton C. Hibben [and C. Hartley Grattan], *The Peerless Leader: William Jennings Bryan* (New York: Farrar & Rinehart, 1929), p. 216. The difference between Bryan's views and pacifism is explored in Merle Curti, *Bryan and World Peace* (Northampton, Mass.: Smith College Studies in History, 1931), p. 183.

6. Charles E. Jefferson, *Christianity and International Peace: Six Lectures at Grinnell College . . . in February, 1915 . . .* (New York: Thomas Y. Crowell Co., 1915), pp. 146, 183–184.

7. On Bryan's nationalism, see also Levine's observations in *Defender of the Faith,* pp. 28–29, 91–92.

8. *Commoner* 15 (July, 1915): 1–2. Bryan's Biblical reference, Second Corinthians 6: 14, was somewhat more appropriate than his earlier one. The full verse reads, "Be ye not unequally yoked together with unbelievers: for what fellowship hath righteousness with unrighteousness? and what communion hath light with darkness?"

9. *Commoner* 15 (July, 1915): 2.

10. Clipping in Taft Papers, Box 313 (Gen. Corr.).

11. *Record,* 63rd Cong., 3rd sess., January 29, 1915, pp. 2688–2689.

12. Roosevelt, "Peace Insurance by Preparedness against War," *Metropolitan* 42 (August, 1915): 11–12.

13. Roosevelt to Jonathan S. Bonner, February 9, 1916, Roosevelt Papers, Letterbook 94.

14. *New York Times,* June 10, 1915; Henry Cabot Lodge, *War Addresses, 1915–1917* (Boston: Houghton Mifflin Co., 1917) pp. 23-43.

15. Taft to Mabel T. Boardman, April 9, 1915, Taft Papers, Series VIII, Letterbook 30; *League to Enforce Peace,* pp. 15–16, 19.

16. Robert E. Osgood, *Ideals and Self-Interest in America's Foreign Relations: The Great Transformation of the Twentieth Century* (Chicago: University of Chicago Press, 1953), pp. 142–143 (hereafter cited as Osgood, *Ideals and Self-Interest*).

17. See, e. g., Roosevelt's comparison of international relations to the Wild West, where every man had to pack a gun because no effective police power existed. *New York Times,* November 8, 1914.

18. See Peterson, *Jefferson Image in the American Mind* pp. 225–226, 333-343. Osgood illuminates the difference between Roosevelt and Wilson in an incisive analogy with Nietzsche's figures of the Warrior and the Priest, and their responses to the Will-to-Power in *Ideals and Self-Interest,* pp. 144–145. Harold Nicolson analyzes the "warrior or heroic" tradition in diplomatic thinking in *Diplomacy* (New York: Harcourt, Brace & Co., 1939), pp. 51–55. It is also discussed with reference to Roosevelt in the pre-World War I context in John P. Mallan, "Roosevelt, Brooks Adams, and [Homer] Lea: The Warrior Critique of the Business Civilization," *American Quarterly* 8 (Fall, 1956): 216–230, and John P. Campbell, "Taft, Roosevelt, and the Arbitration Treaties of 1911," *Journal of American History* 52 (September, 1966): 279–298. Those articles follow Nicolson in finding the basic divergence of international outlook between the "warrior" and "mercantile or shopkeeper's" traditions. Osgood's stress on attitudes toward power, however, seems to touch upon a still deeper divergence. Basic similarities between the views of Roosevelt and Taft or Elihu Root, who were unequalled exemplars of the "mercantile" tradition, suggest that Nicolson's categories have singled out what are simply differences of style, emphasis, and method within a power-affirming attitude. The thought of Wilson and Bryan, with its power-distrusting attitude, drew instead upon religion, which Nicolson considers of little influence on diplomatic thinking. See *Diplomacy,* p. 50.

19. T. Roosevelt to Owen Wister, June 23, 1915, quoted in Owen Wister, *Roosevelt: The Story of a Friendship* (New York: Macmillan Co., 1930), p. 344.

20. Taft to Gus J. Karger, August 26, 1915, Taft Papers, Series VIII, Letterbook 36. Taft did close the letter, however, "I sympathize with him in his trial, for it is a great one."

21. *New York Times,* July 4, 1915.

22. *Who's Who in America, 1914–1915* (Chicago: A. N. Marquis Co., 1915), p. 1766; Samuel P. Orth, "Our State Legislatures," *Atlantic* 94 (December, 1904): 734.

23. Orth, "Our State Legislatures," p. 737; Samuel P. Orth, *The Centralization of Administration in Ohio* (New York: Columbia University Press, 1903), pp. 13–14, 173–175; idem, *Five American Politicians:*

A Study in the Evolution of American Politics (Cleveland: World Publishing Co., 1906), pp. 13–14, 131, 174.

24. Samuel P. Orth, "What of the Individual?", *North American Review* 194 (October, 1911): 524–525; idem, *Socialism and Democracy in Europe* (New York: Henry Holt, 1913), pp. 253, 261–262, 269.

25. Samuel P. Orth, "Democracy in Europe," *North American Review* 196 (September, 1912): 406, 421; idem, "Is Socialism upon Us?", *World's Work* 24 (August, 1912): 459.

26. Samuel P. Orth, *The Imperial Impulse* (New York: Century Co., 1916), pp. iii, 14; idem, "Germany: A Model or a Warning?", *World's Work* 26 (July, 1913): 321; idem, "Germany's Destiny," *Century* 89 (November, 1914): 38.

27. On uses of the contrast to Europe as justifications for reform, see Eric F. Goldman, *Rendezvous with Destiny: A History of Modern American Reform* (New York: Alfred A. Knopf, 1952), p. 234.

28. Samuel P. Orth, "Kaiser and Volk: An Autocratic Partnership," *Century* 95 (November, 1917): 100; idem, *Our Foreigners: A Chronicle of Americans in the Making* (New Haven: Yale University Press, 1921), pp. 142–144; idem, *The Boss and the Machine: A Chronicle of Politicians and Party Organization* (New Haven: Yale University Press, 1921), pp. 15–16, 189.

29. Orth, "Presidential Leadership," *Yale Review* 10 (April, 1921): 465–466; *New York Times,* February 27, 1922.

30. Ellery C. Stowell to ———, November 25, 1914 [fragment]; Stowell to [Robert] Linscott, January 21, 1916, Ellery C. Stowell Papers, Library of Congress, Box 7a (hereafter cited as Stowell Papers).

31. Stowell, "Plans for World Organization," *Columbia University Quarterly* 18 (June, 1916): 227; Stowell to Alpheus H. Snow, November 8, 1916, Stowell Papers, Box 7a.

32. Stowell, "A League of Nations," *Nation* 103 (December 7, 1916): 536–538.

33. Stowell to John Bassett Moore, March 26, 1913, Harvard College transcript to University of Paris, August 29, 1904, Edward B. Hill to Mrs. G. L. Stowell, September 6, 1901, Stowell to James Brown Scott, December 3, 1908, February 22, 1909, Stowell Papers, Box 6; Stowell to Mrs. G. L. Stowell, May 15, 1904, ibid., Box 2.

34. Stowell to Mrs. G. L. Stowell, November 8, December 11, 1903, ibid., Box 2; Stowell to C. R. Nutter, May 5, 1913, ibid., Box 6; Stowell to Frederick A. Woods, February 10, 1916, ibid., Box 7. On the beginnings of international relations study in the United States, see William T. R. Fox, "Interwar International Relations Research: The American Experience," *World Politics* 2 (October, 1949): 69–70.

35. Stowell, "The London Naval Conference," *Independent* 66 (June 10, 1910): 1286; *The Diplomacy of the War of 1914: The Beginnings of the War* (Boston: Houghton Mifflin Co., 1915), p. 451; *New York American,* May 21, 1916.

36. *New York Times,* March 1, 2, 1918; *Columbia Spectator,* March 4, 1918, clipping in Stowell Papers, Scrapbook 1.

37. *Who's Who in America, 1924–1925* (Chicago: A. N. Marquis Co., 1925), p. 3073; George L. Stowell to E. C. Stowell, August 29 [1919 ?], Stowell Papers, Box 21; E. C. Stowell, *Intervention in International Law* (Washington: J. Byrne & Co., 1921), pp. 449–450; E. C. Stowell, *International Law: A Re-statement of Principles in Conformity with Actual Practice* (New York: Henry Holt, 1931), p. 638; *Who Was Who in America, 1951–1960* (Chicago: A. N. Marquis Co., 1960), p. 827.

38. Randolph S. Bourne, "Doubts about Enforcing Peace," Randolph Bourne Papers, Columbia University Library, Box 6 (hereafter cited as Bourne Papers); *New Republic* 9 (December 9, 1916): 138. Bourne had been an early contributor to *The New Republic* and was a friend and admirer of Lippmann, then one of the founding editors. Bourne visited with Lippmann, Harold Laski, and Felix Frankfurter (whom he called "a Jewish trinity which is the wonder of the world, at least of my world") in November, 1916. He and Lippmann may have discussed internationalist programs. See Bourne to Alyse Gregory, November 10 [1916], Bourne to Dorothy Teall, June 14, 1915, Bourne Papers, Box 1; Herbert Croly to Bourne, December 10, 16, 1914, ibid., Box 2.

39. Bourne, "Doubts about Enforcing Peace," Bourne Papers, Box 6.

40. Christopher Lasch, *The New Radicalism in America, 1889–1963: The Intellectual as a Social Type* (New York: Alfred A. Knopf, 1965), p. 81. Cf. Bourne, *Youth and Life* (Boston: Houghton Mifflin Co., 1913), pp. 291–310, 349–353.

41. Bourne to Carl Zigrosser, November 3, 1913, Bourne to Alyse Gregory, August 25, 1914, Bourne Papers, Box 1; Bourne to Elizabeth Shepley Sergeant, June 25, 1915, ibid., Box 2.

42. Bourne, "Continental Cultures," *New Republic* 1 (January 16, 1915): 16; "American Use for German Ideals," ibid., 4 (September 4, 1915): 117.

43. Bourne, "Trans-National America," *Atlantic* 118 (July, 1916): 91–92, 96.

44. There was a striking resemblance between Bourne's remarks and expressions by Roosevelt and Beveridge of envy for the European belligerents' "heroic" experiences. See, e.g., Roosevelt to Arthur Lee, September 4, 1914, in Elting E. Morison, ed., *The Letters of Theodore Roosevelt* (Cambridge, Mass.: Harvard University Press, 1954), 8: 817–818; *New York Times,* October 11, 1914; Roosevelt to Mrs. Cornelius Vanderbilt, March 30, 1915, Roosevelt Papers, Series IV-A, Box 5; Albert J. Beveridge, *What Is Back of the War* (Indianapolis: Bobbs Merrill Co., 1915), pp. 30–31, 410; Beveridge to John C. Shaffer, April 1, 8, 1915, Beveridge Papers, Box 280; *New York Times,* April 14, 1915.

45. Bourne, "International Dubieties," *Dial* 62 (May 3, 1917): 387–388; "The War and the Intellectuals," *Seven Arts* 2 (June, 1917): 139–140.

46. Bourne, "The Collapse of American Strategy," *Seven Arts* 2 (August,

1917): 424; "The State," in Carl Resek, ed., *War and the Intellectuals: Essays by Randolph S. Bourne, 1915–1919* (New York: Harper & Row, 1964), pp. 68–69.

47. On the last year of Bourne's life, see John Adam Moreau, *Randolph Bourne: Legend and Reality* (Washington: Public Affairs Press, 1966), pp. 186–203.

48. See Bibliographical Essay, pp. 241–257.

49. See E. H. Carr, *The Twenty Years' Crisis, 1919–1939: An Introduction to the Study of International Relations* (London: Macmillan, 1939), esp. pp. 104–105, 108–112.

50. See John Dewey, *Characters and Events: Popular Essays in Social and Political Philosophy* (New York: Henry Holt, 1929), 2: 663–665.

51. *Commoner* 15 (October, 1915): 2.

52. See below, pp. 160, 204–205.

53. See Stowell to Scott Nearing, April 20, 1915, Stowell Papers, Box 21.

54. See Leuchtenburg, "Progressivism and Imperialism," *Mississippi Valley Historical Review* 39 (December 1952): 486–487; Fred H. Harrington, "The Anti-Imperialist Movement in the United States, 1898–1900," *Mississippi Valley Historical Review* 22 (September, 1936): 216–220; Manfred Jonas, *Isolationism in America, 1935–1941* (Ithaca, N.Y.: Cornell University Press, 1966), pp. 16, 22, 34–35.

55. See Samuel P. Huntington, "Conservatism as an Ideology," *American Political Science Review* 51 (June, 1957): 454–473. Cf. Karl Mannheim, *Ideology and Utopia: An Introduction to the Sociology of Knowledge* (New York: Harcourt, Brace & Co., Harvest Book edition, n.d.), esp. pp. 229–230.

56. On the conservatism in the progressive ideology, see Richard Hofstadter, *The Age of Reform: From Bryan to F. D. R.* (New York: Alfred A. Knopf, 1955), esp. pp. 200–201, 213–215, and Lippmann's contemporary remarks in his *Drift and Mastery* (New York: Mitchell Kennerly, 1914), esp. p. 130.

57. For gloomy progressive assessments of the situation, see, e.g., *New Republic* 1 (November 7, 1914): 3; ibid. (January 6, 1915): 6; La Follette to Herman Ekern, November 16, 1914, Ekern Papers, Box 16; Raymond Robins to Gifford Pinchot, July 15, 1915, Raymond Robins Papers, State Historical Society of Wisconsin, Box 9. For a correspondingly cheery conservative view, see Taft to Horace Taft, November 8, 1914, Taft Papers, Box 290 (Gen. Corresp.).

3

Support for Isolationist Policies

At the same time that the first isolationist doctrines were being formulated, isolationist policies were attracting support from certain politicians. Renewed controversies over military preparedness at the end of 1915 and beginning of 1916 again disclosed an affinity for idealistic isolationism among agrarian Democrats. Some Middle Western and Western progressive Republicans also showed inclinations toward isolationist idealism in opposition to preparedness. Recurring submarine crises revealed continuing support for noninterventionist policies. This support was based upon the same complex of progressive sentiments and German-American loyalties, which was in turn linked with Middle Western feelings of impartiality. By the beginning of 1916, partisanship also began to affect the support for noninterventionist policies. Yet the coalescence of a firm and extensive isolationist position did not come until the end of 1916. Tensions with Germany relaxed in the spring of that year, so that international issues receded in immediacy and impact until after the Presidential election.

Democrats and the Preparedness Issue

By itself, Bryan's formulation of an isolationist argument suggested a potential source of support for a political position. His reason for leaving the Cabinet, he told his wife and daughter, was that "a great part of America . . . on the other side of the Alleghany Mountains" had vested a trust in him to keep the nation out of war. "By resigning I will be free to assist them in their struggle against entering this heart-breaking conflict on *either* side." [1] The substantial cult-following that Bryan retained, especially in the South and Middle West, lent some validity to his claim. Moreover, reactions of prominent Democrats to the preparedness agitation and the sinking of the *Lusitania* demonstrated the prevalence of views like the Commoner's.

Bryan had been the party's chief spokesman on foreign affairs between 1900 and 1912, and his views had left a strong imprint. According to a leading political scientist writing in February, 1915, the Democrats' record made them the party which "would hold aloof from Europe, would continue to pursue a policy of conciliation with the countries to the south of us, and would not be aggressive in matters pertaining to the Orient." The Republicans, on the other hand, "must favor an aggressive policy of interest, participation, and often interference in affairs beyond our borders and in every corner of the globe." [2]

If the Democrats had been in opposition when Bryan enunciated his isolationist arguments, many of his cohorts might have jumped to second him. But the party was in power. That circumstance constrained Democrats to support Wilson's handling of diplomatic problems, despite both their own previous views and their affection for Bryan. Rather than a chorus of approval from Democrats, the Commoner's isolationist principles gained immediate assent from only one of the party's national officeholders. That was Representative Warren Worth Bailey of Pennsylvania. Born in Indiana in 1855, Bailey was a self-educated printer and journalist who had become an early convert to Henry George's Single Tax doctrines. After serving as president of the Chicago Single Tax Club, Bailey had secured the backing of George and Cleveland mayor Tom Johnson to acquire the Johnstown, Pennsylvania, *Democrat*. As its editor and publisher, Bailey preached the Single Tax philosophy and supported Bryan's repeated Presidential bids. He similarly distinguished himself during his two terms in the House, from 1913 to 1917, as the Commoner's devoted follower and chief lieutenant on Capitol Hill.[3]

Bailey's response to the threat of intervention mirrored Bryan's. "The United States are the light of the world in this hour of darkness," he wrote to Wilson in July, 1915. "Can we afford to dim the splendor of that light by plunging the country into a situation where its identity would be lost in the murk of this awful conflict involving more than half the world?" In the fall of 1915, Bailey rejected internationalist proposals in which "the final appeal is to force." The program of the League to Enforce Peace struck him as wrong on several counts. It would "involve the making of entangling alliances with governments of the old world; . . . involve the abandonment of the Monroe doctrine; . . . drag us willy-nilly into the quarrels of our friends across the sea. . . ." Philosophically, what Bailey regarded "as incongruous is a proposition to enforce peace. . . . I do not believe that the policeman really enforces peace. We secure peace in our communities only through the growth of enlightened sentiment, the spread of the thought that gains final expression in the Golden Rule." [4]

Bailey was the only Democrat to join Bryan immediately in espousing an idealistic isolationist argument. A few of the Commoner's closest associates privately sympathized with his sentiments, but most agrarian Democrats supported Wilson despite misgivings. A former proponent of the arms embargo, Senator Sheppard of Texas, now told the President, "I am doing everything within my power to uphold our government in this critical period and I would not knowingly advocate any course that might embarrass it." Another Texan, Representative James L. Slayden, a personal friend of Bryan's and an antipreparedness stalwart, declared, "I still believe the President will maintain the dignity of the country and the rights of Americans on the sea and avoid war." [5]

Many leading Democrats who tended to share Bryan's views on foreign policy rebuked him for his actions. Representative Robert N. Page of North Carolina would later leave Congress because of his own conflicts with Wilson over the submarine issue, but at this time he considered Bryan's resignation "a great mistake." Page also thought that "by his frequent statements in justification of his act" Bryan was "making an ass of himself. . . . No American with red blood in his veins can subscribe to the ideas of Mr. Bryan at this time." The new Majority Leader in the House, Claude Kitchin, also of North Carolina, likewise expressed irritation at his old friend. Kitchin believed Bryan "too good a Democrat" to divide the party. "But," he asked, "hasn't Mr. Bryan done about enough talking?" [6] These reactions exposed the principal barrier to Democratic support for an isolationist position. Loyalty to the party in power blocked what might otherwise have been a natural political following for isolationism.

Yet isolationist idealism did accord with deep-seated convictions among Democrats. This consonance showed up strikingly in the controversy over military and naval preparedness which wracked the party from the fall of 1915 through the first months of 1916. The controversy opened when Wilson switched his stand on preparedness in the summer of 1915. The President came out for increases in the army, including a new reserve force to be called the Continental Army, and in the battleship and cruiser strength of the navy. Previous Democratic opposition to such increases, especially Wilson's own position of December, 1914, compelled him to move gingerly. The new program, he insisted, was "not for war, but only for defense. . . . The mission of America in the world is essentially a mission of peace and good will among men." [7] Yet opposition sprang up immediately. Bryan charged that the "same old gang" of reactionaries and plutocrats were using "the same old tactics" of seeking to stifle reform and reap profits through preparedness. Congressman Tavenner asserted that "war trafficking firms" were again attempting to enrich themselves by putting "the peace of 100,000,000 people . . . in jeopardy." [8]

On Capitol Hill, a nucleus of opponents formed among a group of about thirty Democratic Representatives, headed by Kitchin and Bailey. Two-thirds of these opponents came from the South, with all but one of the remainder from the Middle West and West. Only Bailey represented a Northeastern district. All were friends of Bryan and members of the agrarian progressive wing of the party. They included such men as

William C. Adamson of Georgia, Oscar Callaway of Texas, and E. Y. Webb of North Carolina, and they comprised basically the same group of Representatives that had organized before the war to press for agricultural relief legislation, stringent antitrust laws, and a variety of advanced progressive measures. Most were long-established opponents of preparedness, with Tavenner, Slayden, Page, and Samuel Witherspoon of Mississippi also among them. Evidently they represented the sentiments of their constituents, because there were reports of large antipreparedness rallies in many of their districts and the North Carolina Farmers' Union officially condemned the President's program.[9]

The antipreparedness faction in Congress lost no time in establishing ties with other opponents. Kitchin and Bailey maintained close contact with Bryan, who blasted away at Wilson's proposals in editorials and on speaking tours throughout the fall of 1915. They were also in touch with Oswald Garrison Villard, editor and publisher of the New York *Evening Post,* the most distinguished journalistic critic of preparedness. Villard launched a press campaign against the Administration's requests and acted as an informal liaison between the Congressmen and various other antipreparedness forces. Perhaps the opposition's greatest stroke of fortune was Bailey's success in securing the backing of the automobile magnate Henry Ford. In November, 1915, at the same time as his peace ship fiasco, Ford espoused the antipreparedness cause. Besides issuing several statements to the press denouncing Wilson's program, Ford contributed substantial amounts of money, particularly for newspaper and magazine advertisements.[10]

The most effective tactic of the opponents lay in attacking the President's military and naval programs in the respective

House committees. As chairman of the Ways and Means Committee, Kitchin wielded his authority over Democratic committee assignments to fill vacancies on the Military and Naval Affairs Committees with members of the antipreparedness faction. Those assignments, along with the public apathy that greeted Wilson's requests, seemed to assure success to the opposition. "Between us, confidentially," Kitchin exulted to a friend in January, 1916, "we have practically defeated his army program." Likewise, even though the navy program was less controversial and seemed destined for eventual passage, Kitchin was sure that they could "greatly modify" it, too.[11] Wilson appeared to be in deep political trouble at the beginning of 1916. "If your leadership in this matter is rejected," cautioned his secretary, Joe Tumulty, "the Democratic party may as well go out of the business of government. Our all is staked upon a successful issue in this matter." [12]

The Democratic wrangle over preparedness revealed the conflicting circumstances surrounding potential support for an isolationist position. On one side, Bryan and Bailey incorporated resistance to preparedness into their isolationist arguments. The Commoner implored Congress to save "this country from a policy of preparedness which would lower the nation's ideals, carry it down to the brute level of the pending conflict in Europe, . . . and give to our nation the swagger of the nations that put their faith in the sword." Bailey admonished, "It is precisely because America is so strong in resources, in courage, in institutions, in geographical position, that she can, before all other powers, afford to be moral and to set the example of a mighty Nation walking the paths of justice and of peace." [13]

A few other antipreparedness Congressmen also presented isolationist arguments. At the beginning of January, 1916,

Isaac Sherwood of Ohio declared, "It is now up to this Congress to decide whether all the sacred history of the past, sacred because humane and successful for over a hundred years of undisturbed peace, shall continue to endure in the purpose and hope of its founders, or whether we shall enter the devious path of world-power exploitation. Militarism and imperialism are a couplet of devious devils that will carry the American people on the down grade speedily." At the age of eighty, Sherwood was the oldest man in the House. He had served as a brigadier general in the Union Army during the Civil War and as a Republican Representative for a term in the 1870s. After converting to the cause of monetary inflation, Sherwood had become one of the more colorful members of the advanced progressive wing of the Democracy. In the same speech he denounced "that powerful group of war exploiters in Gotham who value blood-coined dollars as more vital than orderly self-government." [14]

Two days after Sherwood spoke, Representative James H. "Cyclone" Davis of Texas took a similar isolationist stand. Once a renowned Populist orator, Davis derived his nickname from a dervish-like platform manner. He denounced the "millionaire magi" who were "forming cabals to force upon the country a stupendous program of military preparedness, hoping to put in the White House a dictator to execute it." But Americans must not heed hypocritical appeals to national pride and hobgoblins of foreign invasion." Nor must they believe "that our safety lies in following the unhappy nations of Europe. . . . 'The wages of sin is death' applies to nations the same as to individuals. The nations, now drunk on blood, rioting in ruinous war, are paying the death penalty because their sins have found them out. Given over to ravenous greed with a riotous aristocracy, living in luxury and lust, ruling in rapacity, . . . they are now reaping the harvest of their sowing." [15]

Sherwood and Davis hardly qualified as the most highly regarded members of the antipreparedness faction. A more respectable statement of isolationist principles came from Representative Slayden, a courtly man who was a former president of the American Peace Society and a friend and associate of the multimillionaire philanthropist Andrew Carnegie and of Stanford University President David Starr Jordan. Slayden was also one of the original advocates of a pan-American system of friendship, arbitration, and security, an idea which the Wilson Administration had recently and somewhat halfheartedly swung around to support.[16] After lengthy meditation on Wilson's preparedness program and his policies in the submarine crisis, Slayden began "to suspect the existence of a conspiracy to force our country into a war with Germany." In March, 1916, he decried the "great and influential lobby operating about the Halls of Congress and in the press," seeking to subvert the nation's deepest values.

The conspiracy aimed not only at making Americans "reverse our traditional, nonmilitary policy and . . . build up an army and a navy to the size of those of the European kingdoms" but also at employing "our enlarged forces in Europe." Had Americans, asked Slayden, "forgotten the sound advice of George Washington that we should not meddle in the affairs of other countries; that, above all things, we should avoid entangling foreign alliances?" Apparently they had, since they did not seem to be providing the determined popular resistance through which the "enemies of peace" with their "exhaustless resources" could be thwarted. "Against them we can only array earnest, conscientious, peace-loving people.

They stand for the right, as they see it, against the majority of the newspapers and great commercial interests." [17]

These were further indications of how well idealistic isolationism accorded with established Democratic views. But there were also signs that the attractiveness of isolationist views had limitations. Bailey, Davis, Sherwood, and Slayden were the only antipreparedness Congressmen who took an explicitly isolationist position. The rest merely recited familiar contentions that large-scale armaments were unnecessary and expensive, dangerous to democracy, and detrimental to reform. Like the majority of Americans, the antipreparedness Democrats did not yet appear to believe that overseas involvement was a permanent threat against which a clearly defined ideological defense might be required. Accustomed ways of thinking, embedded in the old consensus of mission and isolation, still seemed adequate, even after the shocks of the World War.

More important, the immediate interests of the party stood in the way of Democrats' becoming isolationists. Though vociferous and committed, opposition to Wilson's program did not extend beyond the inner circle of agrarian progressives. Except for Kitchin, none of the party's Congressional leaders openly opposed the Administration. Senator John W. Kern of Indiana, the Majority Leader in the upper chamber, for example, was repelled by "the sickening twaddle of sensationalists" over preparedness, yet he supported Wilson's requests from the beginning. Similarly, Representative James Hay of Virginia, chairman of the Military Affairs Committee, stood firmly against the Continental Army plan, but otherwise he did "not see how it is possible for us to refuse to take up an administration measure upon which the President's mind seems to be made up." Congressman Dan V. Stephens of Nebraska, a friend of Bryan's, succinctly expressed the quandary of many Democrats: "The truth is I am very distressed over the Administration program. . . . I am equally distressed with the proposition of making a fight against the Administration for to do so would weaken our chances of re-election all along the line." [18]

The limitation on Democratic opposition to preparedness did not automatically improve Wilson's fortunes. Members of the antipreparedness faction held strategic places on the Military Affairs Committee, and the army program appeared to be in for long delay and deep slashes. Many Congressional Democrats preferred procrastination to the unappetizing choice between supporting preparedness and opposing the President.[19] Wilson faced a delicate task. Tumulty and Postmaster General Albert Burleson, his principal political advisors, reminded him that maintenance of his leadership required stimulating public sentiment behind his program. Still, Wilson had to reassert control without siding openly with the Republicans, who were generally stronger in support of preparedness. Also, considering Bryan's popular following and matchless talents on the hustings, the Commoner should not be entirely alienated in the approaching election.[20]

Wilson met the situation deftly. First, he demonstrated his skill as a public educator in a speaking tour of the Northeast and Middle West at the end of January, 1916. His speeches consisted of a few basic themes with variations. As his departure point, Wilson contended that the United States was caught up in international affairs whether Americans liked it or not: "We live in a world which we did not make, . . . which we can not think into a different condition from that which actually exists." The nation was, he further asserted, in a dangerous predicament: "The world is on fire and there is tinder everywhere." A measure of military preparedness was necessary, therefore, "not for war, . . . but for adequate national defense." It must be preparedness in the "American" way. Jefferson, he noted, had favored a comparable combination of an adequate navy and citizen reserve forces. Finally, Wilson invariably reaffirmed his faith in America's mission to promote peace, justice, and freedom in the world. "Without that ideal there would be nothing that would distinguish America from her predecessors in the history of nations." [21]

To some, the President appeared to be pulling wavering Democrats into line. To others, however, he seemed to be precipitating a party split. The antipreparedness group remained obdurate. Kitchin professed to find "a sub rosa sentiment here, even among the preparedness advocates, that the President was a little too war alarming in his speeches—they sounded too much like Roosevelt." Meanwhile, Bryan was dropping ominous public and private hints about opposing Wilson's renomination.[22] Then, at the beginning of February, 1916, the President made a major concession to his opponents on Capitol Hill. The principal bone of contention had always been the Continental Army plan, which raised the specter of a standing army and drew the fire of the well-organized National Guard lobby. Representative Hay told Wilson that the Military Affairs Committee would report out the Administration's program only if the Continental Army were excised. Wilson had never personally cared for either the plan or its sponsor, Secretary of War Lindley Garrison. He decided, therefore, to bow to the Committee and let Garrison resign, as he had several times threatened to do if the plan were dropped.[23]

The decision cleared the air at once. Hay assured the President of the "very great appreciation" of the Committee and of "its desire to work in harmony with you in perfecting a plan which would be of the greatest benefit to the country." The situation improved still further when Wilson appointed Newton D. Baker, a leading Democratic progressive and until recently an opponent of increased preparedness, to be Garrison's successor.[24] After February, 1916, the preparedness issue declined in importance, although Democratic opposition to large-scale armaments persisted in the House. Later, certain Republicans attempted to increase the size of the army and new battleship construction above the levels which the Military and Naval Affairs Committees had approved. Of the 216 Representatives who voted or announced against enlarging the army, 181 were Democrats, with 123 from the South and all but six of the rest from the Middle West or West. Of the 213 opposed to more battleships, 194 were Democrats, 129 from the South, forty from the Middle West, thirteen from the Northeast, and twelve from the West.[25]

Similarly, the hard core of antipreparedness Democrats remained more or less intact. In August, 1916, when the diplomatic situation had calmed and the Presidential campaign was in full swing, fifty-one Representatives voted against final passage of the naval appropriation bill—thirty-six Democrats, fourteen Republicans, and one Socialist. The Democrats were mostly the same group of Southerners and Middle Westerners who had formed the original coteries of opponents a year earlier. The only real changes—portentous ones—lay in the smallness of the vote and in the attrition of a number of Southerners who had hitherto been stalwart foes of preparedness.[26]

Republicans and the Preparedness Issue

During the preparedness controversy of 1915 and 1916, a small band of Middle Western progressive Republican Representatives once more stood with the Democratic opponents of enlarged armed forces. One of these Republican opponents presented an idealistic isolationist argument. In June, 1916, Gilbert Haugen of Iowa, who later became renowned as the author of agricultural relief measures, declared that "by clinging to our traditional policy, the great moral principle of justice to all, equality of man, . . . not by a strong standing Army or Navy," would the United States remain secure. "I believe that if we continue these great moral and political principles and refrain from 'butting in' and strictly attend to our own affairs, as we have in the past, we can conserve all the influence in the past and continue to have confidence, good will, and cooperation of all the nations of the world." [27]

The most important politician to espouse isolationist principles in opposition to increased preparedness was a Republican. It was Senator Works, the California progressive who had earlier championed the arms embargo. Works held the United States responsible for the sinking of the *Lusitania* because the Government permitted the munitions trade to continue. In June, 1915, he became the only national officeholder of either party who publicly praised Bryan's resignation.[28] By the end of 1915, the preparedness controversy brought him to the verge of formulating an isolationist argument. "The European war is forcing a sentiment that is foreign to the free institutions of our government," Works wrote in December. A combination of "army and naval officers and big business engaged in furnishing war materials" was agitating for the creation of armed forces that would destroy American democracy. Their threat could "be met only by the highest degree of patriotism on the part of level-headed people who sincerely believe in preserving the constitution and the institutions of the country in their purity, thus preserving the rights and the liberties of the people." [29]

What caused Works to take a clear-cut isolationist stand was the conjunction of internationalist proposals with the preparedness drive. On March 22, 1916, he declined an invitation to join the California branch of the League to Enforce Peace. Works scorned "the proposal to compel a nation to keep the peace by force of arms. Such an idea is entirely inconsistent with what I think a peace organization should be." Works avowed himself "as anxious—I hope—as anyone in this country to avoid war on our own part and to preserve the peace of all nations but to become a member of an organization of this kind would be entirely inconsistent with my views of the right way of going about it." [30] The next day, Works expanded upon his isolationist argument in an address to the Senate. "This Nation has lost that calm poise that should characterize a just and righteous nation," he asserted. ". . . We seem not to remember the saying of one of the Beatitudes, 'Blessed are the peacemakers for they shall be called the children of God.' "

The preparedness agitation which had warped people's thinking, charged Works, sprang from "the influence of plutocracy, wealth, big business. . . . Plutocracy and militarism are concordant and congenial evils." Together, those influences would inevitably "pervert and sooner or later destroy our free republican institutions." What America really needed "to prepare for is not war but peace. The world is just what the world thinks and what the world thinks it will do, sooner or later, be it good or bad, unless the thought is changed." World peace, therefore, could never "be accomplished by peace plans or regulations. The people of all nations must be brought to love God with all their hearts, . . . to love peace and hate war. . . . Thus will universal peace be established. It can not be established in any other way." America's duty, Works concluded, was "to pacify, soothe, and reassure the public mind, to talk peace and not war. . . . This is a time when the whole Nation as taught by Jesus of Nazareth, the man of love and peace, should join in the universal Christian prayer, 'Lead us not into temptation but deliver us from evil.' "[31]

Works's argument provided another illustration of how idealistic isolationism could be drawn from the domestic views of certain progressives. Like his earlier advocacy of the arms embargo, Works's opposition to preparedness disclosed suspicions that big business was working with ubiquitous stealth to control and corrupt American life. Earlier, in California he had often denounced the Southern Pacific Railroad and politicians who wore "the collar of the railroad without seeming irritation."[32] He explicitly linked his progressivism and isolationism in June, 1916, when he held that Americans needed "moral courage; courage to stand for what is right without regard to the consequences to one's self. . . ." They needed courage in order to resist the subtle influences and temptations of wealth at home and to promote peace and friendship abroad. "Courage such as this would establish true Americanism in our own country. Such courage on the part of all mankind would put an end to war and make courts of international conciliation and arbitration, as well as war, unnecessary."[33]

Works's isolationist idealism also stemmed from a religious

model of personal conduct. As his frequent Biblical allusions suggested, he resembled Bryan in the self-conscious religiosity of his politics. Works was an early convert to Christian Science, having joined the sect shortly after moving to California in the 1880s. He applied his religious beliefs to international affairs through the conviction, which he expressed in September, 1915, that "the only way of securing peace among nations is to regenerate the individual man and make him peaceful and just. . . . The only way that universal and eternal peace can be brought about is through this regeneration of mankind which must come through the teachings and practice of Christian Science."[34] For Works, then, idealistic isolationism was Christian Science applied to international affairs.

His isolationism likewise resembled Bryan's in being pacific but not pacifist. At the age of fifteen, Works had served as a cavalryman in the Union Army, and in the speech containing his first isolationist argument he affirmed that some wars, like the Civil War and the American Revolution, had served noble ends. But, he added, "No war is necessary or justifiable unless it be for the establishment of some great principle of right or justice or humanity." The present European conflict was merely "a war of kings against kings" in which all the participants were caught "in the grip of militarism." America's duties were to remain neutral and impartial and to stop the "nefarious trade" in munitions.[35] Works objected, in short, not to war itself, but to European wars, fought to maintain selfish, despotic power politics.

Works's argument demonstrated the potential attractiveness of isolationism to progressive Republicans. Unlike most reformers of his party, Works had displayed before the war antimilitarist, anti-imperialist attitudes like those of agrarian Democrats. But other progressive Republicans began to move in that direction after the sinking of the *Lusitania.* Several of them in the Senate besides Works joined the opposition to the preparedness program in the fall of 1915. La Follette denounced Wilson's proposals as the product of influences by "the glorious group of multimillionaires who are making such enormous profits out of the European war." Norris feared that an "epidemic" of carefully created hysteria was being used to fasten dangerous and unnecessary forces on the United States. Even Borah, who tended to favor increases, was troubled and believed, "We ought to go slow about this matter of preparedness with a little more deliberation and reflection. . . ." [36]

As a matter of fact, the sharpest resistance in the Senate to Wilson's program came from Republican progressives. These Senators displayed their opposition clearly on four critical votes in April and July, 1916. The votes involved the size of army reserve forces, new battleship construction, and passage of the naval appropriation bill. La Follette, Norris, and Asle Gronna of North Dakota aligned themselves with the agrarian Democrat Vardaman of Mississippi as consistent opponents of bigger armaments. Close behind were Works, Moses Clapp of Minnesota, and Charles Curtis of Kansas, a regular with some progressive leanings, who opposed increased preparedness on three of the four votes.[37] These votes confirmed that a trend existed among at least some progressives away from earlier Republican approval of preparedness and diplomatic assertiveness.

Nor was the change in progressive Republican attitudes confined to these outright opponents of preparedness. Borah, for example, continued to favor a large defense program, but with growing misgivings. He avowed in May, 1916, that he did not want to feed the spirit of "arbitrary power." Uneasiness was evident even among third-party Progressives who had bolted with Roosevelt in 1912. As the Colonel's devoted admirers, most Progressives seem to have originally shared his fondness for preparedness. In August, 1915, however, Representative William Kent of California confided to Gifford Pinchot, "T. R. is, to my mind, talking too much like a war Lord to suit my taste." William Allen White told Roosevelt in August, 1916, that he believed the world mad. "With the street full of lunatics armed, it would seem to [*sic*] the common sense part to play for a sane man . . . not to get out into the street and court trouble."[38] These doubts were part of a general revulsion toward the zestful national assertiveness and rather lighthearted social Darwinist notions about international conflict which had been popular especially during Roosevelt's Presidency.[39]

But the loss of imperialistic innocence could lead to internationalist as well as isolationist conclusions. Norris offered an amendment to the Navy bill calling for the postponement of new naval construction and authorizing the President to seek "the establishment of an international court by an agreement between the leading nations of the world. . . ." The tribunal would be empowered, Norris added, to enforce its decisions with an international navy. "Isolation is no longer possible with any nation," argued another antipreparedness Republican, Representative David Hollingsworth of Ohio. "America, world-renowned for the justness of its conceptions, has outgrown any fear of foreign entanglements. The simplicity and ideals of the Washington era are impossible in the twentieth century; the world must be recognized as a friendly field of common endeavor for all nations, all creeds, and all conditions of mankind." Quoting several statements endorsing the program of the League to Enforce Peace, Hollingsworth called them "words of wisdom, and, like the shots fired at Lexington and Concord, destined to be heard around the world." [40]

A kind of working agreement among idealists of isolationist and internationalist leanings was revealed when the anti-preparedness faction in the House attached an amendment to the Navy bill in May, 1916. This amendment authorized American participation in international conferences on disarmament and judicial settlement of disputes. Its author, Walter Hensley of Missouri, an old-line opponent of preparedness, explained, "We settle differences between men; we have a mechanism whereby disputes between individuals are settled. Why can there not be some sort of machinery whereby disputed international questions may be submitted for settlement?" Kitchin viewed the insertion of the Hensley amendment as his group's signal achievement. It was, he wrote to Villard, "a great moral step toward peace, and strengthens the bill wonderfully, in my judgment." [41]

Interestingly, one opponent of preparedness even switched from an isolationist to an internationalist position during 1916. By November, Representative Slayden found that he had nearly become convinced that he must join the League to Enforce Peace. "I begin to fear that there may be no other method of keeping the peace. . . ." [42] The preparedness controversy caused few idealists to choose irrevocably between internationalism and isolationism. The question of overseas involvement had not yet become the overriding political issue.

Anti-Interventionist Responses to the Submarine Crisis

The submarine crisis with Germany stretched into the spring of 1916, with cycles of relaxing and tightening tensions. At first, during the summer of 1915, Wilson's efforts to preserve peace with honor appeared to satisfy popular desires. His extraction of an ambiguous pledge from the Germans not to sink passenger liners without warning brought an outpouring of public gratitude. Villard, for example, broke a century-old policy to publish Wilson's picture on the front page of the *Evening Post,* with the caption, "THIS IS THE MAN Who . . . won for Civilization THE GREATEST DIPLOMATIC VICTORY OF GENERATIONS." A Western Republican leader informed the party's national chairman that "President Wilson's over-seas policy is approved by the American people generally, except for those of German decent [*sic*]." Secretary Daniels reported to Wilson that on a trip to New England he heard praise everywhere for "your tempered firmness." [43]

The honeymoon did not last long. In the fall of 1915, the Austrian ambassador and the German military and naval attachés were expelled from the country after disclosures of their complicity in efforts to promote sabotage and strikes at munitions factories. Then the Italian liner *Ancona* was sunk by a submarine which was apparently Austrian but actually German, with a loss of twenty-seven American lives. Changes in attitudes quickly became evident. The British ambassador delightedly wrote to London at the beginning of December, "The continued publications as to German plots and German outrages have gradually aroused public opinion and the excitement seems to be growing." Colonel House likewise warned Wilson that public restiveness would make it "increasingly difficult to refrain from drastic action." [44]

The strongest pressures for action pointed, however, in an anti-interventionist direction. Immediately after Congress convened in December, several Democrats resurrected suggestions to warn citizens against travel on belligerent merchant vessels. Senator Stone, the chairman of the Foreign Relations Committee, notified the President in December that several of his colleagues were "quite seriously disturbed" over the diplomatic situation. "I feel obligated to say that the situation in the Senate as I see it is not reassuring." The disquiet broke through to the surface on January 5, 1916. At an anxious moment in the renewed submarine crisis, Thomas P. Gore, the blind Senator from Oklahoma, introduced a resolution to prohibit passports from being issued for travel on belligerent ships. "No single citizen," affirmed Gore, "should be allowed to run the risk of drenching this nation in blood merely in order that he may travel upon a belligerent rather than upon a neutral vessel." [45]

Gore's resolution touched off a brief but spirited debate. Four Senators—Works, Wesley Jones of Washington, a progressive Republican; Robert Owen, Gore's Oklahoma colleague; and James A. O'Gorman of New York, a Tammany Democrat on the outs with Wilson—seconded the proposal to prohibit travel on belligerent ships. Jones declared that a citizen who voyaged on one of those vessels was "utterly lacking in patriotism and wholly regardless of the rights of humanity." As such, he was "entitled to no consideration whatever, and for this country to become embroiled in this trouble on his account would be a colossal crime against humanity." Four other Senators—Lodge, Borah, James A. Reed of Missouri, a Democrat, and Knute Nelson of Minnesota, a progressive Republican—condemned the resolution as both an abridgment of American rights and a diminution of international law. Finally, by insisting upon the regular order of Senate business, Stone shut off the debate, adding that it had offered a "way of feeling out and getting some index of the sentiment of the Senate. . . ." [46]

That debate furnished another sign of potential support for an isolationist position. Two proponents of prohibiting travel on belligerent ships, Owen and Gore, were agrarian progressive Democrats; Gore was also an ex-Populist. Two others, Jones and Works, were progressive Republicans. O'Gorman was an exception. Works's remarks showed how arguments against travel could stem from the larger complex of attitudes that included idealistic isolationism. Works linked his advocacy of this prohibition on travel to stopping the arms trade, once more finding the United States at fault in the sinking of the *Lusitania*. "We did not come to the question in dealing with a foreign nation with clean hands"; rather, by supplying munitions to one side, "we are hypocritical in claiming that we are neutral." [47]

Further indications of attitudes that might contribute to a support for an isolationist position came when several Senators revived the arms embargo scheme at the end of January, 1916. "The jingle of the bloody dollar," avowed William S. Kenyon of Iowa, a Republican progressive, "can not drown the sound of the groans and cries of misery arising from the battle fields of Europe. International law may permit it [the arms trade]; moral law condemns it." Moses Clapp of Minnesota agreed that America was wrong to supply the "instrumentalities with which to make more widows and orphans." James A. Martine of New Jersey, a Democrat close to Bryan, declared that he would "not aid my brother in the slaughter of his fellow man." Henry Ashurst, an agrarian Democrat, wanted the United States to be "the great Sanhedrim of the world— stainless and pure, able truthfully to look all the other nations in the face and say, 'We have not contributed in any way to the perpetuation or the prolongation of your gigantic strife.' " La Follette reasserted his conviction "that history will hold us accountable for our contribution to the general holocaust. . . ." [48]

Behind all these utterances lay the traditional beliefs in American purity and mission to make the world better and more peaceful. These beliefs were coupled with the conviction of progressives that big business was corrupting and destroying basic national values. Kenyon's remark about "the bloody dollar" echoed earlier expressions in support of the arms embargo. An affinity between those beliefs and idealistic isolationism was also plain. Works's subsequent expression of an isolationist position in March, 1916, covered the gamut of these attitudes revolving around the idea of mission. Similarly, Slayden's idealistic isolationist argument derived from the interplay of his antipreparedness views with his support for keeping citizens off ships of warring nations.[49] These debates at the beginning of 1916 illuminated a set of attitudes shared by agrarian Democrats and progressive Republicans, which could lead to support for isolationism.

But few enunciations of clear-cut isolationist arguments actually occurred. Except for the statements by Works and the antipreparedness Democrats, the only formulation of an isolationist doctrine came from Senator Porter J. McCumber, Republican of North Dakota. A quiet, studious man, McCumber was one of his party's financial experts. He was a regular who had avoided the insurgency which had smitten so many of his Middle Western and Western colleagues. But

McCumber sponsored and worked for many progressive measures, particularly the Pure Food and Drug Act, and he was re-elected in 1916 with the tacit approval of North Dakota's Non-Partisan League. McCumber also arrived at an isolationist position by thinking about the travel prohibition in connection with preparedness, which he supported with qualms. What worried him especially, he said in March, 1916, was the "press-created sentiment" that was attempting to excite people and "force upon the country a military and a naval program that would outrival and make insignificant the armaments and militarism of the Old World."

In McCumber's view, the oceans and the exhaustion of the European nations both amply protected the United States. Only aggressive purposes could justify current policies, such as large-scale preparedness or extreme tenacity in asserting the right to travel on belligerent vessels. Americans seemed to be trying to compel "the fighting nations by a show of our teeth to accede to our view as to what commercial rights may be to our financial interests to insist upon, no matter though the insistence upon such rights would sound the death knell of such other nation." Huge armies and navies, apart from their uselessness, would create "a non-producing official aristocracy" and insure the curtailment of freedom. "Americanism and militarism cannot walk hand in hand." In sum, warned McCumber, "We are in danger of sacrificing our ancient policy of aggrandizement in the arts of peace, a policy which our splendid isolation makes possible—we are in danger of surrendering that for the aggrandizement of military prowess. It is the vanity of power gaining mastery over the just pride of a higher, better, and more humane enlightenment." [50]

The outcome of the Congressional debates over travel on belligerent vessels supplied additional signs of political interests and popular feelings that could contribute to an isolationist position. Panic broke out on Capitol Hill on February 23, 1916, when word was leaked that the Administration had withdrawn its "modus vivendi" proposal to Germany. The "modus vivendi" was an ill-considered move conceived by Secretary of State Robert Lansing, who suggested that German modification of submarine warfare be traded for Allied disarmament of merchant vessels. The proposal was being withdrawn to aid Colonel House's secret mediation efforts in Europe. Most Congressmen and Senators, however, knew nothing of the diplomatic background. To them, the Administration appeared to be scuttling a promising overture and risking war over a small point. Loud demands arose for passage of the Gore resolution and a similar measure introduced in the House by Jeff McLemore, Democrat of Texas.[51]

Wilson easily quelled this Congressional revolt. First, in a public letter to Senator Stone he upheld his strict construction of the right of Americans to travel on merchant ships of all nations. He also pledged "that I shall do everything in my power to keep the United States out of war." Then, taking the offensive, he demanded immediate votes on the Gore and McLemore resolutions, as expressions of confidence in his policies. At the same time, he met privately with Congressional leaders to assure them that they would be consulted before any steps were taken toward a diplomatic break with Germany. Finally, on March 2, Wilson sent Burleson and Secretary of the Treasury William Gibbs McAdoo to the Capitol. They carried with them to show to House and Senate Democrats a handwritten Presidential note requesting "an early vote" in order "to clear up the existing situation and relieve the present embarrassment of the Administration in dealing with the foreign relations of the country." [52] Both Houses swiftly complied. The Senate tabled the Gore resolution on March 3, after a confusing series of moves, by a vote of 68 to 14. The House tabled the McLemore resolution on March 7, by a margin of 276 to 142.[53]

These votes indicated several potential sources of support for an isolationist position. The most striking features were the pronounced partisan and sectional alignments. Of the fourteen Senators who opposed tabling the Gore resolution, twelve were Republicans. Only two Democrats, O'Gorman and George Chamberlain of Oregon, joined them. Other advocates of the resolution voted to table it. These included Gore himself, Vardaman, Owen, Stone, and James Clarke of Arkansas. The vote partly reflected the confusion caused by Gore's last-minute amendment, striking out a critical "not," to make the resolution declare that submarine attacks "*would* constitute a just and sufficient cause of war between the United States and the German Empire." Clarke complained that few Senators knew what they were voting for or against. But party loyalty offered the more important reason behind Democrats' failure to support the resolution. Stone, for example, admitted that he was bowing to the need "to bring the Congress with practical unanimity to the support of the President in the conduct of the diplomatic questions involved." [54]

The Republican Senators who voted against tabling the Gore resolution came for the most part from the same group of progressives who supported the arms embargo and cooled toward preparedness. They included La Follette, Norris, Works, Cummins, Clapp, McCumber, and Gronna.[55] Seven of the opponents of tabling were from the Middle West, representing North Dakota, Wisconsin, Minnesota, Illinois, Iowa, and Nebraska. Large German-American populations in several of those states may have influenced their votes. Yet none of these Senators expressed any sympathies for the Central Powers. This vote suggested once again that progressive Republicans might form an important isolationist following. Unlike their Democratic counterparts, they were not restrained by party commitments. For some, German-American constituencies may have supplied additional pressures to follow an ideological inclination toward isolationism.

The House vote on the McLemore resolution revealed these partisan and sectional characteristics even more strikingly. Of the 142 Representatives who voted and the two who announced against tabling the resolution, 104 Republicans were joined by thirty-four Democrats, five Progressives, and one Socialist. Democrats like Kitchin, Webb, Sherwood, and Page, who either publicly or privately favored keeping Americans off belligerent ships, voted for tabling. As in the Senate, their votes partially reflected the immediate situation. The rules adopted forbade any amendments to the poorly drafted, offensively worded McLemore resolution.[56] Again, however, party loyalty exercised the strongest influence over Democrats. Representative Page expressed the predicament of many when he announced that he was retiring from Congress in order to avoid further conflicts between following his judgment and backing the President. Cyrus Cline of Indiana asserted that he wanted to bar travel on belligerent ships, but "the question presented in this context is whether we shall stand by the President in this crisis or not. That is the issue for us to settle, and not whether we want war or whether we do not want war." [57]

The behavior of Democratic Representatives toward the McLemore resolution further exposed the limitations on their attraction to isolationism. By the same token, Republicans confirmed earlier indications of its attractiveness to members of their party. This was as great an embarrassment to some Republicans as the Democrats' behavior was to Bryan, who had rushed to Washington to rally them behind the resolutions. Before the vote on the McLemore resolution, such militant nationalists as Gardner, Lodge, and Stimson had appeared to speak for the Republican party. Roosevelt was talking about returning to the fold to mount a "heroic" campaign against what he considered perfidious, weak-kneed diplomacy. Elihu Root agreed in February, 1916, to be boomed for the Presidential nomination, in order to assure the party's commitment to a strong foreign policy. Now, however, more than half the Republicans in the House had voted against tabling the McLemore resolution, while well over three-quarters of the Democrats voted the other way. For the first time, as some commentators noticed, the two parties had reversed their accustomed postures toward overseas involvement.[58]

The division in Republican ranks was partly ideological and conspicuously sectional. A large number of those who voted against tabling belonged to the progressive wing of the party. They included Charles Lindbergh of Minnesota, Haugen of Iowa, and La Follette's lieutenants from Wisconsin, as well as his cousin William R. La Follette of Washington. Likewise, five of the six Progressives backed the resolution and voted against tabling. On the other side, many of the Republicans who supported tabling were conservatives from the Northeast. But the division was far from perfectly ideological. Such stout conservatives as James R. Mann of Illinois, the Republican leader in the House, Nicholas Longworth of Ohio, and that old party warhorse Joseph G. Cannon, also of Illinois, voted against tabling.

More striking was the sectional nature of the Republican split. Sixty-three of the 104 Republicans voting against tabling were from the Middle West, whereas 67 of the 94 who took the opposite side were from the Northeast. The Middle Western vote against tabling included solid Congressional delegations from Wisconsin, Iowa, Minnesota, Nebraska, and North Dakota. In Nebraska, Wisconsin, and, to a lesser degree, in Iowa and in certain Missouri and Illinois districts, the vote against tabling reflected powerful German-American constituencies. In Minnesota and North Dakota, however, Scandinavian-Americans were the strongest ethnic group. Some prominent Scandinavian-Americans were pro-German, but the most important Swedish-language journal, *Svenska Amerikanaren* of Chicago, strongly favored the Allies, as did Norwegian-born Senator Nelson of Minnesota.[59]

No single factor accounted for the Middle Western preponderance. German-American influences certainly contributed. Yet from Michigan, which also had strong German communities, only one of thirteen Republican Congressmen voted against tabling. This Middle Western position can probably best be explained by a combination of factors. Partisanship, at least to the extent that Republicans were not bound to back the Administration, was linked with some ethnic loyalties and with progressives' predispositions to idealize America and distrust the workings of big business. Several journalistic observers at the time noted that Middle Western feelings of detachment from the World War reflected something in the region's culture, a kind of idealistic self-satisfaction.[60] Certainly, such feelings were not peculiar to the Middle West. Heretofore, the South had provided the greatest resistance to potential overseas involvement. What was peculiar to the Middle West, however, was a conjunction of circumstances best suited to give those feelings political expression.

At the beginning of 1916, there were also further illustrations that idealists had not yet split into firmly established camps of isolationists and internationalists. Senator McCumber reversed himself in April, just a month after delivering his isolationist argument. The World War, McCumber now said, had moved men to ask "why nations, which are but collections of individuals, should not abide by the same code of morals in their international relations that they by law enforce upon their citizens in their individual relations." The difference lay in enforcement. "Every individual, in order to secure protection, is compelled to surrender a moiety of his sovereignty; but in that security he is able to achieve a thousandfold more than would be possible without the surrender and the corresponding security. What is true of the individual is equally true of the nation."

McCumber urged, therefore, that "the nations of the world unite to form an international compact, signed by every great nation of the world, prescribing the rights, duties, and obligations of nations, endowing a court for the settlement of every international question, and the enforcement of the decrees of the court by the combined power of all nations against the offending one." The United States could easily "afford to surrender that little moiety of our sovereignty which would be required to bring us into the family of law-abiding, law-enforcing, right-living nations of the world." This speech marked the beginning of McCumber's career as one of the most steadfast internationalists of his party. In the postwar controversy over joining the League of Nations, he would become the only Republican Senator to vote for membership without reservations.[61]

Interestingly, another Middle Western Republican critic of preparedness and opponent of travel on belligerent vessels moved in the opposite direction. In March, 1916, Representative Philip Campbell of Kansas declared that the world needed to "establish international justice, insure international tranquility, provide national security and promote the general welfare under an international federation and constitution, and I fear that these ends cannot be accomplished in any other way." Yet after the war Campbell became a strident opponent of entering the League of Nations, which he viewed as an instrument of Britain and France for gaining "dominion and control over smaller and weaker nations" through which the United States would be made to share "the burden of policing Europe and maintaining the boundaries of their nations. . . ." [62]

As in the preparedness controversy, Wilson's presentation of a firm front while making an important concession during the armed ships revolt defused an explosive issue. In April, 1916, he finally pushed the submarine crisis to a climax when, after the attack on the Channel steamer *Sussex,* he threatened to break relations with Germany. No Congressional uprising accompanied his action, and the Germans' sullen pledge at the beginning of May to comply with American demands brought the long crisis to a temporary close.

The Campaign of 1916

The seven months that followed the *Sussex* pledge were, in Colonel House's words, "a lull in foreign affairs." The threat of embroilment in the World War had apparently abated, and the main diplomatic difficulties concerned British trade restrictions.[63] The chief political preoccupation in the United States was the Presidential campaign. Only a few men enunciated isolationist arguments during these months, and there was little indication of support for isolationist policies.

One important step toward making overseas involvement a major issue came when Wilson openly stated an internationalist argument. Speaking to the League to Enforce Peace on May 27, 1916, he affirmed "that the peace of the world must henceforth depend upon a new and more wholesome diplomacy." Nations must reach "some sort of agreement as to what they hold to be fundamental to their common interest, and as to some feasible method of acting in concert when any nation or group of nations seeks to disturb those fundamental things." For such fundamentals, Wilson suggested four propositions that he would later incorporate into the Fourteen Points: self-determination, freedom from aggression, territorial integrity, and freedom of the seas. Though declining to discuss specific plans for an international organization, Wilson did insist that soon "some common force will be brought into existence which shall safeguard right as the first and most fundamental interest of all peoples and all governments, when coercion shall be summoned not to the service of political ambition or selfish hostility, but to the service of a common order, a common justice, and a common peace." [64]

The speech appeared to offer a direct challenge to Bryan. Just nine days before, the Commoner had reiterated his isolationist arguments to the Lake Mohonk Conference on International Organization. Stressing the necessity for avoiding power politics and furnishing a righteous example, Bryan had dismissed internationalist proposals with the gibe, "I prefer to have this nation a moral power in the world rather than a policeman." Two of Bryan's friends in the Senate answered the President's speech with isolationist arguments. "I still believe in the policy of no entangling alliances," protested Gore. "I believe our policy of isolation is our best security." Ashurst agreed that America should never contract "any sort of alliances with any country for any reason. It is a dangerous thing, and the admonition of Washington should be religiously followed. The European war, with all its horrors, should serve as a warning of the penalty of alliances." By contrast, two Republican Senators commended the President. Curtis of Kansas, an opponent of preparedness, declared that Wilson's suggestion was not "at all entangling in the sense meant by Washington." Warren Harding of Ohio welcomed "such an alliance as proposed by President Wilson. Peace is an aim commendable enough to justify almost any kind of arrangement with other powers." [65]

Actually, Wilson had not meant to challenge Bryan and his friends. He squelched plans for a Congressional resolution endorsing his position. He believed, he explained to Taft, that "it was most unwise to give those opposed to the principle and [*sic*] opportunity to enlarge upon their objections now." Wilson also highlighted the common assumptions held by idealistic internationalists and isolationists. In attempting to disarm his critics, he asserted on May 30, "I shall never myself consent to an entangling alliance, but I would gladly assent to a disentangling alliance—an alliance which would disentangle the peoples of the world from those combinations in which they seek their own separate and private interests and unite the people of the world to preserve the peace of the world upon a basis of common right and justice." [66]

The Democratic convention of 1916 offered a vivid illustration of the party's divided mind on international affairs. A strong isolationist statement appeared in the keynote address by former Governor Martin Glynn of New York. America was, Glynn declared, "constrained by the traditions of its past, by the logic of its present, and by the promise of its future to hold itself apart from the European warfare." No policy in history had ever "justified itself so completely and entirely as the American policy of neutrality and isolation. . . . It has freed us from the paralyzing touch of Europe's balance of power, leaving to Europe the things that are Europe's and preserving to America the independence, the peace, and the happiness that now are hers." As to proposals for "the reversal of our traditional policy," Glynn concluded, they "would make the United States the policeman of the world." That role Rome, Portugal, and Spain "tried and went down, and the United States proposes to profit by the experience of the ages and avoid ambitions whose reward is sorrow and whose crown is death." [67]

Yet the same delegates who wildly applauded Glynn's speech also renominated Wilson by acclamation and unanimously adopted a platform with a plank written by the President that pledged American membership in an international peace-keeping organization.[68] Rather than schizophrenia, the Democrats were demonstrating that mounting a vigorous, unified campaign was more important to them than arguing about what as yet seemed only academic disagreements over ways of pursuing the nation's idealistic destiny. Literally weeping with joy, Bryan called the convention a "love feast" and declared that Democrats would disregard past differences in their drive to reelect the man who had enacted so much progressive legislation and kept the nation out of war.[69]

The Republicans had comparable disagreements to submerge in their campaign to repossess the White House. By chance, a sort of bipartisanship existed between the Presidential candidates on internationalist proposals. In his acceptance speech of July 31, 1916, the Republican nominee,

Charles Evans Hughes, endorsed the "development of international organization" behind which "there must be the preventive power of a common purpose." Hughes likewise affirmed that "there is no national isolation in the world of the Twentieth Century. If at the end of the present war the nations are ready to undertake practicable measures in the common interest in order to secure international justice, we cannot fail to recognize our international duty." [70]

Other Republicans disagreed. In response to Wilson's address before the League to Enforce Peace, Congressman Gardner had reasserted his ultranationalist isolationist position. Did Americans, he asked, really want an organization with enforcement powers to judge the Monroe Doctrine or possession of the Philippines? After all, such a body "must settle questions which men fight about, not questions which men only argue about." Similarly, the New York *Tribune,* a Republican paper, had uttered almost the only criticism in the press of the President's internationalist ideas. It dismissed them as "only another flagrant illustration of Mr. Wilson's instability as a statesman, his fluid sentimentalism, his servitude to winged phrases." [71]

The needs of both parties for a semblance of unity in their campaigns effectively ruled out nearly all isolationist expressions. Bryan never mentioned his differences with Wilson. He dwelled instead, to an extent, on peace and more on progressivism, prohibition, and woman suffrage.[72] Works ignored both candidates' endorsement of internationalist ideas and focused his opposition on Wilson's "despotic assumption of unconstitutional power" in domestic affairs. Virtually the only attack on internationalist proposals during the 1916 campaign came from Beveridge. Like most of the top-ranking Progressives, Beveridge supported Hughes. He attacked Wilson's internationalist ideas in a speech in Chicago on October 5, 1916. Beveridge observed that the "wisest and most constructive mind of his time, the great Chief Justice John Marshall, avowed time and time again that this nation ought not to make an alliance 'with any nation on earth,' even to avoid war and to insure the safety of the country." Beveridge was no idealist. He had long regarded what he considered the efficiency and wholesome sacrifices of the nations at war with scarcely disguised envy, and in this speech he admonished Americans to build "a broader, deeper, stronger nationalism" to match Europe's "mutual spirit born of that titanic struggle." [73]

The paucity of isolationist utterances during the 1916 campaign also reflected a more general confusion surrounding foreign policy issues. On the surface, militant Republicanism seemed to contrast vividly with pacific Democracy. The major supporting actors, who sometimes eclipsed the candidates themselves, were Roosevelt and Bryan. In substance, however, differences were far from clear. Most of Hughes's talk about diplomatic firmness referred to Mexico rather than the European conflict, while his friendliness toward the "hyphenated loyalties" of Irish- and German-Americans mortified his pro-Allied supporters among patrician Eastern Republicans. Conversely, Wilson stood for peace but stingingly invoked "Americanism" against "disloyal" criticisms from the spokesmen to whom Hughes appealed. By election day the two seemed to William Allen White "a cambric tea candidate as against a kind of a skimmed milk candidate." Westerners voted for Wilson, agreed California's Governor Hiram Johnson, after concluding "that there was little difference between them" and accepting "the one with whom they were familiar, rather than the one of like sort, who might be worse." [74]

The influence of foreign policy on the outcome of the 1916 election was ambiguous. Even the groups in the electorate that should have been most sensitive to war-related issues apparently were not. Nearly all German-American leaders vociferously supported Hughes, but the populace voted in much the same manner as other Americans. Wilson carried such German-American strongholds as Milwaukee, Hoboken, and St. Louis. Likewise, according to a recent study, Irish-American voters went strongly for Wilson because of their concerns at home, with little regard for foreign policy.[75] A number of left-wing antimilitarists also considered domestic issues more important. Amos Pinchot, Gifford's more radical Progressive brother and a founder of the American Union against Militarism, supported Wilson, not because "he has kept us out of war," but because "the Republican party is just what it has always been—the tool of organized wealth." The Socialist John Reed voted for the President "as considerably the lesser of two evils" because "the forces of deadly reaction were behind Hughes." [76] With such people evidently so little concerned about foreign policy, it was hardly surprising that isolationist arguments played no great part in the 1916 campaign.

Only after the election was over did a significant expression of isolationist principles occur in connection with the campaign. At a banquet given in his honor on December 6 by the Democratic National Committee, Bryan again attempted to impose his policies on the party. The Commoner called for a constitutional amendment to "submit every declaration of war to a referendum of the people, except in case of *actual invasion of the country*." Americans must also spurn all thoughts of "our being an international policeman!" Instead of "stepping down" to the level of other nations, the United States "should lift them up to a higher level. . . . There is only one way to lift, and that is the way that is given to us by the author of our religion—'And I, if I be lifted up will *draw* all men unto me.' (Applause.) It is the drawing power of example." Thus would America persuade, but never compel, others to be righteous and peaceful. "The principles of a real democracy, put into practice in a republic, will be more potent for peace than all the armies we could send across the Atlantic, more than all the warships we could build." [77]

Bryan's statement exemplified how an isolationist position had not achieved real political importance. The Commoner remained the single political figure of the first rank who had taken a clear-cut isolationist stand. As yet, no national magazines or large metropolitan newspapers had expressed isolationist arguments. A survey of 763 newspapers in November, 1916, by the League to Enforce Peace found that only a fifth of them had formed any opinion of its program—129 in favor and 38 critical or opposed.[78] Yet at the time that Bryan spoke, events were moving toward the juncture at which the question of overseas involvement would be thrust into the center of American politics. This would occasion the forging of an extensive isolationist position.

NOTES

1. Grace Bryan Hargreaves manuscript biography, Bryan Papers, LC, Box 65.

2. E. F. Robinson, "A Future for the Democratic Party," *New Republic* 27 (February 13, 1915): 47. On Bryan's leadership among Democrats in foreign affairs before 1912, see Glad, *The Trumpet Soundeth*, pp. 79–80.

3. For biographical information on Bailey, see Warren Worth Bailey Papers, Princeton University Library (hereafter cited as Bailey Papers); also, *Who's Who in America, 1914–1915,* p. 92, and *Official Congressional Directory, 63rd Congress, 3rd Session* (Washington: Government Printing Office, 1914), p. 98. See also Charles Barker, *Henry George* (New York: Oxford University Press, 1955), pp. 521, 623.

4. Bailey to Wilson, July 12, 1915, Wilson Papers, Series II, Box 122; Bailey to William H. Short, November 5, 11, 1915, Bailey Papers. Cf. Bailey to Alton B. Parker, October 14, 1915, ibid.

5. Morris Sheppard to Wilson, July 22, 1915, Wilson Papers, Series II, Box 122; Slayden statement, *New York Times,* July 24, 1915. For private approval of Bryan's resignation, see James A. O'Gorman to Bryan, June 8, 1915, and James K. Vardaman to Bryan, June 9, 1915, Bryan Papers, LC, Box 30; William J. Stone to William G. McAdoo, June 10, 1915, Wilson Papers, Series II, Box 121; Henry F. Ashurst diary entry, June 11, 1915, in George F. Sparks, ed., *A Many-Colored Toga: The Diary of Henry Fountain Ashurst* (Tucson, Ariz.: University of Arizona Press, 1962), p. 40 (hereafter cited as Sparks, *Ashurst Diary*).

6. Robert N. Page to Edwin Y. Webb, June 14, 1915, Edwin Y. Webb Papers, Southern Historical Collection, University of North Carolina Library, Chapel Hill, Box 9 (hereafter cited as Webb Papers); *New York Times,* July 26, 1915.

7. Address of November 14, 1915, *Wilson Public Papers,* 3:386. See also *New York Times,* July 24, 1915; Joe Tumulty to Wilson, August 9, 1915, Wilson Papers, Series II, Box 123; Gus J. Karger to Taft, July 27, 1915, Taft Papers, Box 316 (Gen. Corr.).

8. *Commoner,* 15 (July, 1915): 3; *La Follette's Magazine* 7 (August, 1915): 5.

9. See Samuel A. Witherspoon to Kitchin, October 6, 1915, Claude Kitchin Papers, Southern Historical Collection, University of North Carolina Library, Box 3 (hereafter cited as Kitchin Papers); Bailey to Kitchin, October 9, 1915, Bailey to O. G. Villard, November 10, 1915, Bailey Papers; *New York World,* November 7, 1915; *New York Times,* November 19, 1915. The characterization of the antipreparedness group is based upon the letters in the Kitchin Papers, Boxes 3–5, and in the Bailey Papers. Cf. *New York World,* October 11, 13, November 14, 1915. It agrees with Link's estimate in *Wilson* (Princeton, N. J.: Princeton University Press, 1964), 4:27–28. For differing interpretations of the group's prewar domestic activities, see Link, "The South and the 'New Freedom': An Interpretation," *American Scholar* 20 (Summer, 1951): 314–324; and Richard M. Abrams, "Woodrow Wilson and the Southern Congressmen, 1913–1916," *Journal of Southern History* 22 (November, 1956): 417–437.

10. *Commoner* 15 (October, 1915): 1; *New York Times,* November 13, 14, 1915; *Nashville Tennesseean,* September 29, 1915, clipping in Bryan Papers, LC, Box 61; Bailey to Kitchin, October 9, 1915, Bailey to Villard,

November 10, 1915, Villard to Bailey, October 18, November 5, 22, 1915, and Bailey to Ford, September 16, November 4, 1915, Bailey Papers; O. G. Villard, *Fighting Years: Memoirs of a Liberal Editor* (New York: Harcourt, Brace & Co., 1939), p. 308. Villard's antipreparedness articles and editorials were reprinted as a book, *Preparedness* (New York: New York Evening Post Co., 1915).

11. Kitchin to C. O. McMichael, January 26, 1916, Kitchin Papers, Box 7. See also Kitchin to Samuel Witherspoon, October 12, 1915, ibid.; Bailey to Rudolph Spreckels, February 16, 1916, Bailey Papers.

12. Tumulty to Wilson, January 17, 1916, Wilson Papers, Series II, Box 130. Cf. Taft to Gus J. Karger, January 11, 1916, Taft Papers, Series VIII, Letterbook 42.

13. *Commoner* 15 (December, 1915): 5; *Record,* 64th Cong., 1st sess., January 20, 1916, p. 1324.

14. *Record,* 64th Cong., 1st sess., January 4, 1916, pp. 458–463. For biographical information on Sherwood, see *New York Times,* October 16, 1915; Francis P. Weisenburger, "Isaac Ruth Sherwood," in *Dictionary of American Biography* (New York: Charles Scribner's Sons, 1935), 17:100.

15. *Record,* 64th Cong., 1st sess., January 6, 1916, pp. 635–636. For biographical information on Davis, see James H. "Cyclone" Davis, *Memoir* (Sherman, Texas: Courier Press, 1935), esp. pp. 14–15; also, *Official Congressional Directory, 64th Congress, 1st Session* (Washington: Government Printing Office, 1916), p. 109, and *Nation* 102 (April 20, 1916): 435.

16. For biographical information on Slayden, see esp. his wife's witty, acerbic diary, *Washington Wife: Journal of Ellen Maury Slayden from 1897 to 1919* (New York: Harper & Row, 1962). For his role in the Pan-American pact, see Link, *Wilson* (Princeton, N. J.: Princeton University Press, 1956), 2:324–327.

17. *Record,* 64th Cong., 1st sess., *Appendix,* March 8, 1916, pp. 514–516.

18. Kern to Bailey, September 17, 1915, and Stephens to Bailey, October 23, 1915, Bailey Papers; Hay to Kitchin, October 15, 1915, Kitchin Papers, Box 3; Kern to Tumulty, September 9, 1915, Wilson Papers, Series II, Box 124. Cf. Kern to Kitchin, October 4, 1915, Kitchin Papers, Box 3; Kitchin to Bailey, November 1, 1915, Bailey Papers.

19. Kitchin to Bruce Craven, December 11, 1915, Kitchin Papers, Box 6; entry for January 1, 1916, in Sparks, *Ashurst Diary,* p. 44.

20. Tumulty to Wilson, January 17, 1916, Wilson Papers, Series II, Box 130; R. S. Baker interview with Burleson, May 17–20, 1927, R. S. Baker Papers, LC, Series I, Box 22. On Wilson's situation cf. the analysis of the *New Republic* 4 (September 25, 1915): 191, and Bryan's comments, Bryan to Kitchin, October 14, 1915, Kitchin Papers, Box 3.

21. Addresses of January 27, 29, 31, 1916, *Wilson Public Papers,* 4:5, 23, 25, 44, 51.

22. *New York Times,* February 1, 1916; *New York World,* February 7, 1916; *New Republic* 7 (February 5, 1916): 1–2; W. F. Sapp to Tumulty

and August Kopke to Tumulty, February 3, 1916, Wilson Papers, Series II, Box 131; Kitchin to Bryan, February 9, 1916, and Bryan to Kitchin, February 5 [?], 1916, Kitchin Papers, Box 8; Bryan to Daniels, February 4, 1916, Daniels Papers, Box 37; *New York Evening Post,* February 15, 1916.

23. Hay to Wilson, February 5, 8, 1916, Tumulty to Wilson, February 9, 1916, and Wilson to Garrison, February 10, 1916, Wilson Papers, Series II, Box 131.

24. Hay to Wilson, February 11, 1916, and Frank P. Glass to Wilson, February 12, 1916, Wilson Papers, Series II, Box 131; R. S. Baker interview with Garrison, November 30, 1928, R. S. Baker Papers, LC, Series I, Box 34.

25. *Record,* 64th Cong., 1st sess., March 23, 1916, p. 4729; ibid., June 2, 1916, p. 9189. For statistical descriptions of these votes, see Tables 5 and 6 in Appendix.

26. *Record,* 64th Cong., 1st sess., August 15, 1916, p. 12700. For a statistical description of this vote, see Table 9 in Appendix.

27. *Record,* 64th Cong., 1st sess., *Appendix,* June 2, 1916, p. 1096.

28. *New York Times,* June 9, 1915.

29. Works to Nathan Straus, December 23, 1915, Works Papers, Berkeley, Box 1. Cf. *Record,* 64th Cong., 1st sess., December 16, 1915, pp. 318–326.

30. Works to Benjamin Ide Wheeler, March 22, 1916, Works Papers, Berkeley, Box 1.

31. *Record,* 64th Cong., 1st sess., March 23, 1916, pp. 4669–4674.

32. Quoted in George E. Mowry, *The California Progressives* (Berkeley: University of California Press, 1951, p. 94. For Works's role, see ibid., esp. pp. 117–118, 122, and John D. Works manuscript autobiography, John D. Works Papers, Stanford University Library (hereafter cited as Works Papers, Stanford).

33. *Record,* 64th Cong., 1st sess., June 26, 1916, p. 9979.

34. Works to Frederick Dixon, September 27, 1915, Works Papers, Berkeley, Box 1.

35. *Record,* 64th Cong., 1st sess., March 23, 1916, pp. 4670–4671. On Works's early life, see manuscript autobiography, Works Papers, Stanford.

36. *La Follette's Magazine* 7 (November, 1915): 1; *New York Times,* November 13, 1915; Borah to Villard, November 20, 1915, Borah Papers, Box 170. Villard forwarded Borah's letter, which he found "very encouraging," on to Bailey. Villard to Bailey, November 22, 1915, Bailey Papers.

37. *Record,* 64th Cong., 1st sess., April 18, 1916, p. 6359; ibid., July 17, 1916, p. 11192; ibid., July 21, 1916, p. 11379; ibid., July 21, 1916, p. 11384. For statistical descriptions of these votes, see Table 1 in Appendix.

38. *Record,* 64th Cong., 1st sess., May 17, 1916, p. 8126; William Kent to Gifford Pinchot, August 20, 1915, William Kent Papers, Yale University

Library, Box 37; White to Roosevelt, August 27, 1916, Roosevelt Papers, Box 311. Cf. William Allen White, *Autobiography* (New York: Macmillan Co., 1946), pp. 507–508.

39. See Richard Hofstadter, *Social Darwinism in American Thought* (Boston: Beacon Press, revised edition, 1955), p. 203.

40. *Record,* 64th Cong., 1st sess., July 17, 1916, pp. 11185–11186; ibid., *Appendix,* September 7, 1916, p. 2134.

41. *Record,* 64th Cong., 1st sess., June 1, 1916, pp. 9143–9144; Kitchin to Villard, May 24, 1916, Kitchin Papers, Box 11. On the background of the amendment, see Walter Hensley to R. S. Baker, August 3, 1928, R. S. Baker Papers, LC, Series I, Box 36.

42. Slayden to W. H. Short, in *League to Enforce Peace Weekly Bulletin,* no. 9 (November 16, 1916), p. 5.

43. *New York Evening Post,* September 2, 1915; Villard, *Fighting Years,* p. 282; Daniels to Wilson, September 3, 1915, Wilson Papers, Series II, Box 124; E. H. Dewey to Charles D. Hilles, October 12, 1915, copy in Borah Papers, Box 92. Cf. Lodge to Roosevelt, September 25, 1915, Lodge Papers, Roosevelt-Lodge Corresp.; *Current Opinion* 59 (November, 1915): 302–303; Wilson to House, September 20, 1915, House Papers.

44. Spring Rice to Grey, December 9, 1915, in Gwyn, ed., *Spring Rice Letters,* 2:301; House to Wilson, November 19, 1915, Wilson Papers, Series II, Box 127. Cf. [Tumulty] to Wilson, undated memorandum, December [?], 1915, ibid., Box 129.

45. Stone to Wilson, December 13, 1915, Wilson Papers, Series II, Box 128; *Record,* 64th Cong., 1st sess., January 5, 1916, p. 495. See also Hoke Smith's speech, ibid., December 10, 1915, p. 144.

46. *Record,* 64th Cong., 1st sess., January 5, 1916, pp. 505–510. For estimates of Senatorial opinion, see *New York World,* January 6, 7, 1916.

47. *Record,* 64th Cong., 1st sess., January 5, 1916, p. 507.

48. Ibid., January 27, 1916, pp. 1613–1616, 1619.

49. Slayden to Kitchin, January 10, 1916, Kitchin Papers, Box 7; *Record,* 64th Cong., 1st sess., *Appendix,* March 8, 1916, p. 514.

50. Ibid., March 17, 1916, pp. 4278–4287. For biographical information on McCumber, see *New York Times,* May 19, 1933, and W. C. Hunter, "Porter James McCumber," *Dictionary of American Biography: Supplement One* (New York: Charles Scribner's Sons, 1944), 21:525–526.

51. *New York Times,* February 24, 25, 1916; *New York World,* February 24, 1916; Tumulty to Wilson, February 24, 1916, Wilson Papers, Series II, Box 131; Spring Rice to Grey [?], February 26, 1916, in Gwyn, ed., *Spring Rice Letters,* 2:316; E. Y. Webb to C. H. Blanton, February 29, 1916, Webb Papers, Box 11.

52. *New York Times,* February 25, March 1, 2, 3, 1916; *New York World,* March 2, 1916; Irvine L. Lenroot manuscript memoirs, Irvine L. Lenroot Papers, Library of Congress, Box 13; E. Y. Webb to W. W. Aiken, March 11, 1916, Webb Papers, Box 11; Wilson to Burleson and

McAdoo, March 2, 1916, Albert S. Burleson Papers, Library of Congress, Letterbook 16.

53. *Record,* 64th Cong., 1st sess., March 3, 1916, p. 3465; ibid., March 7, 1916, p. 3720. For a statistical description of the House vote, see Table 10 in Appendix.

54. *Record,* 64th Cong., 1st sess., March 3, 1916, pp. 3463, 3470; ibid., March 2, 1916, p. 3406. Italics added.

55. Borah also voted against tabling. He opposed the resolution but protested against being "gagged." Ibid., March 3, 1916, p. 3464.

56. See Kitchin to D. T. Ward, February 28, 1916, and Kitchin to H. Q. Alexander, March 9, 1916, Kitchin Papers, Box 9; Webb to Thomas W. Alexander, February 29, 1916, Webb Papers, Box 11; statements by Representatives Lenroot (R-Wis.) and Charles Fuller (R-Ill.), *Record,* 64th Cong., 1st sess., p. 3697; ibid., *Appendix,* March 7, 1916, p. 487.

57. Page statement, March 6, 1916, Robert N. Page Papers, Duke University Library; *New York Times,* March 7, 1916; *Record,* 64th Cong., 1st sess., March 7, 1916, p. 3706. Cf. remarks of George Huddleston (D-Ala.), ibid., March 7, 1916, p. 3706, and ibid., *Appendix,* March 7, 1916, pp. 455–457; Samuel Tribble (D-Ga.), *Record,* 64th Cong., 1st sess., March 8, 1916, p. 3773; John H. Stephens (D-Tex.), ibid., *Appendix,* March 9, 1916, pp. 495–496; Webb to J. C. Eliott, March 10, 1916, Webb Papers, Box 11.

58. *New York Times,* March 6, 7, 1916; *New York World,* March 7, 1916; Stimson to Philip Roosevelt, December 17, 1915, and Theodore Roosevelt to Stimson, December 22, 1915, Stimson Papers, Box 140; Roosevelt to Arthur Lee, February 18, 1916, Roosevelt Papers, Letterbook 94; Taft to Gus J. Karger, February 20, 1916, Taft Papers, Series VIII, Letterbook 44; Taft to Charles D. Hilles, April 12, 1916, ibid., Letterbook 47; *New York Evening Post,* March 8, 1916; Walter Lippmann, "The Issues of 1916," *New Republic* 7 (June 3, 1916): 107–109.

59. See George M. Stephenson, "The Attitude of Swedish Americans toward the World War," *Proceedings of the Mississippi Valley Historical Association* 10 (1918–1919): 84; Knute Nelson to Peter Shippman, March 10, 1916, Knute Nelson Papers, Minnesota Historical Society, Box 75; *Record,* 64th Cong., 1st sess., January 20, 1916, pp. 1304–1305.

60. See esp. James Davenport Whelpley, "The Middlewest and the War," *Outlook* 110 (August 11, 1915): 870–871; *New Republic* 6 (March 4, 1916): 119–120; *Literary Digest* 52 (March 11, 1916): 625–628; R. S. Baker Diary, March 3, 1916, R. S. Baker Papers, LC, Series II, Notebook 9.

61. *Record,* 64th Cong., 1st sess., April 5, 1916, pp. 5497–5498. On McCumber's position in the League controversy, see ibid., 66th Cong., 1st sess., November 19, 1919, pp. 8786, 8803.

62. Ibid., 64th Cong., 1st sess., March 20, 1916, pp. 4476–4477; ibid., 66th Cong., 2nd sess., April 8, 1920, p. 5345. For biographical information on Campbell, see *Biographical Directory of the American Congress, 1774–1949* (Washington: Government Printing Office, 1950), p. 943.

63. House to Robert Lansing, May 30, 1916, House Papers. On the difficulties with Britain, see House to Wilson, July 5, 1916, Wilson Papers, Series II, Box 138; Wilson to House, July 23, 1916, House Papers; Walter Hines Page interview with Wilson, September 22, 1916, W. H. Page Diary, 1916, Series V, W. H. Page Papers.

64. *Wilson Public Papers,* 4:184–188.

65. *Commoner* 16 (August, 1916): 10; *New York American,* May 29, 1916.

66. Taft to Theodore Marburg, June 6, 1916, Taft Papers, Series VIII, Letterbook 49; *Wilson Public Papers,* 4:195.

67. Official reporter's transcript of Democratic convention, Wilson Papers, Series II, Box 136.

68. See copy of Democratic platform, with Wilson's handwritten corrections (ibid., Box 137); Wilson to House, July 2, 1916, House Papers.

69. Convention transcript, Wilson Papers, Series II, Box 136; *New York World,* June 16, 1916.

70. Address of July 31, 1916, copy in Charles Evans Hughes Papers, Library of Congress, Box 182 (hereafter cited as Hughes Papers).

71. *Record,* 64th Cong., 1st sess., June 1, 1916, pp. 9140–9141; *Literary Digest* 52 (June 10, 1916): 1683.

72. The evidence as to which issues Bryan stressed more is conflicting. David Lawrence, who covered Bryan's campaign in October, observed that his "plea was for peace." (Lawrence, *True Story of Woodrow Wilson,* p. 148; cf. *New York Evening Post,* October 19, 1916) But Mrs. Bryan's recollection and the speeches Bryan himself reprinted in *The Commoner* indicate almost exclusive stress on domestic issues. (*Bryan Memoirs,* p. 444; *Commoner* 16 [October, 1916]: 1–2, 14–15, 22–23) Bryan himself wrote during the campaign, "'He kept us out of war' is our strongest slogan." But he appears to have been referring to Mexico rather than Europe. (Bryan to Thomas J. Walsh, October 6, 1916, Thomas J. Walsh Papers, Library of Congress, Box 167). Bryan's standard speech in the campaign dwelled largely on domestic issues, with more of his attention to foreign policy devoted to his arbitration treaties and Mexico than to the World War. (See sample speech enclosed in ibid.)

73. Works to Republican National Committee, October 5, 1916, Works Papers, Berkeley, Box 1; Beveridge speech of October 5, 1916, copy in Beveridge Papers, Box 305.

74. White to Roosevelt, December 27, 1916, Roosevelt Papers, Box 318; Johnson to Roosevelt, February 7, 1917, ibid., Box 321. Privately, Democrats were also appealing to hyphenate votes. See Stone to Tumulty, September 25, 1916, Wilson Papers, Series II, Box 141; George Sylvester Viereck, *Spreading Germs of Hate* (New York: Horace Liveright, 1930), pp. 241–242.

75. For contemporary analyses of the German-American vote, see *New York Times,* November 12, 1916; Charles R. McCarthy to Lord Bryce, November 18, 1916, Charles R. McCarthy Papers, State Historical Society

of Wisconsin, Box 30. Cf. Thomas J. Kerr, "German-Americans and Neutrality in the 1916 Election," *Mid-America* 43 (April, 1961): 95–105; William M. Leary, Jr., "Woodrow Wilson, Irish Americans, and the Election of 1916," *Journal of American History* 54 (June, 1967): 57–72.

76. Amos Pinchot open letter, October, 1916, Amos Pinchot Papers, Library of Congress, Box 24 (hereafter cited as Pinchot Papers); John Reed to Carl D. Thompson, October 13, 1916, Socialist Party of America Papers, Duke University Library.

77. *Addresses and Proceedings Incident to the Dinner . . . in Honor of Hon. William Jennings Bryan at the Hotel Lafayette, Washington, D. C., December 6, 1916* (n. p., n. d.), copy in Bryan Papers, LC, Box 63.

78. *League to Enforce Peace Weekly Bulletin,* no. 14 (December 21, 1916), p. 3. Among national magazines, only *The Saturday Evening Post* criticized internationalist proposals (188 [Aug. 28, 1915]: 20); later, it warmly supported internationalism. Among newspapers, the failure to espouse isolationist arguments could be seen in criticisms of Wilson's policies by such papers as the *Omaha World-Herald* and the *San Francisco Chronicle.* Both denounced militarism and all ideas of intervention, but without drawing any connections between their positions and the maintenance of isolation. See *Omaha World-Herald,* November 6, December 9, 1915, February 25, 1916; *San Francisco Chronicle,* January 29, February 25, May 6, 1916.

4

Beginnings of an Isolationist Coalition

THE final phase in the formation of an isolationist position opened when the question of forceful commitments outside the Western Hemisphere became a major political issue in December, 1916, and January, 1917. In attempting to end the World War, first through his note to the belligerent countries asking them to state their peace terms and then in the "peace without victory" address, Wilson pledged the United States to membership in an international peace-keeping organization. An isolationist coalition almost immediately began to form in opposition, drawing together idealists and ultranationalists. Senator Borah emerged as the leading spokesman for the idealistic viewpoint. The other outstanding opponent was Senator Lodge, who, without becoming an isolationist himself, exemplified the tendency of ultranationalists to spurn overseas commitments because of the idealistic intentions that were being attached to such commitments. In both cases, Republican opposition to the

Wilson Administration was an important contributing factor, and these partisan interests formed one of the bases of an emerging isolationist political position.

Reactions to the Peace Proposal of December, 1916

As soon as his reelection was assured, Wilson commenced preparations for a diplomatic departure. In October, confidential reports had reached him that pressures were mounting in Berlin for a resumption of submarine attacks on merchant shipping. But the Kaiser, Wilson was also told, hoped that a successful American peace initiative might head off any decisions about undersea warfare. "No such critical circumstances in regard to our foreign policy have ever before existed," Wilson told Lansing on the eve of the election. He considered the situation so grave that if Hughes won the election he planned to appoint the Republican candidate Secretary of State. Then, after receiving the Vice President's resignation, he would resign himself, thereby installing his successor in the White House at once and avoiding the four-month interregnum until the inauguration in March. "It would be my duty to step aside so that there would be no doubt in any quarter how that [foreign] policy was to be directed, towards what objects and by what means." [1]

Immediately after the election Wilson started drafting an appeal to the belligerents to state their respective conditions for ending the war. The note was transmitted on December 18, 1916, and published two days later. Wilson observed that all the nations at war had declared themselves "ready to consider the formation of a league of nations to insure peace and justice throughout the world." The United States, he avowed, was just "as vitally and directly interested" in such a league. "They stand ready, and even eager, to cooperate in the accomplishment of these ends, when the war is over, with every influence and resource at their command." [2] Wilson was staking his internationalist program as a diplomatic commitment for the United States.

At first, the note to the belligerents caused little controversy. Bryan and a number of Congressmen and Senators of both parties hailed the President's action. Only pro-Allied stalwarts like Lodge, Roosevelt, and Gifford Pinchot opposed the move, denouncing Wilson as the Kaiser's catspaw in a trick to avert German defeat.[3] Secretary of State Lansing similarly feared that the note would be interpreted as an anti-Allied maneuver, and he tried to undermine the effort with a deliberate indiscretion. The appeal to the belligerents, Lansing told reporters on December 21, would entail the abandonment of traditional isolation. "I mean by that that we are drawing nearer to the verge of war ourselves." Tumulty promptly sent the President a copy of Lansing's statement, with that sentence underlined. Infuriated, Wilson ordered the Secretary to issue an immediate explanation that his position had been "radically misinterpreted" and "that it was not at all in your mind to intimate any change in the policy of neutrality which the country has so far so consistently pursued in the face of accumulating difficulties." [4]

A volley of qualifying remarks poured out of the White House and State Department. Neutrality was confirmed; the Monroe Doctrine was upheld; the President's ideas about international organization were "nebulous," it was insisted, and not at all based upon the plan of the League to Enforce

Peace.[5] Such hedging was tardy, and these protestations of not contemplating departures from traditional policies were tantamount to an admission that departures were indeed being considered. By raising the specters of war and alliances, Lansing transformed Wilson's internationalist proposal into a heated political issue. "Does the Administration hold that by treaty or otherwise without the consent of Congress," demanded a Republican Representative, "it has the power to commit the United States in an armed international League to Enforce Peace?" [6]

On the same day that Lansing made his statement, Senator Borah started moving toward an isolationist position. When a resolution approving Wilson's appeal to the belligerents was introduced in the Senate on December 21, Borah objected to its receiving immediate consideration. Everyone applauded the President's efforts to achieve peace, Borah observed, but there was "a wide difference of opinion as to how best to effectuate that purpose. So far as I am concerned, I do not want to be placed in the attitude of endorsing a proposition of such tremendous consequences as this, upon which I have had no opportunity to reflect, and about which we have had no facts presented by the President. . . ." Borah's objection, seconded by other Republican Senators, delayed consideration of the resolution until after Congress returned from its Christmas recess.[7]

Borah responded with an isolationist argument on January 5, 1917. The President's internationalist proposals would require, he charged, "an entire change of policy with reference to our foreign affairs. . . . Could a single proposition involving more completely the peace and contentment of this Republic for all time be submitted to this body for consideration?" Wilson was proposing that the nation adopt the program of the League to Enforce Peace. Not only would their scheme prescribe automatic American entry into every foreign war, but it would also "authorize other nations to make war upon the United States if we refuse to submit some vital issue of ours to the decision of some European or Asiatic nations. This approaches, to my mind, moral treason."

Nor were those the most damnable aspects of the matter. "When we agree to enter into an alliance which proposes by means of the military and naval forces of the United States to protect the national integrity of every small nation of Europe we have gone to the storm center of European politics. We have abandoned the policy of nearly a century and a half and entered directly and at once upon that policy which was condemned by the Father of our Country in the very beginning of the Government." This was the nub of Borah's opposition to internationalism. "I want peace," he protested, but the President's proposal would have "my country enter upon that course which, in my humble judgment, is not to promote peace but to promote war. . . . Had it not been for Washington's policy, had he yielded in the fateful hour when urged to form a European alliance, we would have participated in every war which has tormented Europe from that hour to this." [8]

Borah was expounding basically the same principles of idealistic isolationism as Bryan and the three intellectuals had enunciated earlier. National egoism, even a touch of xenophobia, could be seen in Borah's condemnation of the idea of letting other countries decide upon peace or war for America. Yet, for him, too, the overriding consideration was not unfettered sovereignty or national power, but America's fundamental values of peace, freedom, and justice.

Joining an international organization backed by force, Borah told a friend shortly after his speech, "would be practically the end of this Republic." It would mean "our engaging in the family quarrels and dynastic ambitions of Europe, and not only that but it would bring us into alliance with Japan and China. We would be a republic in arms from that time on." [9]

Borah's isolationist position contained both broader political ramifications and personal elements. His enunciation of an idealistic isolationist argument confirmed previous indications that progressive Republicans might be attracted to them. Borah was the most prominent Republican progressive to take an isolationist stand thus far, and his foreign policy views typified those of his Middle Western and Western fellows. Before 1917, his attitudes toward major foreign policy issues had oscillated between sympathy for the antimilitarist, anti-imperialist outlook of the agrarian Democrats and an attraction to the exuberant, assertive nationalism of Rooseveltian Republicans. Exposed to Populism in his youth, Borah had expressed Anglophobic, antimonarchical views in 1896 when, as a Silver Republican, he had supported Bryan. He had become an enthusiastic advocate of imperialism after returning to party regularity in 1898. Once elected to the Senate, however, he had advocated independence for the Philippines and condemned intervention in Nicaragua, although he had also criticized Wilson's reluctance to send forces into Mexico in 1914 and 1915.[10]

Borah displayed comparable ambivalence in his responses to the World War. On the one hand, he favored increased preparedness and a tough line toward Germany both during the *Lusitania* crisis and in opposition to the Gore resolution. He even condemned Senator McCumber's original isolationist statement, declaring that the United States was "a great Nation . . . whose commerce is ramifying all parts of the earth, and which is most likely . . . to have some misunderstandings with different nations of the earth. The best way to insure peace, the best way to insure respect, is to be prepared for war." [11] On the other hand, he supported the arms embargo and entertained serious qualms about greater preparedness. Likewise, he affirmed in September, 1915, that he was "opposed to being drawn into war with any European nation at any time or under any circumstances if it can possibly be avoided with honor to the American people." The war, he stated at the beginning of 1916, had shown that "the old, ugly passions and prejudices and ambitions of men" could still throw civilization "back many a decade." [12]

An experience in March, 1916, finally began to resolve Borah's ambivalence in favor of pacific idealism. Several National Guard lobbyists repeatedly tried to bring pressures on him from Idaho. They wanted Borah to support the section of the Army bill which provided for federalizing the state Guard units. These tactics backfired. As a progressive, Borah was already inclined to suspect lobbyists. Moreover, as a Westerner, he was disposed to dislike the National Guard because of the overbearing ways in which mineowners had used it against labor unions.[13] There was also a peculiarly personal element in Borah's reaction. The lobbyists' attempts to influence him affronted the political role in which he cast himself, that of unfettered follower of conscience and principle.[14]

The incident gave Borah second thoughts about preparedness. He speedily denounced the various National Guards as parts of "a dominant and aggressive military organization,

. . . of profound concern to the communities in which they are situated." On May 17, 1916, he further arraigned the Guard as an agency of "modern militarism" which, by subtly mixing in politics, "supplants the courts and tears down the guarantees of personal liberty." More generally, Borah warned that it would be easy "to relapse and hasten on the back track to the old, brutal, cowardly days of arbitrary power. . . . Arbitrary power is the besetting sin of all nations. It seems to be in the blood, and though for years it may not reveal itself, upon some untoward occasion it breaks out . . . in all its hideous, repulsive, and hellish deformity. I do not want to feed this spirit. I do not want under the guise of preparedness to foster the feeling of contempt for civil government and civil courts which has been manifested so much of late." Borah continued to favor increases in the army and navy, and Works chided him in July by recalling his remarks of May 17.[15] But those remarks did reveal the direction that Borah was taking in his thinking.

Precisely what impelled him to take an isolationist stand at the beginning of 1917 is not entirely clear. Bryan may have provided a critical stimulus. On December 26, 1916, the Commoner wrote to Borah that he had learned "that you are opposed to the plan of the League to Enforce Peace. Am glad to hear it. It would require abandonment of Washington's doctrine—avoidance of entangling alliances—and of the Monroe doctrine. The people will not stand for either." No evidence exists to show that Bryan's encouragement was responsible for Borah's subsequent course. Borah replied three days later that he was "glad that we agree upon this that seems to me perfectly vicious proposition of a league to enforce peace. It has only one virtue that I can see and that is that it is wholly impracticable. But if it should be put into execution it would be vicious, in my judgment to the last degree." [16]

Admitting to being influenced by anyone else would have been contrary to Borah's near-neurotic belief in his absolute independence. But it is conceivable that he may have looked up some of Bryan's arguments against internationalism. The two men knew and respected each other. They were natives of the same section of Illinois, where their fathers had been acquaintances. As a Silver Republican, Borah had campaigned for Bryan in 1896. Also, the Commoner's isolationist views were being prominently displayed in December, 1916. The Democratic banquet in his honor had been a well-publicized affair, and he had just begun a series of syndicated newspaper debates with Taft over the question of an international peace-keeping organization.[17] Borah was likely, therefore, to have been aware of Bryan's arguments at the end of 1916.

It was symbolically fitting that Borah brushed against Bryan on his way to an isolationist position. Borah's basic perspective was also an idealized vision of small-town and rural America applied to international affairs. His domestic views consisted mainly of opposition to economic concentrations of power. "Monopoly is at war with democratic institutions," he had declared in February, 1913, "and the conflict is as irrepressible as was the conflict between freedom and slavery. . . ." Business and financial "centralization" was, he asserted not long afterward, "at variance with self-reliant, self-respecting, free, and independent citizenship—the only guaranty under heaven or among men for a Republic." His outlook was also anti-urban, because, as he had insisted in 1911, cities like New York were where "the criminal hunts . . . where the job is easy, and where if successful, he can become a great political power." [18] In short, Borah resembled Bryan in subscribing to a middle-class social norm, with agrarian and sectional overtones. Both men believed that all dangers to the good society emanated from the top and bottom and from the alien metropolis. Their thinking about foreign policy extended those conceptions to encompass the place of the United States in world affairs.

Oddly, even some of the personal elements in Borah's isolationist position resembled Bryan's. Like the Commoner, he was a political moralist, who championed prohibition and regarded the antitrust issue as "at its base a question of morals." In Borah's view, isolationist policies offered similar means, although without Bryan's overtly religious expressions, of assuring that America would avoid sin. Finally, Borah found in his isolationist doctrines a way of casting the United States in his own political role. He nearly matched Bryan as a believer in the efficacy of unaided talk. In 1912 he had called oratory a statesman's "apostolic" capacity, in which he summoned "forth the invincible moral forces of an entire nation. There is no higher duty than that of arousing to moderate and sustained action the minds of those with whom all power rests." [19] Throughout his career Borah avoided all kinds of ties and commitments that might compromise his principles through the exercise of power. He cast himself, instead, in a political role that allowed him to do little besides talk. For Borah, too, isolationism appears to have been a way of making the United States act like himself.[20]

Borah's isolationist idealism again indicated an appeal to progressive Republicans. Although his faith in oratory was something he shared with few besides Bryan, his political moralism and social ideals were fairly typical of his Middle Western and Western colleagues. Partisanship added to progressive Republican leanings toward isolationism, inasmuch as they were not constrained to support Wilson's internationalist program to anywhere near the same extent as Democrats. At least one Republican interpreted Borah's stand as a party matter. "The Republican party needs leadership," wrote Edward B. Boise. "You have taken a long step in the right direction." [21] As yet, Borah and Works were the only important Republican progressives who had espoused isolationism, but they appeared to represent an increasingly important potential following.

Borah's arguments were part of a broader upsurge of opposition to idealistic internationalism. Roosevelt privately condemned the League to Enforce Peace in December, 1916, for playing "Germany's tune by persuading people that it is all right to refuse to do anything to correct hideous present wrongs if only we agree to make impossible promises as to some nebulous future." At the beginning of January, 1917, he published another article denouncing the League as a "wicked" organization "which interferes with the all-essential movement for spiritual and material preparedness." [22] Lodge now joined Roosevelt in publicly criticizing such internationalist ideas. Although he had called for a "united nations" in June, 1915, Lodge criticized the League to Enforce Peace in the spring of 1916 for wanting "to bind us to all kinds of things which the country would not hold to." He continued to favor an international organization and, ironically, shared the speaker's platform with Wilson in May when the President endorsed internationalism. But at the end of 1916, Lodge told Roosevelt, ". . . I regret that I ever got mixed up in it [the League]. . . . I have become perfectly dissatisfied with it." [23]

Lodge preceded Borah in attacking Wilson's proposals. In asking peace terms, he told the Senate on January 3, 1917, the President was projecting America "into the field of European politics," where "we have no national or legal concern. The terms of peace, as the war now stands, are wholly beyond and outside our national interests." As for the promise to join an international peacekeeping league, Lodge did not wish "to discuss now the merits of our engaging and associating ourselves with the powers of Europe. I merely point out that it is a departure from the hitherto unbroken policy of this country, a departure so important that it does not seem to me that it ought to be hastily taken." Lodge did suggest that membership in such an organization might limit national sovereignty on such matters as immigration restriction and compromise the Monroe Doctrine by making "us a part of the political system of another hemisphere, with the inevitable corollary that the nations of that other hemisphere will become a part of our system." He also accused Wilson of acting out of partiality toward Germany in the peace move.[24]

The juxtaposition of Borah's and Lodge's statements suggested how idealists and ultranationalists could come together in an isolationist coalition. But that coalition had not yet formed. The differences between Borah's and Lodge's positions remained clear. Roosevelt and Lodge had long favored a much larger American role in world affairs, and, as Robert Osgood has pointed out, they did not reject Wilson's internationalist ideas simply for favoring outside ties and commitments. Their concern was with the ends that those ties would serve. They were willing for the United States to contract alliances with the right nations, like Britain, for the sake of enhancing American power within the existing international system. What they scorned was the idea of creating an organization that would replace that system of sovereign concern for national security and prestige.[25] Roosevelt and Lodge themselves represented an ultranationalist position that was hardly isolationist, since they continued to favor various forms of overseas commitments. But the earlier statements of Gardner and Beveridge did indicate that ultranationalists could become full-fledged isolationists in the process of rejecting proposals for an idealistic world organization.

Two incidents in January, 1917, illustrated the differences between Wilson's ultranationalist critics and the idealistic isolationists. One was Roosevelt's writing to congratulate Borah for his attack on Wilson. But Borah's criticisms, Roosevelt added, "did not go nearly far enough." The internationalists erred in prescribing procedures instead of judging "the righteousness or unrighteousness of any action"; the League to Enforce Peace might easily take action "*not against the wrong doer, but against the wronged party!* A more preposterous, a more wickedly preposterous absurdity could hardly be devised." It was even "on a lower level than Mr. Bryan, for at least Mr. Bryan did not propose to go to war in the interest of brutal offenders against those wronged nations which instantly resented wrongs." The whole notion, Roosevelt concluded, was "like that of an individual who in private life should demand that if a ruffian slapped the face of a decent citizen's wife, and if the decent citizen promptly knocked the ruffian down, the Peace League should, in the interest of the ruffian, attack the man who objected to having his wife's face slapped." [26]

At bottom, Roosevelt's objection was that the internationalists sought to prevent the United States from enjoying the benefits of the existing system of international relations. Borah's objection was just the opposite. He believed that an internationalist program would condemn the United States to lose its ideals and suffer all the iniquities of the present system of power politics. The plan of the League to Enforce Peace, Borah replied to Roosevelt, "if it would work at all . . . would be almost fiendish in its results. . . . Its evil effects upon this country would be stupendous." [27] It was, however, a sign of the changing circumstances that these men were writing to each other as if they were in basic agreement.

The other incident that illustrated the difference between idealists and ultranationalists was the outcome of the Senate debate on the resolution endorsing Wilson's peace note. To Lodge's surprise and dismay, Borah closed his speech of January 5 with the announcement that he would vote for the resolution. Since it approved only the President's action in asking peace terms and not the substance of his note, Borah said that he would not "stand in the way of any supposed aid that the passage of the resolution . . . might be to the cause of peace." The Senate then approved the resolution, 48 to 17. All but ten of those voting in favor were Democrats, whereas all but one of the opponents were Republicans. Republican support for the resolution came, with just two exceptions, from Middle Western and Western progressives. Besides Borah, they included Norris, Cummins, Kenyon, Clapp, and Jones; La Follette, who was absent, was announced in favor.[28]

The division among Republicans once more revealed the attraction of progressives to pacific idealism, as opposed to conservatives' more orthodox nationalist position. The alignment was not perfect, because Works and McCumber both opposed the resolution. Yet the break in Republican ranks again highlighted common assumptions held by idealistic internationalists and isolationists. The vote also disclosed how Wilson's program was becoming a partisan issue. Democrats enthusiastically supported his call for peace terms, with Bryan alone objecting to the commitment to join an international organization. Republicans, conversely, were cooling to internationalist schemes. The vote against the resolution confirmed reports that a number of Republican Congressional leaders privately disliked Wilson's action and opposed his pledge of membership in a peace-keeping organization.[29]

Together, the attacks on idealistic internationalism and the partisan Republican distrust of Wilson's proposals portended the imminent coalescence of an isolationist political position. Some distinctions between the idealist and ultranationalist opponents were already becoming blunted. Taft could still joke, "It is a fairly good indication that we are nearly right when both Bryan and Roosevelt are opposed to us." But when veteran Republican diplomats like Henry White and Joseph Choate expressed to Borah their "hearty approval of your eloquent words," it was clear that opposition to Wilson's proposals was obscuring previous differences. This drift of Republican sentiment portended a major shift. Taft was president of the League to Enforce Peace, and earlier one of its officers had boasted to Hughes, "we have had more Republican than Democratic members." [30] Now, however, Republican tendencies to distrust internationalist projects were becoming a facet of the emerging isolationist position.

"Peace Without Victory"

Wilson furthered the alignment of the isolationist position when he clarified his internationalist commitment in the "peace without victory" speech. Rapidly changing diplomatic conditions convinced the President that he must make a more extensive public overture to the belligerents. Accordingly, with the prior knowledge of only House, Lansing, and Senator Stone, he appeared before the Senate on January 22, 1917.[31] He was concerned, he told the Senators, not only with efforts to "end the present war" but also about progress toward "the discussion of an international concert which must hereafter hold the world at peace." It would be "inconceivable that the people of the United States should play no part in that great enterprise. To take part in such a service will be the opportunity for which they have sought to prepare themselves by the very principles and purposes of their polity and approved practices of their Government ever since the days when they set up a new nation in the high and honorable hope that it might in all it was and did show mankind the way to liberty."

Wilson plainly stated that replacement of the present system of international power politics was his fundamental aim. Permanent peace, he affirmed, must be "a peace that is worth guaranteeing and preserving, a peace that will win the approval of mankind, not merely a peace that will serve the several interests and immediate aims of the nations engaged." It would have to "be made lasting or not by the guarantees of a universal covenant" backed by an international force "so much greater than the force of any nation now engaged or any alliance hitherto formed or projected that no nation, no probable combination of nations could face or withstand it." In addition, Wilson declared in the phrase which would characterize the address, it must be "a peace without victory. . . . Only a peace between equals can last. Only a peace the very principle of which is equality and a common participation in a common benefit." He reiterated the conditions of peace which he had proposed earlier and would later incorporate in the Fourteen Points—self-determination, freedom from aggression, freedom of the seas, and disarmament.

Wilson also tried to fend off attacks by showing that he subscribed to many of the same principles as idealistic isolationists. He was proposing, he contended, "that the nations should with one accord adopt the doctrine of President Monroe as the doctrine of the world . . . I am proposing that all nations henceforth avoid entangling alliances which would draw them into competitions of power; catch them in a net of intrigue and selfish rivalry, and disturb their own affairs with influences from without." There could be "no entangling alliance in a concert of power." Rather, by uniting to act "in the common interest" and "under a common protection," all nations would be freed from entanglements. "These are American principles, American policies. We could stand for no others." [32]

This attempt to forestall isolationist criticisms did not succeed. Instead, isolationism attracted greater support in response to Wilson's program. Borah refused to give an immediate comment on Wilson's address, but he privately stated that he opposed "both the propriety and the substance" of the speech. Three days later he introduced a resolution affirming the Senate's "faith and confidence in the permanent worth and wisdom" of traditional isolation and pledging continued efforts "to conform its acts to these time-honored principles so long and so happily a part of our own policy." On January 26, speaking outside the Senate, he warned, "Once in the maelstrom of European politics and it will be impossible to get out. Once involved in the matter of economically boycotting or in the matter of enforcing decrees of military force it will be practically impossible to get back to the policy under which we have lived and strengthened for more than a century." [33] These were foretastes of a major address in which Borah was preparing to denounce the idea of an international organization and expound his isolationist principles more fully.

Before he spoke, another progressive Republican Senator answered Wilson's speech with an idealistic isolationist argument. On January 30, Albert Cummins stated "my belief that if this country shall do what the President proposed we will be involved either in almost continuous war waged all over the world or we will be engaged in almost continuous rebellion against the authority which he proposes to set over us." Cummins insisted that he was heartily in favor of all efforts to eliminate war and promote judicial settlement of international disputes. It was "only when it is attempted to confer upon such a tribunal or league or sovereignty . . . the power to use armies and navies to enforce its decrees or to make contracts bidding us to fight in a quarrel not our own that my opposition begins." Such a plan would "provoke war instead of suppressing it. . . ."

Cummins illustrated what he considered the fundamental flaw in internationalist schemes by reading excerpts from a recent article on world government by H. G. Wells. Wilson's address, he argued, was "a mere paraphrase, in loftier, statelier tones," of that article. "The whole argument presented by Mr. Wells is that the United States must enter into the disputes of Europe or chaos will ensue; a chaos in which we are necessarily involved. That the nations of that continent are incapable of either right thinking or right doing. If this be true, there is no world league, in which the countries of

Europe must be the dominant power, that can either construct or maintain permanent peace." That was why Cummins refused to follow Wilson "when he leads the way toward the world sovereignty which he has proposed." [34]

Another distinguished Republican progressive had espoused isolationism. Cummins was a charter member of the progressive movement. As Governor in 1901, he had fathered the "Iowa idea" of withholding tariff protection from trust-made products. After entering the Senate, he had been like other Republican progressives in vacillating between strident nationalism and pacific idealism. The World War made him begin to question preparedness, which he only lukewarmly supported. In the fall of 1915, he wrote that the nation's "paramount duty is to make all things ready for an advance in the cause of international peace." America must work "to broaden the scope of arbitration, to increase efficacy of mediation, and to secure the high advantages of reflection and delay." [35] Later, Cummins furnished another illustration of how idealistic purposes could lead an isolationist to switch at least part of the way to internationalism. In the postwar controversy over joining the League of Nations, he would become, though with serious misgivings, one of the handful of "mild reservationist" Republican Senators who favored membership with relatively few restrictions.[36]

In responding to the "peace without victory" address, other progressive Republicans provided evidence of the idealistic premises on which many isolationists agreed with internationalists. Reporters noticed that La Follette led the applause when Wilson finished speaking. Afterward, he declared, "We have just passed through a very important hour in the life of the world." Clapp of Minnesota, who also cheered the President, called the speech "a wonderful document."

Norris asserted that he was "in favor of trying to do something, even though we may not accomplish all that any man thinks we ought to accomplish." Even if America attempted to establish a peace organization and failed, "it will be something worthy of a trial and fair consideration of honest men everywhere in the civilized world." [37] Those statements showed again that Republican progressives could also be attracted to idealistic internationalism.

But the clearest indication of a progressive Republican's position was Borah's isolationism. He delivered a full-dress rebuttal to Wilson on February 7, 1917. Opening with a lurid evocation of the horrors of the World War, he declared, "even these are not all there is to this war. After that comes [*sic*] the bitterness and hate, smoldering on through the decades, the demoralization of man's faith in the obligations of treaties, in the ties of international friendship, and even in Christianity itself. . . ." The World War was "the most pronounced threat to return to barbaric methods and brute force in society" since the Moors had been turned back at Tours over a thousand years before. "Its deadening, discouraging, disintegrating effect upon all the vital ties and moral ligaments which bind society together, upon all that the human family cherishes and loves, beggars description." Plainly, the United States had an inescapable duty to help heal the wounds and bring future peace.

But, Borah admonished, those ends could be pursued only by preserving isolation. There must be "no alliances, no leagues, no entanglements. I want this nation to stand alone, . . . in this crash of nations, firm in its purpose to uphold international law, supporting with all its influence international morality, conserving to the utmost of its powers that influence and prestige which will enable it to serve and counsel in the day of reconciliation and readjustment. What this passion-torn world needs and will need are not more leagues and alliances, but a great untrammeled, courageous neutral power, representing not bias, not prejudice, not hate, not conflict, but order and law and justice." If America faithfully maintained isolation, Borah concluded, "the time will come in this very world crisis when we may serve all who recognize that our purposes and policies are just and righteous altogether." [38]

Ultranationalists also attacked Wilson's proposals. "Peace without victory is the natural ideal of the man who is too proud to fight," sneered Roosevelt. "It is spurned by all men of lofty soul, by all men fit to call themselves fellow-citizens of Washington and Lincoln. . . . The Tories of 1776 demanded peace without victory. The Copperheads of 1864 demanded peace without victory. These men were Mr. Wilson's spiritual forbears." Two other former Progressives took an ultranationalist isolationist stand in opposition to Wilson. Beveridge again condemned the idea of a league of nations in an essay which was not published. Senator Miles Poindexter of Washington rejected "the President's proposition that we shall surrender our independence. . . . In such a league the United States would be helpless as against the rest of the world." [39]

The most important ultranationalist reaction came from Lodge, who now explicitly aligned himself with Borah in assailing the President. Although his initial public reaction to Wilson's speech was skeptical but not hostile, Lodge told Taft privately that he did "not at all favor the use which the President has made" of the idea of a league of nations, "and I do not think it ought to be mixed up in any way with the conclusion of the war in Europe." [40] Then, on February 1, he rebuked Wilson at length. Lodge considered all the President's conditions for peace little more than meaningless generalizations. Peace without victory was nonsense, since lasting peace "rests upon justice and righteousness" and could be "based upon the compromises and concessions of treaties or upon victories in the field." Self-determination was fine in theory, but it might have embarrassed the United States in the past if it had been applied to the Louisiana Purchase or the acquisition of Alaska. Freedom of the seas sounded nice, but it could seriously impair national rights in the event of belligerency.

Lodge considered Wilson's internationalist arguments equally specious. He ridiculed the notion of a worldwide Monroe Doctrine; ". . . if we have a Monroe Doctrine everywhere we may be perfectly certain that it will not exist anywhere. . . ." The proposal to create an international body empowered to maintain peace he found attractive but dangerous. "There is no halfway house to stop at. The system must be either voluntary or there must be force behind the agreement. . . ." He had himself formerly advocated establishment of such an organization, "but the more I have thought about it the more serious the difficulties in the way of its accomplishment seem to be." It would require genuine powers of coercion, "and no amount of shouting about the blessings of peace will relieve us from the obligations or the necessities imposed by putting force behind the peace of the world as we put it behind the peace of a city."

Membership in an international peace-keeping league would also entail abandonment of traditional isolation. Lodge avowed that he had "no superstition in regard to Washington's policy," but he did believe "that we should not depart from it without the most powerful reasons and without knowing exactly where that departure would lead." He would not approve of a departure in order to join a league under the terms Wilson proposed. Rather, he favored adoption of Borah's resolution reaffirming faith in isolation, because "I now see in this tortured and distracted world nothing but peril in abandoning our long and well-established policies. . . ." Participation in Wilson's enterprises could never be reconciled with the policies of the Fathers, for they contained "no lurking place" for his league but were "as clear as the unclouded sun at noonday, and are not collections of double-meaning words under which men can hide and say they mean anything or nothing." Maintaining their policies was, Lodge concluded, the best course. "This war will end; the passions of mankind will die down; . . . but the Republic and the American people will endure." [41]

Lodge clearly wished to serve opposite ends from Borah in his reaffirmation of traditional isolation. For Borah, isolation was the means of pursuing America's mission to promote peace and virtue in a benighted world. For Lodge, isolation appeared for the moment to be the way to safeguard the nation's interests and security. The two men's views of the World War and America's relation to it were almost totally opposed. Borah, like the majority of Americans, regarded the war as an unmitigated disaster from which the United States must stay as far away as possible. Lodge, along with Roosevelt and the small group of patrician Republican partisans of the Allies, felt neither revulsion from the war nor horror at the thought of American intervention.[42] Yet it was a sign of the changed circumstances that they glossed over their fundamental differences in common opposition to Wilson's proposals.

For the first time, these two basically dissimilar bases for an isolationist position might be confused with each other. No longer would the differences between them be as sharp as when Roosevelt and Bryan had been the principal critics of idealistic internationalism. The blurring of the distinction also reflected in part the growing appeal of isolationist principles within progressive Republican circles. Borah and Cummins had once supported imperialism, and Borah sometimes used rhetoric which made him appear closer to the ultranationalists than he really was. On the other side, Lodge had temporarily shifted from the role of challenger of traditional isolation to that of its ostensible defender. Hitherto, egoistic nationalists like Roosevelt and Lodge had either implicitly or openly advocated the abandonment of isolation, so that the United States could exercise its power more actively throughout the world. In the future, Lodge would again favor overseas alliances, such as the proposed security pact with Britain and France in connection with the peace settlement at the end of the World War. But at this point, in February, 1917, Lodge seemed willing to reject greater international involvement altogether rather than accept it on Wilson's terms.

Lodge's reactions revealed an important inclination of opinion that gained force from an intimate connection with partisanship. The "peace without victory" address precipitated a sharply partisan division over foreign policy. Mounting Republican opposition to Wilson's proposals was evident. Except for progressives like La Follette, Clapp, and Norris, Republican Senators greeted the President's speech with uniformly bitter comments. Jacob Gallinger of New Hampshire called it "ill-timed and utterly impossible of accomplishment." Francis Warren of Wyoming gibed that Wilson "thinks he is President of the world." Lawrence Sherman of Illinois sneered that the address "will make Don Quixote wish he had not died so soon." [43]

Following Wilson's speech, two prominent Republicans promptly severed their connections with the League to Enforce Peace. Senator James Wadsworth of New York wrote to Taft that he had changed his mind about joining the League because he could not "agree to the proposal that the United States shall become a member of a concert of powers such as has been suggested by the President." Wadsworth feared "that it would lead to embarrassments and difficulties for this country and would eventually deprive us of our peculiarly advantageous position amongst the great powers." Henry Lane Wilson, a former Republican diplomat and president of the Indiana branch of the League, indignantly resigned from the organization. The President, he explained to Taft, had "not only upset the announced program of the League but connected it, in an apparently authoritative way, with new doctrines involving the entanglement of this nation in European questions and the abandonment of the Monroe Doctrine as a continental and hemispherical [*sic*] policy, and its enlargement by the ipse dixit of the chief executive of this nation to cover the field of Europe and the world." [44]

Not all Republicans turned against internationalism in the wake of the "peace without victory" speech. Taft affirmed that all members of the League to Enforce Peace "rejoice sincerely" at the President's statements. On February 1, Senator McCumber announced that he did "not wish to be classed with those who scoff at the idea of a world-enforced peace, in the maintenance of which this country shall take an honored part." McCumber criticized Wilson for minimizing the difficulty of attaining self-determination and for overlooking the perplexities of colonialism and the "color question." But he agreed that joining an international organization would be "no more an entangling alliance than the compact of our States for a general government, because for the one purpose, the specific purpose of enforcing international morality, it is a world government." Five days before, Congressman Frederick Gillett of Massachusetts, who would become the next Republican Speaker of the House, declared himself "in thorough accord" with the President's position, "for it seems to me it is the best practical step toward the permanent end of warfare, which we all desire." [45]

But support for the idea of international organization was exceptional among Republicans. Nearly all of the party's leaders who commented on Wilson's plan either condemned it or were skeptically noncommittal, like Elihu Root, who observed laconically that peace must always be built upon justice. Most observers recognized that the Republicans were forsaking their accustomed advocacy of a larger American role in world affairs. The party which had elevated the United States to imperial power was proposing, in the words of the *New Republic,* "to crouch at its own fireside, build a high tariff wall, arm against the whole world, cultivate no friendships, take no steps to forestall another great war, and then let things rip. The party which was inspired by the American union is becoming a party of secession and states' rights as against world union. There is nothing in the party, nothing in its tradition to justify this policy." [46]

That was an overstatement. Earlier Republican support for overseas involvement had been neither so widespread nor so well-considered as was thought. Some of the progressives had begun to embrace a pacific idealism like that of the agrarian Democrats even before the World War. Moreover, Republican support for assertive foreign policies had always had a radically different basis from idealistic internationalism, as indicated by the various positions taken by Roosevelt, Lodge, Beveridge, and Gardner. Yet a major shift of positions was occurring, and it owed less to ideological predilections than to the simple fact of which party was in power. The Republicans, as Herbert Croly observed to Wilson, appeared to be in a mood to "oppose the participation of the United States in a League of Nations under any conditions. They seem to have decided to try to make party capital out of it." [47]

The election of 1916 had relegated the Republican party for the first time in its history to longer than four years out of the White House. This happened just at the moment when the issue of commitments outside the hemisphere assumed major political proportions. Being out of power naturally instilled in Republicans a need to differentiate their own positions from those of the Wilson Administration. An isolationist stand became, therefore, almost inescapable for many of them. Not all Republicans would become isolationists. Taft, McCumber, and others would remain staunch internationalists. Roosevelt and Lodge, too, would call for overseas ties. But the basic interest of the party ran in the direction of opposition to internationalism.

This Republican shift was one side of the reversal of the established pattern of responsibility for the conduct of American foreign policy. Conversely, Democrats were closing ranks in support of the President's internationalist program. The "peace without victory" address drew acclaim from almost every Democratic Senator, including several former critics of Wilson's submarine policy. Stone rushed up to shake his hand after the speech, exclaiming, "That was a great state paper, Mr. President." Hoke Smith of Georgia called it "a masterful expression of the highest ideals of international relations. . . . It points the way to an end of the present war and to permanent peace." Shafroth of Colorado introduced a resolution calling for establishment of an international court empowered to enforce its decisions. "This is revolutionary," admitted Shafroth, ". . . but at the same time if we are going to stop these horrible catastrophes that are happening we have to invoke something more effective than has been employed in the past." [48]

Some Democrats did oppose Wilson's proposals. Senator James A. Reed of Missouri angrily vowed, "I will never give my consent to an international army big enough to conquer the United States when there are ninety-nine chances out of a hundred that the world court and the leaders of the army will be picked by the monarchs of Europe." Senator Thomas of Colorado praised the "peace without victory" address but doubted whether much could be done to achieve permanent peace. "Human nature is the same as it has always been," Thomas commented. "Man is a fighting animal. . . . As the units, so the nations are. The things which have caused war in the past are the things which will cause war in the future." William Randolph Hearst's chain of newspapers, which were nominally Democratic, took a similar line. The New York *American* held that "since human nature changes little, and since governments are full of jealousy and greed, . . . we do not have any faith that another alliance for the enforcement of permanent peace, organized at this time, would result any better than the effort at The Hague or the effort of the Holy Alliance." [49]

But Democratic opposition was also exceptional. Other than those Senators and Hearst's editors, none of the party's spokesmen took issue with Wilson. Most who had earlier expressed isolationist opinions, like Bailey, Sherwood, "Cyclone" Davis, and Kitchin, who privately agreed with Bryan in opposing internationalism, stayed silent.[50] Bryan's conduct presented the most striking evidence of the conversion of Democrats to support for internationalism. On January 26, he lauded Wilson for "your brave and timely appeal to the war-mad rulers of Europe" but reiterated that "I have not reached the same conclusion you have in regard to the wisdom of joining a league to enforce peace." The mild description of their differences was portentous. On February 2, Bryan declared that although he and Wilson had disagreed over means of pursuing peace, "I rather prefer to leave the question until he himself has presented his views more in detail in the hope that when he does so present them we may find that there is no reason for difference." [51] The most prominent isolationist was getting ready to defect.

Supporting an internationalist position marked as much of a reversal for the Democrats as opposing it did for the Republicans. Previous resistance to Wilson's preparedness and submarine policies had shown how much weight the legacies of anti-imperialism and antimilitarism still carried in the party. Yet, as with the Republican nationalists, the basic issue before now had not been overseas involvement but conceptions of American identity and values. It was, in part, a tribute to Wilson's dialectical skill that he had justified overseas involvement on idealistic grounds that most Democrats could readily accept. Yet, again as with the Republicans, partisan interest furnished a more compelling reason for their course. Few Democrats were likely to want to differ with their first President to win a second consecutive term since Andrew Jackson.

The stiffening of party lines was only one sign of the

growth of an isolationist position. Another indication could be seen in two new statements of isolationist principles in response to the "peace without victory" address. Albert Jay Nock, a philosopher of Jeffersonian agrarianism, wrote to his friend Secretary of War Baker that he disagreed with the President's contentions. Apart from setting a good example, Nock could "see little that we can do for permanent peace." Exemplarism, however, was essential, "in the way of showing that we have our finger on the weak place in our theory of government." Mrs. Joseph Fels, the widow of the benefactor of the Single Tax Movement, was more explicit in her rejection of internationalist ideas. Membership in an international organization, she argued, "means the abandonment of our isolation," which was "the very essence of American effectiveness in the future councils of the nations." Instead, America must "preserve her integrity by preserving her isolation and take the lead by herself standing for a clean foreign policy." [52]

Representative Meyer London of New York, the lone Socialist in the House, also took an isolationist stand. "There is nothing more dangerous," stated London, "than the entry of the United States into an international alliance if membership in the alliance would involve the use of the armed forces of the United States in the joint enterprises of the alliance. I certainly favor a league of nations, but my contention is that as long as each member in the international league maintains an army and navy, and as long as the nations of the world have the power to loose these forces, just so long will there be no opportunity for international peace. It is the possession of armies by nations which have conflicting interests that is bound to lead to war." [53] London's statement again demonstrated that rejection of forceful overseas commitments was the essence of isolationism.

Yet one element was still lacking in the emergence of an isolationist position. Support, though present, was limited. The alignment of attitudes and partisan interests around Wilson's program disclosed lines of a larger political conflict, but only a few leaders took part in these debates at the beginning of 1917. The great majority of Senators and Representatives refrained from committing themselves. Few newspapers or magazines spoke forthrightly either for or against the President's assertion of internationalist convictions. Apparently, most Americans still did not perceive a need to take clear positions toward involvement beyond the hemisphere. What was lacking was the threat of being dragged into the World War. These debates did not have the sense of urgency that had existed earlier and would again be required to evoke widespread public concern.

In fact, a renewed threat of embroilment in the war was about to be foisted on the United States. While Wilson was preparing the "peace without victory" address, the German Government secretly decided to resume unrestricted submarine warfare against Allied and neutral shipping. On January 31, 1917, the German ambassador informed the State Department of the decision, which was to be implemented the following day. As the Kaiser and his advisors recognized, this resumption of submarine warfare would probably plunge the United States into the World War.

NOTES

1. Wilson to Lansing, November 5, 1916, Woodrow Wilson Papers, Princeton University Library. (All other references to the Wilson Papers

are to the collection in the Library of Congress.) This letter, outlining Wilson's plan, is quoted in full in Link, *Wilson* (Princeton, N. J.: Princeton University Press, 1965), 5:155–156. For the German communications to Wilson see House to Wilson, October 18, 20, 1916, Wilson Papers, Series II, Box 141.

2. *Wilson Public Papers,* 4:404.

3. *Commoner* 16 (January, 1917): 2; *New York Times,* December 21, 24, 1916, January 4, 1917; Champ Clark to Wilson, December 25, 1916, Wilson Papers, Series II, Box 144; Lodge to T. Roosevelt, December 21, 1916, Roosevelt Papers, Box 316. For Root's reaction, see entry of December 24, 1916, Chandler P. Anderson Diary, Library of Congress, Vol. 2.

4. Entry of December 3, 1916, Robert Lansing Diary, Library of Congress, Notebook 1 (hereafter cited as Lansing Diary); entries of January 21, 24, 1917, ibid., Notebook 2; *New York Times,* December 22, 1916; Robert Lansing, *War Memoirs* (Indianapolis: Bobbs, Merrill Co., 1935), pp. 188–190; Tumulty to Wilson, December 21, 1916, Wilson Papers, Series II, Box 144; Wilson to Lansing, December 21, 1916, R. S. Baker Papers, LC, Series I, Box 8.

5. *New York Times,* December 24, 25, 27, 1916. The League's Secretary believed, however, that Wilson's note "could not have set forth our platform more definitely if it had been written by our Executive Committee or in this office." W. H. Short to Taft, December 22, 1916, Taft Papers, Box 363 (Gen. Corr.).

6. John Jacob Rogers (R-Mass.) to Lansing, December 26, 1916, Wilson Papers, Series II, Box 144.

7. *Record,* 64th Cong., 2nd sess., December 21, 1916, pp. 635–636; December 22, 1916, p. 668.

8. Ibid., January 5, 1917, 892–895.

9. Borah to Ed Dewey, January 8, 1917, Borah Papers, Box 180.

10. On Borah's early foreign policy views, see Claudius Johnson, *Borah of Idaho* (New York: Longmans, Green & Co., 1936), pp. 39–40, 191–193; Marian McKenna, *Borah* (Ann Arbor, Mich.: University of Michigan Press, 1961), pp. 35–38; *Record,* 61st Cong., 1st sess., June 15, 1909, p. 3237; ibid., 63rd Cong., 3rd sess., January 3, 1915, pp. 1500–1503.

11. See William E. Borah Scrapbooks (microfilm copy in Library of Congress, reel 1); *Record,* 64th Cong., 1st sess., March 17, 1916, p. 4282.

12. Borah to Mrs. L. H. Payne, March 6, 1915 and Borah to F. W. Rochelle, September 6, 1915, Borah Papers, Box 173; *Record,* 64th Cong., 1st sess., January 24, 1916, p. 1439.

13. P. H. Crow to Borah, March 30, 1916, James H. Ray to Borah [undated], and Borah to Gardiner L. Harding, March 9, 1916, Borah Papers, Box 178; Borah to Calvin Cobb, July 12, 1916, and Borah to J. H. Peterson, July 13, 1916, ibid., Box 176; Lodge to Roosevelt, April 11, 1916, Roosevelt Papers, Box 298.

14. On his political role, see Cooper, "Borah, Political Thespian," esp. 147–148 (Chapter 1, note 56).

15. *Record,* 64th Cong., 1st sess., April 4, 1916, p. 5411; May 17, 1916, pp. 8126–8127; ibid., July 17, 1916, p. 11185.

16. Bryan to Borah, December 26, 1916, Borah Papers, Box 183; Borah to Bryan, December 29, 1916, Bryan Papers, LC, Box 31.

17. See Solon J. Fieldman to Bryan, November 25, 1916, Bryan Papers, LC, Box 31; contract, December 7, 1916, Taft Papers, Box 362 (Gen. Corr.). On Borah's family connections with Bryan, see Johnson, *Borah of Idaho,* pp. 3–4.

18. Speech of February 12, 1913, in William E. Borah, *Bedrock: Views on National Affairs* (Washington: National Home Library Foundation, 1936), p. 11; *Record,* 63rd Cong., 2nd sess., December 17, 1913, p. 1071; speech of January 4, 1911, quoted in Johnson, *Borah of Idaho,* p. 98.

19. Borah, *Bedrock,* p. 11; speech of February 12, 1912, in Horace Green, ed., *American Problems: A Selection of Speeches and Prophecies by William E. Borah* (New York: Duffield & Co., 1924), p. 32.

20. The stress on oratory and its relation to his isolationism are discussed in Cooper, "Borah, Political Thespian," pp. 151–152.

21. Edward B. Boise to Borah, January 28, 1917, Borah Papers, Box 182. Cf. Arthur H. Vandenberg to Borah, January 11, 1917, ibid., Box 183.

22. T. Roosevelt to St. Loe Strachey, December 5, 1916, Roosevelt Papers, Letterbook 98; T. Roosevelt, "The League to Enforce Peace," *Metropolitan* 45 (February, 1917): 72.

23. Lodge to Sturgis Bigelow, April, 5, 1916, Lodge Papers; Lodge to T. Roosevelt, December 21, 1916, Roosevelt Papers, Box 316.

24. *Record,* 64th Cong., 2nd sess., January 3, 1917, pp. 792–797.

25. See Osgood, *Ideals and Self-Interest,* p. 249.

26. T. Roosevelt to Borah, January 15, 1917, Roosevelt Papers, Letterbook 101.

27. Borah to T. Roosevelt, January 18, 1917, Borah Papers, Box 183.

28. *Record,* 64th Cong., 2nd sess., January 5, 1917, pp. 896–897; Lodge to T. Roosevelt, January 6, 1917, Roosevelt Papers, Box 318. The sole Democratic opponent was the erratic Martine of New Jersey, who had been defeated for reelection the preceding November.

29. See Bryan to Kitchin, January 2, 1917, Kitchin Papers, Box 16; *Commoner* 17 (January 2, 1917): 2; *New York Times,* January 2, 1917; *New York World,* Jan. 6, 1917.

30. Taft to Horace Taft, Jan. 6, 1917, Taft Papers, Box 365 (Gen. Corr.); Henry White to Borah, Jan. 9, 1917, Borah Papers, Box 182; A. Lawrence Lowell to Hughes, June 24, 1916, Hughes Papers, Box 3-B.

31. House Diary, January 11, 1917, 10:15–17; Wilson to Lansing, January 12, 1917, R. S. Baker Papers, LC, Series I, Box 8; Wilson to House, January 16, 19, 1917, House Papers; Wilson to Herbert Croly, January 25, 1917, Wilson Papers, Series II, Box 146.

32. *Wilson Public Papers,* 4:407–414.

33. *New York Times,* January 23, 27, 1917; Gus J. Karger to Taft,

January 22, 1917, Taft Papers, Box 336 (Gen. Corresp.); *Record,* 64th Cong., 2nd sess., January 25, 1917, p. 1950.

34. *Record,* 64th Cong., 2nd sess., January 30, 1917, pp. 2231–2235.

35. Albert B. Cummins, "Defense and Revenue in the Next Congress," *Review of Reviews* 52 (November, 1915): 555. On his earlier views, see Elbert W. Harrington, "A Survey of the Political Ideas of Albert Baird Cummins," *Iowa Journal of History and Politics* 39 (October, 1941): 339–386.

36. *Record,* 65th Cong., 3rd sess., February 26, 1919, pp. 4309–4315; ibid., 66th Cong., 1st sess., September 26, 1919, pp. 5952–5957.

37. *New York Times,* January 23, 1917; *Record,* 64th Cong., 2nd sess., January 24, 1917, p. 1883.

38. *Record,* 64th Cong., 2nd sess., February 7, 1917, p. 2749.

39. *New York Times,* January 23, 29, 1917; Beveridge to John C. Shaffer, January 31, 1917, Beveridge Papers, Box 281; Beveridge to George C. Lorimer (Jan., 1917); ibid., Box 272. Beveridge's article was turned down by *The Saturday Evening Post* and *Colliers.* (See Lorimer to Beveridge, February 1, 1917, ibid., Box 272; Beveridge to Mark Sullivan, February 3, 1917, ibid., Box 208). No copy of this article has survived, but an essay of December, 1916, condemning the League to Enforce Peace gives an indication of Beveridge's position. (See ibid., Box 306).

40. *Record,* 64th Cong., 2nd sess., January 24, 1917, pp. 1885–1886; Lodge to Taft, January 23, 1917, Taft Papers, Box 366 (Gen. Corresp.).

41. *Record,* 64th Cong., 2nd sess., February 1, 1917, pp. 2364–2370.

42. See Lodge to Roosevelt, January 15, 1915, Roosevelt Papers, Box 281; Lodge to Lord Channing, January 25, 1915, Lodge Papers. On this pro-Allied group, see Hermann Hagedorn, *Leonard Wood: A Biography* (New York: Harper & Bros., 1931), 2:179; Richard W. Leopold, *Elihu Root and the Conservative Tradition* (Boston: Little, Brown & Co., 1954), p. 98.

43. *New York Times,* January 23, 1917.

44. James Wadsworth to Taft, January 26, 1917, Henry Lane Wilson to Taft, January 26, 1917, Taft Papers, Box 367 (Gen. Corr.).

45. *New York Times,* January 27, 1917; *Record,* 64th Cong., 2nd sess., February 1, 1917, pp. 2361–2364; ibid., January 27, 1917, p. 2131.

46. *New York Times,* January 23, 1917; *New Republic* (February 3, 1917): 1–2.

47. Croly to Wilson, January 23, 1917, Wilson Papers, Series II, Box 146.

48. *New York Times,* January 23, 1917; *Record,* 64th Cong., 2nd sess., January 24, 1917, pp. 1881–1882, 1885.

49. *New York Times,* January 23, 1917; *Record,* 64th Cong., 2nd sess., February 1, 1917, pp. 2370–2373; *New York American,* January 29, 1917.

50. See Kitchin to Bryan, January 8, 1917, Bryan Papers, LC, Box 31.

51. Bryan to Wilson, January 26, 1917, Wilson Papers, File VI-A,

Folder 2400; speech of February 2, 1917, *Commoner* 17 (March, 1917): 8.

52. Albert Jay Nock to Newton D. Baker, January 27, 1917, Newton D. Baker Papers, Library of Congress, Box 3. Mrs Joseph Fels, "The Enforcement of Peace," *Public* 20 (February 9, 1917): 131–132.

53. *Record,* 64th Cong., 2nd sess., *Appendix,* January 27, 1917, p. 391.

54. Most journals praised the address without endorsing Wilson's position. See *Literary Digest* 54 (February 3, 10, 1917): 231–232, 324.

5

Coalescence of the Isolationist Position

A SUBSTANTIAL isolationist political position coalesced in response to the threat of intervention posed by the resumption of submarine warfare in February, 1917. Reluctantly, Wilson took the successive steps of first breaking diplomatic relations with Germany, then arming American merchant vessels, and finally entering the war itself. Each of these moves he justified with idealistic internationalist appeals. Correspondingly, opponents answered with idealistic isolationist arguments, and at each stage they broadened their following. The bulk of support for the isolationist position now clearly reflected the nexus of attitudes that had been forming since 1915; these included the originally agrarian progressive view of the relation between foreign policy and domestic reform, more recent partisan dispositions toward the Wilson Administration, and some ethnic influences of German-American ties. By the time the United States entered the First World War in April, 1917, a sizable isolationist position had emerged.

Responses to Renewed Submarine Warfare

Bryan injected idealistic isolationist arguments into the public debate even before the decision was made to break relations with Germany. On February 2, the Commoner asserted in a speech in New York that the World War was "not OUR war. . . . God forbid that we shall ever entangle ourselves in the quarrels of the Old World." He preferred to see whether the Germans would carry out their threats, but even if they did he was still not "willing that one single mother's son shall be carried across an ocean to march under the banner of any European monarch or die on European soil, in the settlement of European quarrels." Bryan urged the Government to warn citizens not to travel on belligerent ships, keep American vessels out of the war zone, postpone settlement of all disputes until after the war ended, and require a popular referendum for a declaration of war. "The most important thing is that officials in Washington shall know that the people at home protest against entering this war on either side . . . that they are not willing to surrender the opportunity to render a supreme service to the world as a friend of all and peacemaker when peace is possible." [1]

Wilson's reaction to the renewal of submarine warfare was scarcely more belligerent. In view of his threat during the *Sussex* crisis the previous April, he could not avoid severing relations with Germany. Yet Wilson feared that the break would lead to war. "I hope with all my heart," he told Bryan, "that something can be worked out that will assure the world of peace and justice." Wilson dreaded the consequences of intervention for America and the world. At a Cabinet meeting on February 2, 1917, he betrayed a rather common racist concern by asking what effect would "the depletion of man power" resulting from American entry into the war "have upon the relations between the white and yellow races?" When Lansing contended that the interests of civilization might demand joining the Allies, he replied, "I am not so sure of that." [2]

Wilson publicly exposed his internal conflict when he explained his decision to sever relations to a joint session of Congress on February 3. Although he called the break the only "alternative consistent with the dignity and honor of the United States," he insisted that he did "not desire any hostile conflict with the Imperial German Government." If "actual overt acts" did result from the Germans' threats, then he might have to request authority to arm American vessels. But, he protested, "We shall not believe that they are hostile to us unless and until we are obliged to believe it. . . ." Then, in a pained conclusion, Wilson invoked his internationalist ideas in an attempt to justify his action. "We wish to serve no selfish ends. We seek merely to stand true alike in thought and in action to the immemorial principles of our people which I sought to express in my address to the Senate only two weeks ago,—seek merely to vindicate our right to liberty and justice and an unmolested life. These are the bases of peace, not war. God grant that we may not be challenged to defend them by acts of wilful injustice on the part of the Government of Germany!" [3] In spite of his pacific desires, Wilson already seemed to be transforming his internationalist idealism into a case for intervention.

Isolationist idealism became, in turn, the chief justification for opposition to the break with Germany. After a resolution of approval was introduced in the Senate, Works denounced the move on February 7, as "a first and long step toward war. . . . Have we the moral courage to do the things now that will avoid war?" Observing that both sets of belligerents had violated American neutral rights, Works argued that the government should simply keep citizens and ships out of the war zone. "To avoid the horrors of war this act of prudence on the part of our Government would be a great act of moral courage by a great country that should be a worthy and patriotic example to all the nations of the world." [4]

William F. Kirby, a newly elected Democrat from Arkansas, likewise asserted that severing relations was "a preliminary declaration of war." He refused, therefore, to "vote for this resolution, which is to commit us to granting the power to enforce by war our own views of what international law is by the power of the United States." Borah also presented an isolationist argument in this debate by delivering his rebuttal to the "peace without victory" address. Although he endorsed the diplomatic break, Borah insisted that his creation did not imply "moving to the side of either of the belligerent forces." He wrote to a constituent on February 6 "that we should remain neutral, exerting our influence as a mediator whenever it is possible to be of any service in putting an end to this conflict or any future conflict." [5]

The resolution approving the severance of relations with Germany passed by a vote of 78 to 5. Besides Works and Kirby, the dissenters were La Follette, Gronna, and Vardaman. Harry Lane of Oregon, a Democrat, announced the following day that he would have voted against the resolution if he had been present. Though slight, this opposition indicated some of the sources from which isolationist support was being drawn. Ethnic influences did not appear strong, since only La Follette and, to a lesser degree, Gronna, represented states with large German-American communities. The opponents were evenly divided between three Bryanite Democrats and three of the best known progressive Republicans. The division illuminated a confluence of interests and attitudes that had begun to form the core of the isolationist position.[6]

Bryan and La Follette had, meanwhile, thrown themselves into the task of organizing opposition to all moves toward entering the war. La Follette listened to Wilson's explanation of the rupture with Germany in deepening gloom and secluded himself for several hours afterward. Bryan, who had hurried to Washington that morning, conferred with La Follette later in the day to plan ways of resisting intervention. The Commoner characteristically suggested a mass meeting, but La Follette convinced him that they should concentrate instead on lining up Congressional opposition. The two men spent the next few days "plugging away," as La Follette put it, to "get some fellows braced up to resist being rushed into war." Bryan told Senator Ashurst that "he would flood Congress with telegrams against war except in case of *actual* invasion." La Follette likewise said that he was "beginning to stir things up" among "the constituents of this flock of congressional sheep." [7]

Progressivism clearly lay behind their responses to the situation. La Follette viewed the matter as another round in the struggle between progressives and conservatives. "The Old Line Republicans are all eager" over the prospect of going to war, he told his family, whereas "all of the Progressive Republicans & Democrats were sick at heart." La Follette also revived the familiar contention that preparedness and foreign affairs were deliberately being used as distractions from pressing concerns at home, like skyrocketing food prices. "Since the outbreak of the war," he wrote in his magazine, "the trusts and combinations have had a mad revel. Taking advantage of a people stunned by a world catastrophe and flaunting a government laboring under the strain of international affairs, the financial barons and food kings opened wide the flood gates of exploitation." Senator Vardaman of Mississippi similarly argued that it would be a "calamity" for the United States to "be drawn into this vortex of blood and plunder to satisfy the greed and cupidity of those who would coin the blood of the murdered soldier and the tears of the broken-hearted women into dollars." [8]

As the crisis deepened, a number of new isolationist arguments were presented. In the House, Bailey, who had been defeated for reelection, restated his position in a valedictory address on February 17. The United States, he asserted, could enter the war "and help the kings and princes of the Old World in their mad struggle to strengthen their thrones and extend their dominions. We can get into it and underwrite the securities which Wall Street has taken for the billions loaned the Allies." "Cyclone" Davis, who had lost his bid for renomination, advanced similar contentions in a farewell speech two days later. By harking to "the advice of Washington's Farewell and Jefferson's glorious teachings," declared Davis, America could "refuse to become a part of that ravenous war which demands that the law of God must give way to the law of lust and loot while the continent runs red with human blood and reeks in cruel and criminal corruption." [9]

Three Middle Western Republican representatives also took up idealistic isolationist arguments. Frank Reavis of Nebraska averred on February 17 that the nation's real loss on entering the war would be "the sacrifice of ideals that have controlled America for 150 years." The United States would then become "a party to the intrigues of Europe, . . . rearranging the boundary lines of Europe, . . . and irretrievably and eternally becoming a party to European affairs." Horace Towner of Iowa recalled the Farewell Address on Washington's birthday, warning that entering the war would ensnare America in "the pleasing task of supporting king and czar and emperor against either foreign aggression or domestic insurrection. We would thus guarantee the perpetuity of tyranny forever." Burton Sweet, also of Iowa, likewise avowed on February 22 that Americans "as a Republic can not afford to ally ourselves with the monarchies of Europe, whose civilization has been constructed upon a wrong basis, and which has irresistibly led to one of the most terrible conflicts of all ages." Europe's civilization had "ignominiously failed. Ours must and shall succeed." [10]

Meyer London, the Socialist Congressman, reiterated an isolationist argument on February 17. America, he admonished, must continue to "be the one great neutral power, the one great Republic, the repository of the ideals of democracy and liberty." Entering the war would make the United States just another "sharer in its spoils," instead of "promoting democracy. . . . I do not hesitate to declare my faith and my hope in the greatness and glory of America as long as she pursues her ideals." Like most American Socialists, London subscribed to the neo-Marxist conviction that the expansive needs of highly developed capitalist economies generated the commercial rivalries which caused wars. Yet it was interesting that his isolationist arguments referred less to the economic interpretation of war than those put forward in the House a week later by Charles Lindbergh of Minnesota.[11]

Lindbergh was a radical progressive Republican who harbored a fierce hostility to big business based upon concern for the small, independent producer. He charged on February 24 that the nefarious dealings of the "money trust" had brought the United States "to the very verge of war, which may come at any day." Americans must not "for the sake of vainglory plunge this Nation into the maelstrom of hell. If we do we shall because of needless sacrifice come out with less power than we enter and destroy for a time our ability to conquer the world by the establishment of an economic system that will appeal to all humanity and be accepted for its justness. Everybody must admit that the existing civilization has proved an absolute failure. The battered continent of Europe supplies the gruesome evidence of it." Rather than imitate the misguided nations of that continent, America must "now establish the economic system that will make war unnatural." [12]

These statements indicated that an isolationist following was being attracted from the groups which had earlier appeared to provide sources of support. Those were principally agrarian Democrats and progressive Republicans, with some possible influences from German-American communities. There were also indications that a wider backing for isolationism might be growing among the public at large in response to the new crisis. Mass rallies were held in several cities to protest against the prospect of intervention. At one meeting in Chicago, Representative Oscar Callaway of Texas, a Democrat close to Bryan, denounced the "munitions makers, capitalists, American Admirals, Generals, Captains . . . leagued together to force the United States into war." [13]

The Armed Neutrality Controversy

One positive alternative to intervention was proposed in the debates following the resumption of submarine warfare. Recalling the experiences of European neutrals at the end of the eighteenth century, Professor Carlton J. H. Hayes of Columbia recommended armed neutrality for the United States. Intervention would mean, Hayes believed, that "we are far more likely to be drawn into an alliance with the Entente Powers" and to become "last and least on the long list of belligerents." Armed neutrality, by contrast, would be "a noble service to humanity" which promised "much that is hopeful for the future. In this case, the United States will be the first and foremost among all neutral powers. And a league of neutrals is a better harbinger of future world solidarity than a league of belligerents." [14]

Armed neutrality quickly became the rallying point for many anti-interventionists. The Committee for Democratic Control, a New York group headed by Bourne, Amos Pinchot, the noted radical Max Eastman, and social justice crusader Winthrop Lane, ran advertisements calling for armed neutrality as the most stringent measure that might be needed. Of those opponents of intervention, Bourne had already presented isolationist arguments, and Pinchot joined him when he asserted on February 16 that "the honor and glory of this country lies [*sic*] in a different direction from that indicated by our friends who make money out of war. I think Washington and Jefferson had the right idea, when they refused to be pulled into the European conflict, because they realized that no nation actually at war can preserve her power for good abroad and her democracy at home." [15]

But other anti-interventionists resisted armed neutrality as a step toward war. During the second week of February, La Follette started to construct a case to show that "the sinking of an *armed merchantman without warning*—even if attended with the loss of American life" was "*not a cause* for war." Bryan warned privately that he would stand in opposition "if the President should go to Congress for further powers." Wilson shared the qualms about armed neutrality. Even after he decided in favor of arming merchant ships, he rebuked the advocates of armed neutrality in the Cabinet for "trying to push us into war." Wilson likewise suspected that efforts then being conducted by Lodge and other Republican leaders to force a special session of Congress after March 4 were intended to hasten intervention. "The President believes, I think," wrote Secretary of the Interior Franklin K. Lane, "that the munitions makers are back of the Republican plan." [16]

Again, however, Wilson took a stiff line toward Germany and buttressed it with internationalist idealism. On February 26 he addressed another joint session to ask Congressional sanction for arming merchant vessels. Wilson vowed that he was not seeking war powers. "No course of my choosing . . . will lead to war. War can come only by the wilful acts and aggressions of others." America wished simply to defend "those rights of humanity without which there is no civilization." Those were "no selfish material rights" but the objects of "that righteous passion for justice upon which all law, all structures alike of family, of state, and of mankind must rest, as upon the ultimate base of our existence and our liberty." [17] Wilson had used his internationalism to justify another step toward intervention.

Two simultaneous events insured that armed neutrality would be considered entirely in light of the prospect of intervention. On February 25, a German submarine sank the British liner *Laconia,* causing the death of two American women passengers. The news reached the United States while the President was addressing Congress, and a wave of editorial indignation swept from coast to coast.[18] Then, on February 28, the State Department released a communication from Arthur Zimmermann, the German Foreign Minister, to his ambassador in Mexico. The British had intercepted this message and turned it over to the American ambassador in London four days before. The Zimmermann telegram offered the Mexicans, in the event of war between Germany and the United States, "Joint conduct of the war. . . . Ample financial support and an agreement on our part that Mexico shall gain back by conquest the territory lost by her at a prior period in Texas, New Mexico, and Arizona." However far-fetched it might seem, this was a direct threat to American territory. Moreover, it offered dramatic evidence that involvement in the war's consequences was far from completely a matter of the United States' own volition. Editorial anger not only flared at the Zimmermann telegram, but for the first time a large segment of the press called for war.[19]

Fear of entering the war formed the backdrop to Congressional consideration of the President's request for authority to arm merchant ships. On February 28, an antiwar delegation led by Jane Addams and Amos Pinchot went to Washington to urge the President and leaders on Capitol Hill to scorn all thoughts of intervention. Bryan arrived in the capital the same day to confer with other opponents of war. The first remarks in Congress about the President's request were addressed to the matter of intervention. Senator Stone, the chairman of the Foreign Relations Committee, broke with the Administration to oppose arming merchant vessels. "I am against this country entering into this war," announced Stone, "—I do not disguise that—and shall use whatever power I have to prevent it. . . . Upon that declaration I take my stand."[20]

A number of Representatives espoused idealistic isolationist views in opposing the idea of intervention. Stanley Benedict, Republican of California, warned that America must not surrender its position as "the hope of the oppressed and the refuge of all liberty-loving people" for the sake of "fighting to maintain the oppression of monarchies." William J. Cary, Republican of Wisconsin, said succinctly, "The example that we have set to the world by our Government and political and social life will be nullified forever if we take sides in this quarrel of conflicting dynasties." Another Wisconsin Republican, John M. Nelson, charged that the "Steel trust" was behind war agitation and admonished the nation to remain at peace and "follow the precepts of the Christ in the spirit of Christianity as it was exemplified in its early history before the Christian church was contaminated by the war spirit of the nations of the earth." [21]

Two Southern Democrats also took isolationist stands. George Huddleston of Alabama contended that business interests were seeking war "for its promotions, its profits, and its influence on our social and political life." Huddleston particularly feared intervention "on account of the entanglements which may result from it. I fear that the United States may be committed to alliances which will plague us through generations to come. . . . Now is the time to heed the advice of the fathers of the Republic." Claude Kitchin began to make public the isolationist convictions that he had hitherto kept strictly private. The European conflict, he asserted, "threatens the faith of mankind in Christianity—" and for the United States to enter it "would seem to challenge the right of Christianity to exist." By staying out, America could "make its blessings to shine out to mankind through the coming ages as an example of the divine reward of peace." [22]

The denunciations of big business in these arguments gave further evidence that a major source of support for the isolationist position lay among progressives. Of the Republicans, Cary and Nelson were long-time associates of La Follette in Wisconsin, while Benedict had followed Hiram Johnson in the California Progressive movement. The two Democrats were well-known as friends of Bryan and former antipreparedness stalwarts. Also, the Wisconsin Representatives may have been influenced by the presence of strong German-American communities in their districts.

Voting in the House on the arming of merchant vessels revealed this pattern of support even more clearly. The armed ships bill itself was approved after only a few hours of debate on March 1, the day after the publication of the Zimmermann telegram, by the overwhelming margin of 403 to 14.[23] Half the opponents had already espoused an isolationist position, including Cary, Nelson, London, Lindbergh, Benedict, and Sherwood of Ohio. Most of them were progressives or radicals of one persuasion or another. The grouping of nine of the votes in the Middle West partially reflected German-American concentrations. That was certainly true of the four votes from districts in the heavily German southern section of Wisconsin. The two votes from Minnesota and one from North Dakota, however, came from Congressmen who represented largely Scandinavian-American districts.

Another vote, on an amendment to the armed ships bill offered by Congressman Henry Allen Cooper of Wisconsin, disclosed the same pattern more broadly. Drawing upon the arms embargo scheme, the Cooper amendment would have prohibited armed American merchant vessels from transporting munitions to the belligerent countries. It was defeated, 125 for, 293 against.[24] Those favoring the amendment included virtually every Congressman who had used an isolationist argument, not only the ones who voted against the armed ships bill, but also others who did not, like Bailey, Slayden, "Cyclone" Davis, Huddleston, and Towner.

Three features of the group of Representatives supporting the amendment were particularly evident. One was progressivism. The Republicans included La Follette's followers from Wisconsin, of whom Cooper was the most notable, La Follette's cousin William from Washington, and all but one of the California ex-progressives. A number of regular Republicans also voted for it, as did most of the agrarian Democrats who had earlier spearheaded the antipreparedness drive.

The second feature of the vote was sectionalism. Half the Representatives favoring the amendment were Middle Westerners. In a number of their districts, particularly in Wisconsin, Nebraska, and Illinois, there was a correlation with the strength of German-Americans. But, once more, other Middle Western districts either were largely Scandinavian or featured no single prominent ethnic element. Of the districts in other sections, only a few in Pennsylvania and Missouri contained substantial numbers of Germans.

The final noteworthy feature of the vote was partisanship. Nearly two-thirds of those approving the amendment were Republicans. Well over one-third of the party's Representatives voted for the Cooper amendment, whereas only about a quarter of the Democrats joined them. Those proportions reflected the more general alignment of partisan interests. Several anti-interventionist Democrats in the House, like Kitchin, who did not vote for the amendment, and Bailey, who did, affirmed their faith in Wilson. Likewise, Bryan left quietly on March 1, after only one day in the capital. Later, he issued an ambiguous statement in which he neither entirely approved nor precisely condemned the armed ships bill.[25]

The Armed Ships Filibuster and the Pattern of Isolationist Support

The pattern of support for the isolationist position was largely one of progressivism, influenced by ethnic and partisan ties. Senate opposition to the bill revealed much the same alignment. Resistance was much stronger there than in the House, since the opponents had organized in advance. Norris, La Follette, and Stone were cooperating with Lodge and the Republican leadership. The latter were filibustering to force the calling of the next Congress because they feared Wilson might respond too mildly to the crisis. This alliance of opposites succeeded in postponing consideration of the armed ships bill until March 3, the last day before the expiration of the Sixty-fourth Congress. "We've got them beaten," Norris exulted to La Follette. "We can hold them now: we've got enough speakers to filibuster from tomorrow on." [26]

Nearly all the Senators who spoke against the armed ships bill used idealistic isolationist arguments. Vardaman charged that interventionist sentiment stemmed from "the shrewd manipulator of governmental functions for personal pecuniary profit, on the one side, the partisan patriot on the other, and mingled with it all the militarist, the imperialistically inclined element, whose natural sympathies are with a strong centralized government as against democracy." Cummins believed that by entering "the quarrels of Europe" Americans were "drifting away from the democracy of our forefathers, and we are atoning now for some of the sins of recent years." Clapp of Minnesota considered it "a sad spectacle, that this great Nation of ours, with its splendid history in the past, is so thoroughly to-day in the hands of commercialism that we propose to lend ourselves to a war for commercialism, born of commercialism, feeding upon commercialism, and fattening upon the commercialism of our own land." [27]

The most important isolationist utterance during the armed ships debate came in a speech which was never given. Administration supporters revenged themselves on La Follette by consuming the final hours and refusing to allow him to deliver the major address with which he planned to close the debate. Printing the speech later in his magazine, La Follette attacked the armed ships bill as a measure of "the evil system of one-man power and secret diplomacy in government that plunged the helpless peoples of Europe suddenly and hopelessly into the awful war that has been raging for the past three years. . . ." Rather than imitate that system, the United States should strive "toward prevention of war and the establishment of permanent peace" by giving "the people, who must bear the brunt of the war's awful burden more to say about it." America's proper course in the present crisis was "TO SUBMIT TO THE SACRIFICE OF UNDISPUTED RIGHTS FOR THE SAKE OF GREATER SERVICE TO THE COUNTRY AND TO HUMANITY."

La Follette insisted that he was no pacifist. The United States could enter the World War for the sake "of carrying food to the hungry in Europe." But the current interventionist agitation stemmed from J. P. Morgan's desire to protect his investments, and the nation was already in such straits because of the trusts "that we should not enter an aggressive war for humanitarian ends, much less for commercial profits, in carrying munitions." The real question, La Follette concluded, was, "Shall we bind up our future with foreign powers and hazard the peace of this nation for all time by linking the destiny of American democracy with the ever menacing antagonisms of foreign monarchies?" La Follette regarded "Europe as cursed with a contagious, a deadly plague, whose spread threatens to devastate the civilized world." The obvious recourse was to cast aside "all thought of material loss, or commercial inconvenience . . . before the necessity of protecting our people from being stricken with the dread disease." [28]

Behind La Follette's statement lay many of the most important strains of thought and political inclinations that were converging to produce support for an isolationist position. La Follette formulated his isolationist argument by extending his domestic political views to the international scene. He had begun the operation with his opposition to imperialism and preparedness, and had continued it with his advocacy of the arms embargo and nationalization of the manufacture of munitions. In the process, La Follette came to hold an almost Marxian view of international conflict. He asserted in July, 1916, for example, "Back of all modern war is practically the one policy, financial imperialism—the scheme of using the surplus wealth wrung unlawfully from the people of the country by the financial interests that dominate the country, the use of that surplus wealth through investments in the weaker undeveloped Governments of the world . . . it is the underlying cause of that which has converted almost all of Europe into a human slaughter pen." [29]

La Follette's view of America's place in the world similarly derived from his domestic beliefs. Like Bryan and Borah, he was applying an idealized image of the common people to the role of the nation in world affairs. The preceding October he had written, "In the agricultural districts, where the day is spent by the farmer following his plow or his harvester, mixing his thinking with his work, in the quiet and hush of country life, where the blast of the bugle and the roll of the drum is [*sic*] not disturbing the serenity, there is a wiser judgment, a truer test." So, too, in the "shops, and factories, and mines," men were not "deceived by a counterfeit call to serve selfish interests." Although La Follette seemed to differ from earlier isolationist idealists in using medical rather than religious metaphors, he also considered the basic problem one of morality analogous to personal conduct. "States are but aggregations of individuals," he declared in 1915. Just as a "deadly weapon within easy reach of the hand breeds a murderer," so "nations armed to the teeth quickly resort to killing as a means of settling their differences." [30]

La Follette differed chiefly from earlier spokesmen in that his views had not immediately led him to isolationist conclusions. Previously, he had been attracted to internationalist ideas. Unlike Bryan or Borah, he now rejected internationalism, not as an abstract argument about America's role in world affairs, but because it was used to justify intervention. The difference was perhaps not so great as it appeared. The implicit threat of entering the World War had lent immediacy to earlier isolationist arguments. But the sequence of La Follette's reactions—first approving internationalist propositions in the abstract, then balking at their practical consequences—was significant because it anticipated both his own and many American liberals' conduct during the controversy over joining the League of Nations at the end of the war. La Follette would initially favor League membership in principle but later become an "irreconcilable" opponent because the organization was bound to what he considered an unjust settlement.[31] This was an indication that disillusioned internationalists might become a significant source of isolationist support.

The immediate considerations which led La Follette to become an isolationist in March, 1917, pointed to the political interests which were contributing to the position. One of these was probably ethnic. Wisconsin contained the strongest German-American community in the country. La Follette, for all his moral stridency and genuine independence, always remained carefully attuned to the sentiments of his electorate. His opposition to prohibition would soon attest further to his sensitivity to the German element.[32] Still, the exact influence of such pressures was far from certain. La Follette was not pro-German. He openly disapproved of that nation's militarism and had never belonged to the school of progressives who admired the Teutonic combination of national strength and social reform. Ironically, the progressives who did were close to Roosevelt and had become a strongly pro-Allied faction, mainly out of revulsion at the conquest of Belgium. Only Beveridge and, in a milder way, George W. Perkins, favored the Central Powers. Beveridge privately disliked, but never publicly opposed, intervention. He both admired German militarism and believed that an Allied defeat would enhance American power in the world. Beveridge's thinking was, of course, exactly the opposite of idealistic isolationism.[33]

For La Follette, the ethnic ties of his constituents were part of a larger political picture. His chief concern lay with the prospects of progressivism. A year earlier, he had denounced preparedness for fostering a "militaristic spirit" which would distract "public attention to such an extent that other matters of moment go unnoticed. Just so surely as we enter upon an extravagant program of preparedness will all the movements for human welfare be paralyzed." This reflected a long-established conviction that war was inimical to reform. Several years before, Tom Watson had said of the Populists, "The Spanish war finished us. The blare of the bugle drowned the voice of the Reformer." In October, 1916, La Follette contended that after the Civil War "the great political parties put uniforms on their voters and marched them in torch light parades" in order to produce an "emotional effect" which would keep them from thinking about "the new economic issues—trusts, transportation, industrial and social justice; problems that grew up in the country following the Civil War. . . ." [34]

La Follette's suspicions were widely shared. The progressive movement had visibly faltered since the elections of 1914, and many blamed the setbacks on the World War. William Allen White wrote in June, 1916, that the trouble with progressivism was that "it hit war. Kaiser Bill blew it up. You cannot get humanitarian progress on the first page when humanitarian retrogression is occupying the headlines." Others feared that intervention would prove progressivism's final undoing. "Every reform we have won since 1912 will be lost," Wilson reportedly told Daniels in January, 1917. ". . . When the war is over those whose privileges we have uprooted or started to uproot will gain control of the government and neither you nor I will live to see government returned to the people." [35]

Partisanship also seems to have marginally influenced La Follette's isolationist stand. Being in power forced Wilson and the Democrats to regard foreign affairs as at least equal in importance to domestic reform. La Follette felt no such constraints. Instead, he could retain primary concern with progressivism as he confronted the question of intervention. In the past La Follette had been one of the least partisan of progressive Republicans. He had tacitly supported Wilson in 1912 and 1916, hailing the President's reelection as a victory of "the plain people" who lived "outside of the great financial and industrial centers of the nation." Yet as soon as the submarine crisis resumed in 1917, he sniffed that the Democrats were "just waiting for orders." [36]

The partisan factor weighed more heavily with other progressive Republicans. Wilson's success in enacting reform legislation created a special need to find ways to differentiate themselves from the Democrats. Hiram Johnson insisted at the beginning of 1917 "that while the President may have shown progressive tendencies the Democratic party is much more hopeless than the Republican for progressivism. . . ." [37] The progressives would have to oppose the Democrats in other areas, like foreign policy, in order to demonstrate the degree of party loyalty necessary to afford the slimmest chances of justifying faith in the Republicans. These various strains of idealistic thinking, ethnic pressures, fears for progressivism, and partisan need were the major factors which were converging to form the isolationist position.

The alignment of Senators against the armed ships bill further confirmed this pattern of support. The twelve opponents included La Follette, Norris, Stone, Clapp, Works, Cummins, Vardaman, Kirby, Lane, Kenyon, Gronna, and O'Gorman.[38] Seven were Republicans, comprising nearly all of the leading progressives, and four were Democrats close to Bryan. Only O'Gorman was an exception. It should also be noted that O'Gorman's opposition to the submarine policies of the Wilson Administration in 1916 and 1917 offers virtually the only evidence that Irish-American Anglophobia contributed to the isolationist following. On the other side, the sole isolationist in the Senate to favor the armed ships bill was Borah, who privately admired the courageous stand of the opponents. Several of those in opposition represented states with large German communities, but ethnic influences hardly explained the positions of all of them. Similarly, partisanship may have contributed to the slight preponderance of Republicans. A number of Democrats told Norris that they privately opposed the bill but were afraid to break with the Administration.[39]

There was also evidence that the armed ships controversy converted more people to isolationism outside of Congress. Contrary to Wilson's dismissal of the Senatorial opponents as "a little group of willful men, representing no opinion but their own," most of them appeared to have strong backing from their constituents. La Follette reported that letters to him, "at a rate of about 500 per day," ran four to one "strong and beautiful in their support." Norris received a great deal of mail from Nebraska applauding his actions, and he encountered an enthusiastic reception when he returned home later in March to explain his stand. Several of the Representatives who voted against the bill also had warm support from their districts.[40]

Amos Pinchot repeated his isolationist argument in response to the armed ships controversy. The United States, he asserted, must stay out of the war for the sake "of coming to the aid of, of emancipating the millions of men and women whom their own governments have enslaved, perhaps had to enslave, for the purpose of destroying each other. . . ." Royal W. France, a progressive New York lawyer whose brother was a newly elected Republican Senator from Maryland, similarly affirmed that intervention would "be contrary not only to the traditions and spirit of our government, but would cause us to forfeit the great position of leadership along the lines of peace and humanity which it should be our sublime mission to assume." [41] These statements offered further indications that the revival of the submarine crisis had advanced the coalescence of an isolationist political position.

The Decision to Intervene

The debates of March and April, 1917, over whether the United States should enter the World War completed the formation of the isolationist position. Acceptance or rejection of intervention required nearly all men in places of responsibility to face the question of reconciling American ideals and interests with overseas involvement. Wilson stated the problem in his second inaugural address on March 5, 1917. Although he observed that the "war inevitably set its mark from the first alike upon our minds, our industries, our commerce, our politics, and our social action . . . all the while we have been conscious that we were not part of it" and that "the part we wished to play was the part of those who mean to vindicate and fortify peace." Nothing, pledged Wilson, "will alter our thought or our purpose" to continue along the lines that he had laid down in the address of January 22. Americans must be "but true to ourselves—to ourselves as we have wished to be known in the counsels of the world and in the thought of those who love liberty and justice and the right exalted." [42]

Stating the problem was easier than solving it. Wilson's thinking appeared to grow more deeply divided as the crisis quickened in March, with more German sinkings of American vessels and with the heartening but unsettling events of the

Czar's overthrow in Russia. On March 19, he told both Lansing and Daniels that he was still not convinced that he should seek either broader measures of armed neutrality or intervention. That same day Wilson unburdened himself about his fears to Frank Cobb, editor of the New York *World*. Entering the war would, he believed, destroy America's moral position in the world. "It means an attempt to reconstruct a peacetime civilization with war standards, and at the end of the war there will be no bystanders with sufficient power to influence the terms. There won't be any peace standards left to work with. . . . If there is any alternative, for God's sake let's take it." [43]

Wilson's doubts vividly illustrated that his idealism had much in common with the isolationism espoused by anti-interventionists. Brent Dow Allinson, a Harvard student, held that America's neutrality was "the very basis of international law. As there can be no civil law without invoking the judgment of a 'reasonable man,' so there can be no international law without invoking the judgment of a neutral." Entering the war, contended Allinson, would leave "no saint in Israel," because as long as wars persisted, "there must be future neutrals or the game of civilization is up." The United States must be "too great to deal in resentments, and too profoundly conscious of American principles and precedent ever to abandon the great task for which an especial Providence has reserved us—the founding of a temple of Jupiter Serenator after the downfall of the Titans." [44]

Similarly, at the end of March, the *Commercial and Financial Chronicle,* a New York business journal, asked, "If, now, we enter into a war overseas, and invade the old realm of government-by-force from which we escaped, what will be the effect upon our own people and nation, and what upon the peoples of the earth, now struggling to be free, or restive under the yoke of monarchy or imperialism?" The *Commercial and Financial Chronicle* worried whether the United States could remain "the palladium of liberty" if it chose to employ the "bad" methods of the Old World to promote the "good" ends of the New. "Can we do this and preserve that democracy which we have exalted and which hitherto has exalted us? It may be that this is our mission, . . . but must we not admit that we are bringing into existence a new republic that is unlike the old?" [45]

The reactions of ultranationalists to the renewed submarine crisis were mixed. In most cases the distinction between them and idealists at least temporarily regained some of its sharpness. On one side, Roosevelt was more than ever the ardent interventionist. He scoffed at Wilson's quandaries as efforts to fight "feeble war—war of the peace-without-victory type. The difference between him and La Follette and Stone is utterly trivial compared to the abysmal difference between him and all honest and patriotic and courageous men." On the other side, Beveridge disliked going to war with Germany. He also maintained his stand against an "alliance with any particular foreign power and against the League to Enforce Peace plan." He likewise looked forward to "universal military training, the biggest navy in the world, NOT the second biggest navy, etc., etc., etc." The *Chicago Tribune* specified those same measures as "the price of isolation. We must be as strong as we are lonely." [46]

Interventionist sentiment grew appreciably toward the end of March. On March 19, Senators McCumber, Poindexter, and Duncan U. Fletcher of Florida called for war. On March 23, the *San Francisco Chronicle,* which up to this point had consistently opposed greater preparedness and tough diplomacy, declared itself resigned to entering the European conflict. The following day the *Chicago Tribune* came out not only for intervention but also for sending American troops to Europe to fight alongside the Allies until Germany was utterly defeated. Two Western Senators who had thus far held back from contemplating war, Nevada's Key Pittman and Hiram Johnson, now Works's successor from California, pledged support for war during the last week of the month. Anti-interventionist sentiment increased, too, with most of it linked to the isolationist position. Representative Webb of North Carolina feared that entering the war would cause "our country to become Prussianized or Russianized" with a "vast standing army" which would "bring about a condition from a military standpoint close akin to that which has existed in Europe for the last fifteen or twenty years." Senator Stone deplored any thought of departing "from the policy long supported by our ablest statesmen, beginning with Washington. Are we to be as successful in the internal affairs of European nations as we have been in Mexico?" [47]

But the opinion of the great majority of Americans evidently found accurate reflection in Wilson's doubts and hesitation. Most newpapers, magazines, and politicians did not commit themselves firmly either for or against war. A number of contemporary observers, with radically different viewpoints, discovered a singular lack of fervor for intervention in Congress, particularly in the House.[48] Not that the bulk of Congressmen were strongly opposed to war, but, like the President and probably like most Americans, they found themselves torn between repugnant alternatives. It is almost certain that Wilson could have carried majorities in Congress and among the public with him in virtually any direction he chose.

Why Wilson decided upon intervention at the end of March, 1917, still remains something of a puzzle. He continued to express misgivings even after issuing a call for Congress to meet to consider further action in the crisis. Once his decision was made, however, Wilson used the assumptions that he shared with idealistic isolationists to justify his choice. He vindicated entry into the World War in two steps. First, he accepted the idealistic isolationists' basic contention. Before the resumption of submarine warfare, Wilson had stood with most internationalists in disputing the argument that participation in international politics would damage the nation's moral position. But in his private apprehensions of February and March, 1917, he acknowledged the validity of that argument. Likewise, he publicly conceded the isolationists' point on April 2, in his address requesting that Congress declare that a state of war existed between the United States and Germany. He confessed his "profound sense of the solemn and even tragical character of the step I am taking." [49]

Then, however, Wilson used the concept of tragedy to answer the contention of the idealistic isolationists. The leitmotif of the war address, which too many interpreters have mistaken for a call for a crusade or holy war, was that of painful, unsought, uncertain choice.[50] The United States desired, he declared early in the speech, "only the vindication of right, of human right, of which we are only a single champion." The decision to intervene, he reiterated near the end, was "a distressing and oppressive duty. . . . It is a fearful thing to lead this great peaceful people into war, into the most terrible and disastrous of all wars, civilization itself seeming to be in the balance." The ends which America pursued were still those of assuring "that the same standards of conduct and of responsibility for wrong done shall be observed among na-

tion to the Diet of Worms: "God helping me, I can do no other."[52] The sentence probably occurred to Wilson by chance. It combined phrases near the end of the "peace without victory" address and at the close of the speech explaining the severance of relations with Germany, in which he had used "God grant" and "We could stand for no others." Yet, in view of Wilson's strongly Protestant upbringing and education, it was scarcely possible that he did not know that he was echoing Luther's declaration. Rather, it appears that the phrase came to Wilson as an inspiration. The Lutheran concept of Christian conduct furnished him with his answer to isolationist idealism.

The American idea of mission was based upon an analogy between international relations and the behavior of individual Christians. The United States was cast in the role of a Christian living in a community of sinners, facing the problem of what kind of relations to maintain in order to uplift and convert them. Isolationists prescribed the avoidance of sin, for the sake of conversion through example and evangelism. They drew upon the model of Christian conduct that Protestant fundamentalists preached. Internationalists, on the other hand, sought immediate betterment of conditions through active involvement in world affairs, and their arguments perhaps owed something to the ideas of liberal Protestantism associated with the Social Gospel. Since it was assumed in both positions that it was possible to avoid sin, Wilson was departing equally from each when he invoked the Lutheran concept of Christian conduct.

Luther had held that the individual believer, since he was a man, was incapable of avoiding sin. He must, instead, "sin boldly" as he sought to live a Christian life and humbly carry out God's will. This concept allowed Wilson to overcome the objections posed by the idealistic isolationists. He agreed with them that involvement in international affairs was fraught with evil consequences and was, properly speaking, sinful. But his answer was that the United States, despite its ideals, could not avoid entrapment in the wrongful acts that were the inescapable lot of nations. By accepting intervention, America would "sin boldly" in an effort to ameliorate world politics. This was the vision of Christian tragedy through which Wilson reconciled himself to entering the war.

Resistance to Intervention

For opponents, intervention remained a sin, which promised to be fatal to America's moral character. Wilson's justification of intervention through his internationalist idealism impelled almost every opponent to respond with an idealistic isolationist argument. Resistance to entering the war finally transformed isolationism into an extensive political position. Isolationist idealism constituted the major stand taken against intervention and thereby attracted the support of all but a few of those who opposed entry into the World War. The contention that embroilment in power politics would betray the nation's ideals was put forward in the first opposition speech during the Congressional debate over the request for war. Senator Vardaman applauded Wilson's ideas for future international order. "But," he warned, "the world will not take his big ideas by force of arms. . . . Moral reform must come by virtue of inherent merit and not by force of standing armies." [53]

Most of the Senators who spoke against going to war used idealistic isolationist arguments. Stone called intervention "the greatest national blunder of history." La Follette ridiculed Wilson's claims of defending democracy by joining the Allies. Except for France and "newly revolutionized Russia" all the Allies were "still of the old order—and it will be generally conceded that no one of them has done as much for its people in the solution of municipal problems and in securing social and industrial reforms as Germany." Besides, he asked, "Are the people of this country being so well represented in this war movement that they need to go abroad to give other people control of their governments?"

Norris similarly blamed intervention on moguls "concealed in their palatial offices on Wall Street, sitting behind mahogany desks, covered up with clipped coupons . . . coupons stained with mothers' tears, coupons dyed in the lifeblood of their fellow men." Americans, he charged, were "going into war upon the command of gold" at a time when they "ought to remember the advice of the Father of our Country and keep out of entangling alliances." [54]

Norris's argument disclosed most of the same strains of thought and political inclination as La Follette's. It was a transparent extension of progressive beliefs in the wickedness of Eastern big business. For Norris, too, an idealized picture of rural life underlay those beliefs. At the beginning of his Congressional career Norris had affirmed, "It is at the rural fireside that virtue, morality, and patriotism have reached their highest state," while "the highest and truest type of contentment and human happiness can be found in the country home." That view of life outside the metropolitan centers now formed the conception of American society that went into his isolationist argument. Ethnic influences from his electorate may also have disposed him to oppose intervention, since Nebraska had a large German-American population.

Norris did not, however, express any sympathies for the Central Powers. In February he had approved the severance of relations with Germany, and at one point in March he had said that he might favor war.[55]

The most interesting part of Norris's espousal of isolationism was his previous adherence to internationalist views. Even more clearly than La Follette, he took an isolationist stand by rejecting the specific actions which internationalist principles were being used to justify. In July, 1916, Norris had proposed creation of a world court to arbitrate disputes among nations and empowered to enforce its decisions with an international navy. In the postwar controversy over the League of Nations, he too approved of American membership in principle, only to become another "irreconcilable" opponent when the organization was tied to a peace settlement which he found unjust.[56] Norris would epitomize the attitude of many American liberals as he shuttled back and forth from internationalism to isolationism during the next twenty-five years. In the 1920s he favored joining the World Court, while in the 1930s he again became a staunch isolationist, but advocated aid to the Allies after the outbreak of the Second World War.[57]

The Senate vote against going to war once more revealed the pattern of isolationist support. The six Senators who opposed the war resolution were Gronna, La Follette, and Norris, three well-known Republican progressives, and Lane, Stone, and Vardaman, three Democrats from the Bryanite wing of the party. Influences of German-American constituencies may have played some part in the cases of Stone and Gronna, as well as La Follette and Norris. Partisanship had entered in, too, when Democrats from Missouri and Mississippi attempted to persuade Stone and Vardaman not to break with the President over intervention. Both men had confessed that having to vote as they did pained them deeply.[58]

Partisan influences could also be seen among some of the Senators who voted for war, along with the failure of several isolationists to hold their ground. Kirby called Wilson's request "a departure from all the policies of the Government heretofore," but he declined to vote against the war resolution since it was sure to pass anyway. Other Democrats who had earlier espoused isolationist convictions, like Thomas, Ashurst, and Gore, favored the resolution. The unwillingness of some isolationists to oppose intervention also extended to Republicans. Cummins believed that war could be avoided but supported the resolution because he thought that the country should not be divided. According to Norris, Kenyon, the other progressive Republican from Iowa, privately opposed intervention. "If this resolution committed our nation to any foreign alliances," Kenyon stated publicly, "I could not support it." [59]

Another isolationist Senator who voted for war was Joseph Irwin France, a progressive Republican from Maryland and the brother of the lawyer who had advanced an isolationist argument during the armed ships controversy. France had written to Wilson on March 28 to urge him not to enter the war. People did not want war, he claimed, "because they do not feel that American ideals and truly American principles are at stake. They attribute materialistic motives to those who have been so loudly clamoring for war." Neutrality was the way to "save this, the only Democracy in the world. . . ." France later became another of the "irreconcilable" opponents of membership in the League of Nations, which he condemned as a pious front cloaking the imperialistic conquests of the European victors. In his subsequent career France never publicly repudiated intervention, but he did deplore its consequences for the United States and the world.[60]

The sorriest performance of an isolationist in the Senate was Borah's. Although he had approved the break with Germany and the arming of merchant vessels, Borah also repeatedly stated that it would be "one of the greatest calamities that could happen to us to get into this war." As late as March 30 he insisted that "I shall not knowingly do anything for the sake of bringing on war." Yet behind those declarations, Borah had begun what appears to have been nothing less than a betrayal of his political role of the unfettered follower of conscience. On March 29, he asked a close friend in Idaho to "tell me what you think of the foreign situation and what people generally think we ought to do. Of course in these matters we all have our convictions and views but it is nevertheless a very wholesome thing to have the light of public opinion shed upon the program." [61]

Borah did "not find it possible on my part to vote against" the war resolution. Yet he also protested, "I join no crusade; I seek or accept no alliances; I obligate this Government to no other power. I make war alone for my countrymen and their rights, for my country and its honor." He finished the speech explaining his stand with a plea against impugning the loyalties of German-Americans. Characteristically, Borah never publicly expressed any regrets over his position, but he reportedly did say privately many times that he wished he could go back and change his vote.[62]

In the House, most of the opponents of the war resolution likewise employed idealistic isolationist arguments. Meyer London expressed their basic contention when he asserted, "The issue is not between Germany and America. The issue is between two Americas—between those who believe that it is the mission of America to influence the world for the better by being a free democracy, by growing into a genuine democracy, by marching unhindered on the road toward nobler and more beautiful ideals, and the group of men who believe that the United States must follow in the footsteps of the European countries and adopt the jargon of European diplomacy about national honor and national dignity." Kitchin agreed that America must not "throw away the only remaining compass to which the world can look for guidance in the paths of right and truth, of justice and humanity, and . . . leave only force and blood to chart hereafter the path of mankind to tread." [63]

Most of the Congressmen who opposed the war resolution also appealed for the maintenance of traditional isolation. Ernest Lundeen, a progressive Republican from Minnesota who later became a Farmer-Laborite, declared that in place of "Washington's policy of absolute neutrality" Wilson was attempting to "chart a new national course. . . . Our fixed determination is to thrust democracy with loving bayonets down the throats of unwilling peoples." Reavis of Nebraska told of how, having just returned from a walk on the Capitol portico, "I was not surprised to note that the towering monument, erected to him who advised against entangling alliances, had hidden its head in the mist and fog." [64]

The vote in the House against the war resolution clearly exposed the configurations of support for the isolationist position. Fifty-four Representatives opposed the resolution, thirty-five Republicans, eighteen Democrats, and one Socialist, London. The most readily apparent feature of the bulk of the antiwar Congressmen was their position on the left side of the political spectrum. Although the Republicans included some conservatives, eight of La Follette's followers from Wisconsin made up the largest single faction among the members of that party who opposed intervention. They were joined by other Republican progressives, like Lundeen, Haugen, William La Follette, and Jeannette Rankin of Montana, the first woman elected to Congress. The Democrats were nearly all members of the Bryanite wing of the party, most of whom had previously made up the hard core of opponents of preparedness. They included Kitchin, Webb, Sherwood, McLemore, Hensley of Missouri, Edward Keating of Colorado, Clarence Dill of Washington, and Carl Van Dyke of Minnesota. Former isolationist spokesmen from both parties like Lindbergh and Bailey, now no longer in Congress, similarly opposed entering the war.[65]

The sectional distribution of the votes may have partially reflected ethnic influences. Thirty-two of the Congressmen were from the Middle West, with twelve from the South, nine from the West, and only one, London, from the Northeast. Many of the Middle Western districts contained concentrations of German-Americans, particularly in Wisconsin, Illinois, Nebraska, and Iowa. Other districts in the Middle West, however, as well as nearly all of those outside it, did not have particularly large numbers of Germans. Many Middle Western Congressmen with substantial German-American communities in their districts nevertheless voted for war. Interestingly, two Representatives from strongly German areas stood against intervention without referring to the idealistic isolationist argument. William Igoe, Democrat of Missouri, said that he simply was expressing the wishes of his St. Louis constituents. Fred Britten, a Republican who represented a German section of Chicago, used ultranationalist arguments. He recommended the institution of universal military training, to "arm our whole Nation for its own defense and keep clear of any entangling alliances with European or Asiatic governments." [66]

Partisanship was partially reflected in the preponderance of Republicans among the antiwar Representatives. Democrats who had espoused isolationist views but voted for war, like Huddleston and Slayden, clearly bore the marks of party conformity. Slayden admitted that the United States would be entering into "an absolutely entangling alliance." But, he explained, "I shall try to comfort myself with the thought that whatever additional perils we are bringing to America may be compensated in the development of a world-wide democracy." [67] As in the Senate, however, the failure of isolationists to oppose intervention did not spring wholly from partisan causes. Republicans who had taken isolationist stands, such as Benedict of California and Sweet and Towner of Iowa, also voted for the resolution.

In all, from the beginnings of the preparedness controversy in 1915 through American entry into the war in 1917, the most striking aspect of isolationist support in Congress was its ideological complexion. The great bulk of exponents of isolationism in both the Senate and the House were progressives who followed an idealistic line. Their arguments showed that the most readily apparent motive for embracing isolationism was the application of a kind of originally agrarian progressive thinking to international affairs. This influence had been obvious in the views of Bryan and Democrats who shared his beliefs, like Bailey, Sherwood, "Cyclone" Davis, and Slayden. Such an outlook was also evident among Republican progressives from the Middle West and West, notably Borah, La Follette, and Norris. The ideological attraction which they displayed can properly be traced to "populism," especially in view of the continuities that existed between this support for isolationism and the original Populist movement. "Cyclone" Davis and Senator Gore had been members of the People's Party, while Bryan had become the principal political heir of the Populists. The most prominent surviving Populist, Tom Watson, likewise vociferously denounced intervention and took up idealistic isolationism.[68]

What caused the greatest following to be drawn from the Middle West was the subsequent influence of ethnic ties and party allegiance. A number of Congressional isolationists represented areas with large numbers of German-Americans. Partisanship also plainly affected the sectional locus of support for isolationism because, on the basis of a populistic ideology alone, the South should have furnished at least as extensive a following as the Middle West. The votes on preparedness in 1915 and 1916 had reflected a Southern antimilitarist and anti-imperialist heritage and revealed the section's potential for attraction to idealistic isolationist views. In addition, the South was the only part of the United States that had directly experienced a major war within the recollection of living men. Congressman John Burnett of Alabama declared that his childhood memories of the Civil War prevented him from backing the President on intervention. Webb similarly stated, "I was born almost amid the embers and smoke of fierce Civil conflict. In my youth I have often heard the horrors of war depicted from my sainted mother's lips." [69]

Yet athwart the attractiveness of isolationist views to Southerners lay the overriding fact of loyalty to the Democratic party, which was for them the least alterable of all commitments. It was heightened by Wilson's being the first Southern President since the Civil War. Perhaps nothing illustrated the impress of partisanship upon the isolationist position more strikingly than the conduct of the Great Commoner in the face of intervention. Bryan did oppose entering the war. He warned Congress by telegram on March 28 against "the signing of the death warrant of thousands, even millions of your countrymen, and the laying of grievous burdens upon future generations." Yet in that message Bryan also called himself "one who expects to live up to a citizen's duties, if war comes." As soon as the war resolution passed, he telegraphed Wilson to offer his services. He could do so, he explained privately, "with a consciousness that the blood that may be shed will not be upon my hands." [70]

The Commoner's opposition was ritualistic at best. To an appeal by David Starr Jordan that he come to Washington, he replied that he had "reached the conclusion that I was embarassing [*sic*] my friends there." His telegram, he said, "will do more good than I could do at a public meeting." Coming from one normally as sanguine as Bryan, that amounted to an admission of defeat. Considering his justification for leaving the Cabinet, this reasoning came close to being a repudiation of his own political role. A spark from the old fire did glow when he said to Jordan, "If I could speak before the Senate or House I would be delighted to come at a moments [*sic*] notice but I have no idea that such a thing is possible. Am doing all that I can following my best judgment as to what is wise." It seemed wise for him to announce as soon as war was declared, "The people are one—they all stand behind the President and Congress. . . ." As for himself, he added shortly afterward, in his last newspaper debate with Taft, he would take a "wait and see" attitude toward a postwar international peace-keeping organization.[71]

The bonds of party fealty which restrained agrarian Democrats help to account for the preponderance of progressive Republicans among the Congressional isolationists. They were able to express their distrust of the influence of foreign affairs on domestic reform more freely. "Everything here is war," reported Hiram Johnson upon taking his Senate seat in April, 1917. ". . . That which has been so intimate a part of our lives in California during the past seven years, governmentally, could not get the slightest hearing." [72] Though initially a supporter of intervention, Johnson grew steadily more critical of Wilsonian diplomacy. By the end of the war he emerged as another "irreconcilable" opponent of membership in the League of Nations. For Middle Western progressive Republicans in Congress, too, the presence of substantial German-American communities in many of their states seems to have had some effect, though usually indirect or secondary, in increasing dispositions toward isolationism.

Resistance to intervention outside Congress appeared to follow the same general lines, at least as far as the evidence uncovered in the research for this book has been able to show. Many of the Senators and Representatives who opposed going to war evidently had strong backing from their districts. Several received large numbers of letters and telegrams commending their stands. La Follette claimed that nine out of every ten communications to him, not only from Wisconsin but also from forty-three other states, gave "unqualified" endorsement to his position. He also reported that a North Dakota Congressman had found people there uniformly opposed to war. Newspaper polls in Sheboygan and Manitowoc, Wisconsin, two strongly German-American cities, showed heavy majorities against intervention. A similar poll in Minneapolis, which was more Scandinavian, also registered overwhelming opposition to entering the war.[73]

The subsequent fortunes of the Congressional opponents offer only spotty indications about whether their constituents were behind them. The evidence from the Senate is unclear. Of the six members who voted against the war resolution, only one, Vardaman, lost his seat in an election which prominently featured war-related issues. Lane and Stone both died within a few months after intervention. Norris was reelected easily in 1918. La Follette did not face reelection until 1922. Gronna failed in his bid for renomination in 1920 largely because of local issues. In the House, twenty-eight of the fifty-four opponents were reelected in 1918. Fourteen were defeated. Several of their losses apparently turned on issues that were not related to their opposition to intervention. On the other side, a significant turnover also occurred in the 1918 elections among Senators and Representatives who supported the war resolution, again mainly because of domestic issues.[74]

There were signs that idealistic isolationist principles formed the most important anti-interventionist platform outside Congress. The American Union against Militarism, which was headed by a group of independent progressives, including Amos Pinchot, contended in a newspaper advertisement, "We cannot bring democracy to Europe by going to war. *We can preserve democracy in the western hemisphere* by staying out." The editor of a newspaper in Canton, Ohio, wrote to Randolph Bourne urging him to "keep it up" and continue "trying to keep a little bit of light alive in the darkness. . . ." [75] These utterances, together with the statements made in February and March, 1917, indicated that isolationist views had begun to spread among the public at large. If these views had not exactly penetrated to the grass roots level, they were certainly prevalent among a number of informed citizens. Moreover, by employing isolationist arguments, the Congressional opponents of war served to spread their views among like-minded constituents. Though the signs were still sparse, a substantial isolationist position did appear to have formed.

NOTES

1. *Commoner* 17 (February, 1917): 2, 10.

2. Wilson to Bryan, February 2, 1917, Bryan Papers, LC, Box 31; William B. Wilson to R. S. Baker, September 17, 1932, R. S. Baker Papers, LC, Series I, Box 58; entry of February 4, 1917, Lansing Diary, LC, Notebook 2. For other accounts of the Cabinet meeting, see Houston, *Eight Years with Wilson's Cabinet,* 1:229–231 (See note 86, Chapter 1.); Daniels, *Wilson Era,* 1:591; Franklin K. Lane to George W. Lane, February 9, 1917, in Anne W. Lane and Louise H. Wall, eds., *The Letters of Franklin K. Lane* (Boston: Houghton Mifflin Co., 1922), pp. 233–235 (hereafter cited as Lane and Wall, *Lane Letters*); Daniels to Wilson, February 2, 1917, Wilson Papers, Series II, Box 147.

3. *Wilson Public Papers,* 4:422–426.

4. *Record,* 64th Cong., 2nd sess., February 7, 1917, pp. 2729–2731.

5. Ibid., February 7, 1917, pp. 2737, 2749; Borah to O. W. Newman, February 6, 1917, Borah Papers, Box 182.

6. *Record,* 64th Cong., 2nd sess., February 7, 1917, p. 2750; ibid., February 10, 1917, pp. 2809–2810. Cf. Lodge's description of the opponents, Lodge to T. Roosevelt, February 7, 1917, Lodge Papers, Roosevelt-Lodge Corresp.

7. La Follette to family, February 3, 4, 6, 1917, quoted in Belle Case La Follette and Fola La Follette, *Robert M. La Follette* (New York: Macmillan Co., 1952), 1:593–594, 595 (hereafter cited as *Robert M. La Follette*); February 3, 1917, entry in Sparks, *Ashurst Diary,* p. 54. Cf. Louis Lochner to Henry Ford, February 4, 1917, Louis Lochner Papers, State Historical Society of Wisconsin, Box 52 (hereafter cited as Lochner Papers).

8. La Follette to family, February 2, 3, 1917, quoted in *Robert M. La Follette,* 1:593–594; *La Follette's Magazine* 9 (February 1, 1917): 1; *Record,* 64th Cong., 2nd sess., February 7, 1917, p. 2734.

9. *Record,* 64th Cong., 2nd sess., Feb. 17, 1917, p. 3523; ibid., *Appendix,* Feb. 19, 1917, pp. 398–402.

10. *Record,* 64th Cong., 2nd sess., Feb. 17, 1917, p. 3525; ibid., Feb. 22, 1917, pp. 3913–3916, 3952–3953.

11. *Record,* 64th Cong., 2nd sess., February 17, 1917, p. 3528. On the Socialists' view of war, see David A. Shannon, *The Socialist Party of America: A History* (New York: Macmillan Co., 1955), pp. 81–82.

12. *Record*, 64th Cong., 2nd sess., February 24, 1917, p. 4202.

13. *New York World*, February, 1917. See also *New York Times*, February 5, 6, 10, 13, 1917.

14. Carlton J. H. Hayes, "Which?: War without a Purpose? Or Armed Neutrality with a Purpose?", *Survey* 37 (February 10, 1917): 538.

15. *New York Times*, February 13, 1917; *New Republic* 10 (February 17, 1917): 82; Pinchot to C. E. L. Wingate, February 16, 1917, Pinchot Papers, LC, Box 30.

16. La Follette to family, February 11, 1917, quoted in *Robert M. La Follette*, 1:599; F. H. Dixon to House, February 15, 1917, House Papers; Daniels, *Wilson Era*, 1:594; Lane to G. W. Lane, February 25, 1917, in Lane and Wall, *Lane Letters*, pp. 239–240.

17. *Wilson Public Papers*, 4:428–432.

18. For editorial reactions to the sinking, see *New York Times*, February 27, 1917; *New York World*, February 27, 1917; *Chicago Tribune*, February 27, 1917; *Omaha World-Herald*, February 27, 1917; *San Francisco Chronicle*, February 27, 1917; *Literary Digest* 54 (March 10, 1917): 605–607.

19. Zimmermann to Bernstorff, January 16, 1917, in Reichstag Committee of Inquiry, *Official German Documents Relating to the World War* (New York: Oxford University Press, 1923), 2:1337. For editorial reactions to the Zimmermann telegram, see *Milwaukee Journal*, March 1, 1917; *Atlanta Constitution*, March 2, 1917; *Baltimore Sun*, March 2, 1917; *New York World*, March 2, 1917; *New York Times*, March 2, 1917; *Chicago Tribune*, March 2, 1917; *Literary Digest* 54 (March 17, 1917): 687–690; *New Republic* 10 (March 10, 1917): 151–153; *Nation* 104 (March 8, 1917): 255–258.

20. *New York Times*, March 1, 1917; *Record*, 64th Cong., 2nd sess., March 1, 1917, p. 4603.

21. *Record*, 64th Cong., 2nd sess., *Appendix*, March 2, 1917, pp. 747–748, 893; ibid., March 3, 1917, p. 831–832.

22. *Record*, 64th Cong., 2nd sess., March 1, 1917, p. 4640; ibid., *Appendix*, March 3, 1917, pp. 817–819. For Kitchin's private isolationist statement, see Kitchin to Bryan, January 8, 1917, Bryan Papers, LC, Box 31.

23. *Record*, 64th Cong., 2nd sess., March 1, 1917, p. 4692. For a statistical description of this vote, see Table 14 in Appendix.

24. *Record*, 64th Cong., 2nd sess., March 1, 1917, p. 4691. For a statistical description of this vote see Table 12 in Appendix.

25. *Record*, 64th Cong., 2nd sess., March 1, 1917, p. 4640, 4688; *New York Times*, March 2, 1917; *Commoner* 17 (March, 1917): 3.

26. Norris to Fola La Follette, February 15, 1939, quoted in *Robert M. La Follette*, 1:609.

27. *Record*, 64th Cong., 2nd sess., March 2, 1917, pp. 4777–4778; ibid., March 3, 1917, pp. 4908–4912; ibid, March 4, 1917, p. 5002.

28. *La Follette's Magazine* 9 (March, 1917): 2–4. On the plot to keep La Follette from speaking, see *Robert M. La Follette*, 1:615–624; George

W. Norris, *Fighting Liberal: The Autobiography of George W. Norris* (New York: Macmillan Co., 1945), pp. 180–181.

29. *Record,* 64th Cong., 1st sess., July 20, 1916, p. 11340.

30. *La Follette's Magazine* 8 (October, 1916): 1; *Record,* 63rd Cong., 3rd sess., February 12, 1915, p. 3633.

31. *Robert M. La Follette,* 2:914–915; *Record,* 66th Cong., 1st sess., November 6, 1919, p. 8433.

32. See *Record,* 65th Cong., 1st sess., August 1, 1917, p. 5660. For a good characterization of La Follette as a politician in the context of an earlier brush with the opponents of alcohol, see David P. Thelen, "La Follette and the Temperance Crusade," *Wisconsin Magazine of History* 47 (Summer, 1964): 291–300.

33. For Beveridge's thinking, see, e.g., Beveridge to Albert Shaw, February 13, 1917, Beveridge Papers, Box 203; Beveridge to W. H. Stayton, March 17, 1917, ibid., Box 210; on Perkins, see Chester Rowell to Hiram Johnson, December 15, 1915, Johnson Papers, Part II, Box 29; Edward W. Hungerford, "After the War: An Interview with George W. Perkins," *Colliers* 58 (January 6, 1917): 5–6, 19. Victor Berger, the Socialist mayor of Milwaukee, also favored the Central Powers because he believed that their victory would advance socialism. See Berger to Morris Hillquit, June 3, 1916, Morris Hillquit Papers, State Historical Society of Wisconsin.

34. *La Follette's Magazine* 8 (March, 1916): 15, (October, 1916): 1; Watson statement, October, 1910, quoted in Woodward, *Tom Watson: Agrarian Rebel* (New York: MacMillan Co., 1938), p. 334.

35. White to Rodney Elward, June 24, 1916, in Walter Johnson, ed., *Selected Letters of William Allen White, 1899–1943* (New York: Henry Holt, 1947), p. 169; Daniels, *Wilson Era,* 1:582.

36. *La Follette's Magazine* 8 (November, 1916): 1; La Follette to family, February 2, 1917, quoted in *Robert M. La Follette,* 1:593.

37. Hiram Johnson to Chester Rowell, January 26, 1917, Chester Rowell Papers, Bancroft Library, University of California, Berkeley, Box 17.

38. The list of opponents is drawn from those Senators who did not sign or approve the round robin supporting the bill (*Record,* 64th Cong., 2nd sess., March 4, 1917, pp. 4988–4989). Cf. *New York Times,* March 5, 1917; Lodge to T. Roosevelt, March 6, 1917, Roosevelt Papers, Box 323.

39. See Borah to Ed Dewey, March 29, 1917, Borah Papers, Box 180; Norris, *Fighting Liberal,* pp. 178–179.

40. La Follette to family, March 8, 1917, quoted in *Robert M. La Follette,* 1:633; letters and telegrams to Norris, February–March, 1917, George W. Norris Papers, Library of Congress, Tray 10, Box 1 (hereafter cited as Norris Papers); R. G. Thomas to J. R. McCarl, Mar. 27, 1917, ibid., Box 3; Norris, *Fighting Liberal,* pp. 183–187; letters and telegrams to Henry Allen Cooper, February–March, 1917, Henry Allen Cooper Papers, State Historical Society of Wisconsin (hereafter cited as

Cooper Papers); Louis Lochner to John M. Nelson, March 6, 1917, John M. Nelson Papers, State Historical Society of Wisconsin. Wilson's remark is in *Wilson Public Papers*, 4:435.

41. Pinchot to La Follette, March 5, 1917, Pinchot Papers, Box 27; Royal W. France letter to editor, *New Republic* 10 (March 10, 1917): 162. Cf. Pinchot letter to editor, *New York Evening Post*, March 27, 1917.

42. *Wilson Public Papers*, 5:2–5.

43. Lansing to House, March 19, 1917, House Papers; entry for March 19, 1917, in Cronon, *Daniels Cabinet Diaries*, p. 117; entry for March 20, 1917, Lansing Diary, Notebook 2; J. L. Heaton, ed., *Cobb of the "World": A Leader in Liberalism* (New York: E. P. Dutton & Co., 1924), pp. 268–270. This conversation, as Arthur Link has pointed out, took place on March 19 and not, as Cobb erroneously remembered, the night before Wilson asked Congress for war. Link correctly observes that its occurrence at this earlier time adds to the significance of the conversation, since these fears represented the considered position which Wilson had to answer in his own mind, rather than last-minute qualms. See Link, *Wilson*, 5:399, n.33. More recently, Jerold Auerbach has raised searching questions about the authenticity of much of Cobb's recollection of the interview. He does concede, however, that the statements about international order were probably accurate. See Auerbach, "Woodrow Wilson's 'Prediction' to Frank Cobb: Words Historians Should Doubt Ever Got Spoken," *Journal of American History* 54 (December, 1967): 608–617.

44. Brent Dow Allinson letter to editor, *New Republic* 10 (March 31, 1917): 264. Allinson later became a conscientious objector to the war and was arrested in 1918 for refusing to serve in the armed forces. See *New York Times*, April 21, 22, 1918.

45. *New York Commercial and Financial Chronicle* 104 (March 31, 1917): 1196–1197.

46. T. Roosevelt to Lodge, March 10, 1917, Lodge Papers, Roosevelt-Lodge Corresp.; Beveridge to Mark Sullivan, March 18, 1917, Beveridge Papers, Box 208; *Chicago Tribune*, February 25, 1917. Cf. T. Roosevelt to Hiram Johnson, March 18, 1917, Johnson Papers, Part II, Box 208.

47. *New York World*, March 20, 1917; *San Francisco Chronicle*, March 23, 1917; *Chicago Tribune*, March 24, 1917; Pittman to Wilson, March 27, 1917, Wilson Papers, Series II, Box 148; Johnson speech of March 31, 1917, scrapbook clippings, Johnson Papers, Part III, Box 19; Webb to Arthur J. Draper, March 31, 1917, Webb Papers, Box 13; *New York Times*, April 1, 1917.

48. See, e.g., Gus J. Karger to Taft, April 6, 1917, Taft Papers, Box 374 (Gen. Corresp.); David Starr Jordan to Jessie Jordan, April 6, 1917, David Starr Jordan Papers, Hoover Institution for the Study of War, Peace, and Revolution, Stanford University (hereafter cited as Jordan Papers); Jordan, *Days of a Man*, 2:733, n. 1; Arthur W. Dunn. *From Harrison to Harding: A Personal Narrative Covering a Third of a Century*

(New York: G. P. Putnam's Sons, 1922), 2:357; Fiorello H. La Guardia, *The Making of an Insurgent: An Autobiography: 1882–1919* (Philadelphia: J. B. Lippincott, 1948), pp. 138, 140.

49. This and following references to the war address are from *Wilson Public Papers*, 5:6–16. For expressions of his continued misgivings, see entry of March 24, 1917, *House Diary*, 10:83; *New York Times*, March 28, 1917.

50. For the "holy war" interpretation see, e.g., Osgood, *Ideals and Self-Interest*, pp. 192–194; John M. Blum, *Woodrow Wilson and the Politics of Morality* (Boston: Little, Brown & Co., 1956), pp. 130–131. Eric Goldman has interpreted the decision much more perceptively by illustrating how Wilson answered his own objections to war in his *Rendezvous with Destiny*, pp. 249–251 (see note 27, Chapter 2).

51. Speech of May 15, 1915, *Wilson Public Papers*, 4:171–172.

52. See, e.g., Sullivan, *Our Times*, 5:285.

53. *Record*, 65th Cong., 1st sess., April 4, 1917, p. 209.

54. Ibid., April 4, 1917, pp. 210, 212–214, 228.

55. Ibid., 58th Cong., 2nd sess., March 14, 1904, pp. 3257–3258; *New York World*, March 20, 1917.

56. *Record*, 64th Cong., 1st sess., July 13, 1916, pp. 10931–10933; Norris, *Fighting Liberal*, pp. 203–204, 208–213; *Record*, 66th Cong., 1st sess., September 6, 1919, pp. 4960–4963.

57. See Norris, *Fighting Liberal*, pp. 390–395. On his international positions, see also Norman L. Zucker, *George W. Norris: Gentle Knight of American Democracy* (Urbana, Ill.: University of Illinois Press, 1966), pp. 127–148.

58. *Record*, 65th Cong., 1st sess., April 4, 1917, p. 261. On Stone and Vardaman, see James A. Reed to Fola La Follette, April 28, 1939, quoted in *Robert M. La Follette*, 1:654; Henry V. Watkins' commemorative address on Vardaman, May 17, 1936, quoted in Albert D. Kirwan, *Revolt of the Rednecks: Mississippi Politics, 1876–1925* (Lexington, Ky.: University of Kentucky Press, 1951), p. 280.

59. *Record*, 65th Cong., 1st sess., April 4, 1917, pp. 219, 220–221, 250; Norris, *Fighting Liberal*, p. 198.

60. Joseph Irwin France to Wilson, March 28, 1917, Wilson Papers, Series II, Box 148. On France's role in the League controversy see *Record*, 66th Cong., 1st sess., October 9, 1919, pp. 6598–6599; *Pittsburgh Gazette-Times*, October 3, 1920, in Joseph Irwin France Scrapbooks, University of Maryland Library.

61. Borah to P. M. Beers, February 12, 1917, Borah Papers, Box 184; Borah to A. W. Rompe, March 30, 1917, ibid., Box 183; Borah to Jonathan W. Hart, March 29, 1917, ibid., Box 181. For other antiwar statements, see Borah to Arthur Condit, March 8, 1917, Borah to L. Schuler, March 13, 1917, and Borah to G. E. Simpson, March 30, 1917, ibid., Box 184.

62. *Record*, 65th Cong., 1st sess., April 4, 1917, pp. 252–253; Claudius Johnson to author, January 4, 1965.

63. *Record,* 65th Cong., 1st sess., April 5, 1917, pp. 330, 332.

64. Ibid., April 5, 1917, pp. 357, 363–364.

65. Ibid., April 6, 1917, p. 413; Charles A. Lindbergh to Eva L. Christie [April, 1917], Charles A. Lindbergh Papers, Minnesota Historical Society, Box 2; Bailey to Kitchin, April 6, 1917, Kitchin Papers, Box 18. For a statistical description of the vote, see Table 15 in Appendix.

66. *Record,* 65th Cong., 1st sess., April 5, 1917, pp. 317, 322–323.

67. Ibid., April 5, 1917, pp. 385–386.

68. See Woodward, *Tom Watson,* pp. 452–455. "Coin" Harvey, the free silver propagandist of the 1890s, had also expressed antimilitarist, anti-imperialist views as part of his anti-British, antimonarchical, anti-international banker ideology. See Richard Hofstadter's introduction to the reissue of William H. Harvey, *Coin's Financial School* (Cambridge, Mass.: Harvard University Press, 1963), esp. pp. 30–31, 32–34, 69–72.

69. *Record,* 65th Cong., 1st sess., April 4, 1917, p. 372; Webb to S. H. Farabee, April 10, 1917, Webb Papers, Box 13.

70. Bryan telegram, March 28, 1917, Bryan Papers, LC, Box 31; Bryan to Wilson, April 6, 1917, Wilson Papers, File VI-A, folder 2400; Bryan to Louis Lochner, April 2, 1917, Lochner Papers, Box 52.

71. Bryan to Jordan, March 28, 1917, Jordan Papers; *Commoner* 17 (April, 1917): 3; Taft and Bryan, *World Peace,* pp. 154–156.

72. Johnson to Chester Rowell, April 10, 1917, Chester Rowell Papers, Box 17.

73. *Record,* 65th Cong., 1st sess., April 4, 1917, pp. 223–224; *New York World,* April 4, 1917. For antiwar mail, see letters and telegrams to Norris, April, 1917, Norris Papers, Tray 10, Box 3; letters and telegrams to Kitchin, April, 1917, Kitchin Papers, Box 18; letters and telegrams to Henry Allen Cooper, April, 1917, Cooper Papers.

74. See Kirwan, *Revolt of the Rednecks,* pp. 284–289; *New York Times,* July 3, October 17, 1920, May 5, 1922; Seward W. Livermore, *Politics Is Adjourned: Woodrow Wilson and the War Congress, 1916–1918* (Middletown, Conn.: Wesleyan University Press, 1966), esp. pp. 181, 227–235.

75. *New Republic* 10 (March 31, 1917): 275; Burton Knisely to Bourne, May 28, 1917, Bourne Papers, Box 4.

Conclusion

THIS book does not pretend to be a comprehensive history of twentieth-century American isolationism, but it does seem appropriate to conclude with a few observations on how the character of the isolationist position was fixed in its emergence during the First World War. Most of the essential features revealed then remained intact over the next twenty-five years. Isolationist arguments, for example, showed little variation. Idealists continued to advocate rejection of overseas commitments in order to provide a righteous example. Ultranationalists upheld the contention that the nation's self-interest required aloofness from all ties outside the hemisphere. Isolationist policies underwent almost no change, either. The expedients first introduced between 1914 and 1917—keeping American citizens and ships out of war zones, prohibiting loans and munitions shipments to belligerents, and requiring a popular referendum for a declaration of war—all formed the isolationist program of the 1930s. Most of these measures saw Congressional enactment in the successive Neutrality Laws.[1]

The isolationist personnel, both leaders and followers, also stayed basically the same. During the postwar controversy over American membership in the League of Nations, Borah and Lodge again stepped forward as the foremost spokesmen for their respective positions in a coalition of idealistic and ultranationalist isolationists. The Middle Western and Western progressive bloc supplied most of the isolationist leadership on Capitol Hill in the 1920s and 1930s. Borah and Hiram Johnson remained active throughout those decades. They were joined by such younger progressives as Senators Gerald Nye of North Dakota and Burton K. Wheeler of Montana. In the cases of Senator Robert M. La Follette, Jr., who succeeded his father in 1925, and Representative Maury Maverick, Slayden's nephew, outspoken isolationism came by way of family descent.[2] Congressional voting in the 1930s showed much of the same partisan, sectional, and ethnic complexion as it had during the First World War. One striking difference, however, lay in a growing conservatism among isolationist elements. This change appears to have stemmed partly from the heated partisan atmosphere of the late thirties and early forties. It also came as part of an internal revolution of American reform, which impelled many former progressives to oppose New Deal liberalism.[3]

One other continuity lay in the comparative strength of idealism and ultranationalism within the isolationist ranks. Clearly, idealism provided the greater following during the First World War. The balance continued in favor of the idealists during the '20s and early '30s, when progressives dominated the isolationist position. Even a great deal of the subsequent conservatism of isolationists on the eve of the Second World War can be traced in part to idealism. As Richard Hofstadter has pointed out, the New Deal era witnessed a trading of rhetoric and perspectives between the two sides of the political spectrum. Liberals came to affect the claims of cold realism that had heretofore characterized the right; conservatives tended to adopt the formerly progressive style of strident devotion to moral principles.[4] The preponderance of idealists did not mean that isolationists were free from self-interest. Many of them undoubtedly cared much more about saving their own skins than the world's soul. But the strength of idealism did signify that the thinking of most isolationists continued to fall within the confines of the American idea of mission.

That idealism should not be surprising. The idea of mission, after all, has been merely a propagandized expression of the optimistic middle-class liberalism that, as a number of interpreters have argued, has formed virtually the exclusive tradition of American politics.[5] Ultranationalists' frank avowals of self-interest and power-seeking have always been rare in the United States. They were probably more prevalent during the First World War than at most other times because a kind of aristocratic, quasi-militarist critique of industrial society was prominent in the progressive era.[6] After the League controversy of 1919 and 1920, ultranationalism declined steadily within the isolationist position. It almost completely disappeared in the 1930s, when Hitler and Mussolini made aggression and militarism understandably unpopular. Interestingly, the version of ultranationalism associated with the Republican right wing in the 1950s and 1960s has featured militant interventionism overseas, and it has been linked with a fervent, though perhaps perverted, devotion to traditional American ideals.

Recent uses of the term "isolationism," especially in debates over the war in Vietnam, raise a final question of whether the position has, in fact, been resurrected. The answer based upon the interpretations presented in this book would be no. True, some signs have pointed to a revival of aspects of isolationism. The often heard contention that involvement in Vietnam has undermined American ideals does hark back to earlier isolationist arguments. Likewise, as in the isolationist heyday, liberals have comprised the bulk of opponents of the war. Increasing numbers of them have apparently accepted the contention that overseas commitments prevent the achievement of needed domestic reforms. Yet few critics of Vietnamese involvement have called for global disengagement. Many have deplored the venture because of its effects on other American commitments, especially in Europe. The clearest difference between the current controversy and the debate which surrounded isolationism is a shift in focus. The central concern is no longer whether the United States should be involved beyond the hemisphere but, rather, what should be the methods, directions, and priorities in pursuing such involvement.

The isolationist position that formed during the First World War and lasted until the Second belonged to a particular moment in American history. Both isolationism and the internationalist challenge that evoked it arose in response to the breakdown of "free security." Acceptance or rejection of overseas commitments became matters of constant, conscious choice. The triple combination of the idea of mission, the preceding century of inattention to international politics, and the unprecedented violence and destruction of the twentieth century produced extravagance in the expectations and claims of nearly everyone involved. If one can say that anything has been proven in the years since the end of the Second World War, it is that both isolationists and internationalists have been wide of the mark in their predictions. Worldwide commitments on the part of the United States have not inaugurated a millennium of peace and freedom through the abolition of power politics. Nor have such commitments caused the downfall of American liberties and values.

Probably the best indication that isolationism will not be revived is that its whole context has been rendered outmoded. The experiences of the 1960s have raised serious questions about the applicability of America's experiences and ideals to the upheavals sweeping through Africa, Asia, and Latin America. Somber assessments are being advanced about how much the United States can either accomplish in those parts of the world or avoid being embroiled in their troubles. Such doubts and questioning serve to dispel what has been the final hangover of isolationism. That is the still-prevalent morality-play account of the controversies over foreign policy in the era of the two world wars. Until recently most Americans still appeared to accept the view that wise, responsible, high-minded internationalists had vied with ignorant, prejudiced, selfish isolationists for control of the nation's foreign policy. That account, of course, simply reversed the roles assigned by the isolationists themselves during their ascendancy in the 1930s. They then portrayed themselves as the Children of Light and the internationalists as the Children of Darkness. If unwillingness to accept such interpretations continues and grows, their demise may become America's one happy casualty of the 1960s.

NOTES

1. On isolationist thought in the 1930s, see Jonas, *Isolationism in America* (page 85n54 85); on the Neutrality Laws, see Robert M. Divine, *The Illusion of Neutrality* (Chicago: University of Chicago Press, 1962).

2. On the isolationists in Congress in the '30s, see John C. Donovan, "Congressional Isolationists and Roosevelt's Foreign Policy," *World Politics* 3 (April, 1951): 299–316.

3. For analyses of voting on foreign policy issues in the '20s and '30s, see George L. Grassmuck, *Sectional Biases in Congress on Foreign Policy, 1921–1941* (Baltimore: Johns Hopkins Press, 1951). The shift in progressive attitudes is explored in Otis L. Graham, Jr., *An Encore to Reform: The Old Progressives and the New Deal* (New York: Oxford University Press, 1967).

4. Hofstadter, *Age of Reform,* pp. 315–316.

5. See Louis Hartz, *The Liberal Tradition in America: An Interpretation of Political Thought since the Revolution* (New York: Harcourt, Brace & Co., 1955).

6. See above, pp. 62, 82n18.

APPENDIX

Statistical Descriptions of Congressional Voting on Preparedness and Foreign Policy, 1915–1917

SOME statistical descriptions of voting in Congress on questions of military preparedness and issues relating to the World War help to indicate patterns of isolationist support. For the Senate, inferences are relatively easy to draw. Table 1 "scores" Senators on opposition to increased preparedness.[1]

The most striking characteristic of this group is progressivism. All the Republicans except Curtis, a regular with some reform leanings, were progressives. All the Democrats belonged to the Bryanite or agrarian reform wing of their party.[2] Hints of partisanship might be detected in the majority of eight Republicans to six Democrats, and even more so in the preponderance of six Republicans to only one Democrat among those opposing greater preparedness on all or three of the four votes. Sectionalism also shows up clearly in the fact that none of these Senators was from the Northeast. Twelve of the fourteen represented states west of the Mississippi, while the other two were from just across the river.

TABLE 1

Senators Opposed to Two or More of Four Measures for Increased Preparedness

	Percent Opposed		*Percent Opposed*
Gronna (*R-N. Dak.*)	100	Cummins (*R-Iowa*)	50
La Follette (*R-Wis.*)	100	Hitchcock (*D-Nebr.*)	50
Norris (*R-Nebr.*)	100	Kenyon (*R-Iowa*)	50
Vardaman (*D-Miss.*)	100	Lane (*D-Oreg.*)	50
Clapp (*R-Minn.*)	75	Myers (*D-Mont.*)	50
Curtis (*R-Kans.*)	75	Robinson (*D-Ark.*)	50
Works (*R-Calif.*)	75	Thomas (*D-Colo.*)	50

Table 2 similarly scores opposition to potential overseas involvement.[3]

Before drawing any inferences from this table, a cautionary note should be sounded. The votes considered were hardly equal in importance. Political costs for the thirty-seven Senators who opposed tabling the amendment to bar munitions shipments or the fourteen who opposed tabling the Gore resolution were negligible compared to those for the six who opposed breaking relations with Germany, the twelve against the armed ships bill, or the six opponents of the war resolution. By themselves, votes can often be misleading. McCumber appears in this table because he opposed the first two measures before becoming an internationalist. His presence does, however, underscore the common idealism of many isolationists and internationalists. Borah, on the other

TABLE 2

Senators Opposed to Two or More of Five Measures Involving Closer Contact with the World War

	Percent Opposed		*Percent Opposed*
Gronna (*R.-N. Dak.*)	100	Clapp (*R-Minn.*)	40[a]
La Follette (*R-Wis.*)	100	Gallinger (*R-N. H.*)	40
Lane (*D-Oreg.*)	80	Jones (*R-Wash.*)	40
Norris (*R-Nebr.*)	80	Kenyon (*R-Iowa*)	40
Vardaman (*D-Miss.*)	80	Kirby (*D-Ark.*)	40[a]
Works (*R-Calif.*)	80[a]	McCumber (*R-N. Dak.*)	40
Cummins (*R-Iowa*)	60	Sherman (*R-Ill.*)	40
O'Gorman (*D-N. Y.*)	60[a]	Stone (*D-Mo.*)	40
Borah (*R-Idaho*)	40		

[a] Not serving in Senate for all five votes.

hand, appears only because of the quirk that he voted against tabling the Gore resolution in protest over procedures. Another isolationist Senator, Thomas of Colorado, does not appear at all. These problems indicate the general limitation of Congressional voting statistics: Inferences should not be drawn from them without close attention to debates and all other evidence which might disclose the thought and motives of the participants.

With those limitations pointed out, certain observations can be made about the pattern of isolationist support in the Senate. Again, progressivism is the most striking characteristic. Among the Republicans, only Gallinger, a staunch conservative, and McCumber, a middle-of-the-roader, were not progressives. Except for the Tammanyite O'Gorman, all the Democrats were agrarians. Partisanship also stands out, since twelve of the seventeen were Republicans. Republicans likewise accounted for four of the six who opposed potential involvement on four or all of the five votes. Sectionalism appears almost as clearly. Only two of the opponents came from the Northeast, whereas twelve represented states west of the Mississippi. The one influence which does not seem to manifest itself in a noteworthy way is German-American constituencies. Although some of these Senators had German communities in their states, so did others whose names do not appear. Scandinavian-Americans were stronger in several states represented by these men.

Table 3 lists states that were above the national averages in 1920 in either German- or Scandinavian-born populations.[4] These percentages naturally do not afford a complete picture of the strength of ethnic elements in these states, since they include only those *born* in Germany or Scandinavia, not all citizens of German or Scandinavian extraction. But the percentages should furnish a reliable, if rough, indication of the strength of these groups.

Another insight afforded by these statistics on Senatorial opposition to preparedness and overseas involvement comes when the two tables are compared. There is a good deal of overlap. Nine Senators, over half of each table, appear on both. Significantly, too, the greatest interchangeability occurs precisely among those who offered the highest degree of opposition: La Follette, Norris, Gronna, Vardaman, and Works. This overlap between opposition to preparedness and overseas involvement suggests forcefully that progressivism—with a sectional thrust of opposition to Northeastern influences and at least some agrarian overtones—formed the strongest basis for the isolationist following. The greater number of Republicans tends to confirm a secondary influence of partisanship. Likewise, the ideological, sectional, and partisan

TABLE 3

States with German- and Scandinavian-Born Populations Above National Average in 1920

	Approximate Percent Born in Germany (Including Austria)	*Approximate Percent Born in Scandinavia (Including Norway, Sweden, and Denmark)*
Ohio	3	([a])
Illinois	4	2.5
Michigan	3	1
Wisconsin	9	3.5
Minnesota	3.5	9
Iowa	3	2.5
North Dakota	2	9
South Dakota	3	5.5
Nebraska	3.5	2.5
Montana	2	4
Wyoming	1	2
Utah	1	3.5
Nevada	2	2
Washington	2	5.5
Oregon	2	8
California	2.5	2
National average	2	1

[a] Less than 1 percent.

alignments of all the Senators in the two tables reveals the same basic pattern of support.

Inferences which can be drawn from voting in the House are less definite. For the Senate, the prominence of its members and close study by historians allow fairly reliable identification of political allegiances. But in the House few Representatives can be identified beyond their party affiliation and geographical location. What is lacking is a precise identification of who progressives and conservatives in the House really were. No one has yet done the close study of the *Congressional Record* and comprehensive roll-call analysis, of the kind done by Joel Silbey and Thomas Alexander for pre-Civil War Congresses, which are necessary to give meaningful identification to any but the most prominent Representatives. The best that can be done here is to offer some rather tentative observations based upon partisan and sectional alignments.

Table 4 shows the composition of the vote in favor of reducing battleship construction in February, 1915.[5]

This vote reveals the basic prewar alignment against pre-

TABLE 4

Sectional Distribution of House Vote to Cut Battleship Construction

	Percent of Total Vote	*Percent of Democratic Vote*	*Percent of Republican Vote*
Northeast	5.8[a]	6.5	0.0
South	60.6	66.2	6.7
Middle West	31.0	25.2	93.3
West	2.6	2.1	0.0
Number of votes	(155)[a]	(139)	(15)

[a] Includes one Socialist vote.

paredness. The dominance of Democrats confirmed earlier partisan positions. The sectional distribution followed previous lines. Gulf Coast and interior Southern districts combined with those from the Middle West to furnish the great bulk

TABLE 5

Sectional Distribution of House Vote against Army Increase

	Percent of Total Vote	*Percent of Democratic Vote*	*Percent of Republican Vote*
Northeast	3.2[a]	3.3	0.0
South	57.8	67.8	5.9
Middle West	31.8	22.1	82.4
West	7.2	6.8	11.7
Number of votes	(216)[a]	(181)	(34)

[a] Includes one Socialist vote.

of the votes. Fourteen of the fifteen Republicans who crossed party lines also came from the Middle West. A few ideological inferences may be drawn on impressionistic evidence. Prominent among the Democrats were the agrarians who later spearheaded opposition to Wilson's program. Generally, too, most of the Democratic votes came from rural districts. The Republicans featured two of La Follette's associates, as well

TABLE 6

Sectional Distribution of House Vote against Increased Battleship Construction

	Percent of Total Vote	*Percent of Democratic Vote*	*Percent of Republican Vote*
Northeast	6.6[a]	6.7	0.0
South	61.0	66.4	5.5
Middle West	25.8	20.6	83.3
West	6.6	6.3	11.2
Number of votes	(213)[a]	(194)	(18)

[a] Includes one Socialist vote.

as two or three others who can with some assurance be identified as progressives.

Tables 5 and 6 show alignments against increased preparedness in 1916.[6]

These tables show quite clearly how the antipreparedness forces in the House remained the same as they had been earlier. It is interesting to note, also, in Tables 7 and 8, the

TABLE 7

Sectional Distribution of House Vote for Army Increase

	Percent of Total Vote	*Percent of Democratic Vote*	*Percent of Republican Vote*
Northeast	56.2[a]	76.7	53.7
South	6.5[a]	6.7	6.0
Middle West	29.2[a]	16.6	30.2
West	8.1[b]	0.0	10.1
Number of votes	(185)[c]	(30)	(149)

[a] Includes one Progressive vote.
[b] Includes three Progressive votes.
[c] Includes six Progressive votes.

corresponding sources of support for greater preparedness.

As much as the opposition, this support for increased preparedness conforms to prewar partisan and sectional configurations. Republicans furnished most of the votes, with slightly over half from the Northeast. At the same time, more than three-quarters of the Democrats who broke ranks also came from the Northeast. There was little indication of cleavage along progressive-conservative lines, since many reform Republicans and the little band of Progressives favored bigger armaments. The circumstances surrounding

TABLE 8

Sectional Distribution of House Vote for Increased Battleship Construction

	Percent of Total Vote	*Percent of Democratic Vote*	*Percent of Republican Vote*
Northeast	53.9[a]	80.8	51.1
South	7.8[a]	3.8	7.8
Middle West	29.1[a]	15.4	31.6
West	9.2[b]	0.0	9.5
Number of votes	(206)[c]	(26)	(174)

[a] Includes one Progressive vote.
[b] Includes three Progressive votes.
[c] Includes six Progressive votes.

these votes may have heightened conformity to earlier patterns. Both measures were Republican attempts to raise the levels of military and naval forces above those requested by the Wilson Administration. This struck a partisan note which probably worked against any shifts of opinion.

TABLE 9

Sectional Distribution of House Vote against Naval Appropriation Bill

	Percent of Total Vote	*Percent of Democratic Vote*	*Percent of Republican Vote*
Northeast	3.9[a]	2.8	0.0
South	39.0	55.5	0.0
Middle West	51.0	36.1	92.9
West	6.1	5.6	7.1
Number of votes	(51)[a]	(36)	(14)

[a] Includes one Socialist vote.

The only indication of changes on preparedness came with the final vote on the naval appropriation bill in August, 1916, described in Table 9.[7]

The partisan and sectional differences are clear. Although Democrats still supplied over two-thirds of the opposition, their numbers were sharply reduced. Roughly the same knot of Middle Western Republicans remained. Also, that section for the first time contributed more heavily than the South to opposition to greater preparedness.

The most striking changes of all, however, had already occurred in the House vote on tabling the McLemore resolution. Table 10 describes the opposition vote.[8]

TABLE 10

Sectional Distribution of House Vote against Tabling McLemore Resolution

	Percent of Total Vote	*Percent of Democratic Vote*	*Percent of Republican Vote*
Northeast	20.8[a,b]	20.7	20.2
South	16.0	35.3	16.3
Middle West	52.8	35.3	60.6
West	10.4[c]	8.7	2.9
Number of votes	(144)[a,d]	(34)	(104)

[a] Includes one Socialist vote.
[b] Includes one Progressive vote.
[c] Includes three Progressive votes.
[d] Includes five Progressive votes.

The composition of this vote is far different from that of the antipreparedness votes. The partisan distribution is almost exactly reversed, with Republicans supplying three-quarters of the votes. Most of the Progressives also switched sides. Likewise, the sectional distribution reflects both much stronger Middle Western and much weaker Southern backing. These changes can be observed equally well in Table 11, which describes the vote in favor of tabling.

TABLE 11

Sectional Distribution of House Vote for Tabling McLemore Resolution

	Percent of Total Vote	*Percent of Democratic Vote*	*Percent of Republican Vote*
Northeast	33.0	13.3	71.2
South	43.5[a]	64.6	3.2
Middle West	17.0	17.7	16.0
West	6.5	4.4	9.6
Number of votes	(276)[a]	(181)	(94)

[a] Includes one Progressive vote.

Several inferences can be drawn from these alignments. The shift of party positions from the preparedness issue demonstrated the respective pressures put on Democrats by officeholding and on Republicans by opposition. Many Democrats who favored the principle behind the McLemore resolution voted to table it out of loyalty to the Administration. Party ties held Southerners in particularly tight rein, with even Kitchin and Page joining in the substantial Southern vote for tabling. The Democratic holdouts were almost all radical agrarians, including Bailey, Slayden, and "Cyclone" Davis. The Republicans presented a mottled picture. Some ideological division was evident both in Republican support for tabling, which came primarily from Northeastern conservatives, and in the opposition, which included most of the party's well-known progressives. Yet such redoubtable conservatives as Cannon, Longworth, and Mann also opposed tabling.

The most difficult matter upon which to draw inferences is ethnic influence. On the one hand, for a number of districts in Wisconsin, Illinois, Iowa, Nebraska, and Missouri, a correspondence did exist between concentrations of German-Americans and votes against tabling.[9] Considering the vociferous support for warning citizens off belligerent ships given by German-American organizations and the German-language press, a measure of ethnic influence was almost certainly reflected in those votes. Yet, on the other hand, many districts of Representatives opposed to tabling contained no great German concentrations. Rather, for a number of Middle Western districts there was almost as much correspondence between Scandinavian-American centers and votes against tabling. Furthermore, several Representatives from districts with strong German communities voted to table the resolution.

The exceptions do not contradict ethnic influences, but they do show that they were hardly simple or clear-cut. This problem deserves close study, with particular attention to how opinions toward the World War actually developed within various communities. Except for a few striking examples in Wisconsin and in cities like Chicago and St. Louis, few Congressional districts which produced votes against tabling contained majorities or even really sizable minorities of German-Americans. Instead, Germans were usually mixed with "natives" and other ethnic groups, often Scandinavians. The kind of considerations that need to be examined include the relations between Germans and other elements in those communities, reactions of the rest of the community to the war, and the political complexions of the communities.[10] Only when such considerations have received careful attention can German and Scandinavian ethnic influences on support for isolationism be satisfactorily gauged.

Another matter that needs further study is the behavior of Irish-Americans. In view of later Irish support for isolationism during the League controversy and in the thirties and forties, it is remarkable that almost no evidence suggests any influence from this quarter during the First World War. Senator O'Gorman is noteworthy because he provides almost the sole example of the ancient Irish grudge against Britain possibly contributing to the isolationist position. Among the questions that should be considered are how much Democratic loyalties restrained the Irish from becoming isolationists. Also, one must ask whether the growing cultural conflict over religious and "nativist" issues may have kept Irish-Americans apart from other groups in the isolationist following.

Table 12 describes the vote in favor of the Cooper amend-

TABLE 12

Sectional Distribution of House Vote for Cooper Amendment

	Percent of Total Vote	*Percent of Democratic Vote*	*Percent of Republican Vote*
Northeast	11.2[a]	8.3	13.2
South	22.4	50.0	5.3
Middle West	50.4	25.0	67.1
West	16.0[b]	16.7	14.1
Number of votes	(125)[a,b]	(48)	(76)

[a] Includes one Socialist vote.
[b] Includes one Progressive vote.

ment of March 1917, to the armed ships bill, which would have prevented munitions shipments.[11]

In nearly all basic features this vote duplicated the vote against tabling the McLemore resolution. The partisan distribution again included a Republican majority, while the Middle West once more supplied half the votes. Intraparty divisions were partially ideological as before, with most of the prominent Republican progressives and a large number of agrarian Democrats favoring the amendment. Also, roughly the same picture of ethnic influences appeared. Several Representatives favoring the amendment had strong German elements in their districts, and a number of Middle Western districts of supporters were predominantly Scandinavian.

The similarity between the votes in favor of the Cooper amendment and against tabling the McLemore resolution can also be seen in Table 13, which describes the opposition.

TABLE 13

Sectional Distribution of House Vote against Cooper Amendment

	Percent of Total Vote	*Percent of Democratic Vote*	*Percent of Republican Vote*
Northeast	35.2[a]	16.8	62.4
South	39.6[a]	61.6	7.7
Middle West	21.1[a]	18.6	24.8
West	4.1[a]	3.0	5.1
Number of votes	(293)[b]	(172)	(117)

[a] Includes one Progressive vote.
[b] Includes four Progressive votes.

Democrats again supplied nearly two-thirds of the votes, with those coming predominantly from Southerners. The

Republican vote was heavily Northeastern and featured virtually all of the party's best-known conservatives. One shift was that those conservatives now included Middle Westerners like Mann, Longworth, and Cannon. Another change was that most of the Progressives likewise opposed the amendment.

The last two House votes during the controversy preceding intervention reveal a measure of coalescence between antipreparedness and anti-interventionist elements. Table 14 describes the vote against the armed ships bill.[12]

TABLE 14

Sectional Distribution of House Vote against Armed Ships Bill

	Percent of Total Vote	*Percent of Democratic Vote*	*Percent of Republican Vote*
Northeast	14.3[a]	0.0	10.0
South	14.3	66.7	0.0
Middle West	64.3	33.3	80.0
West	7.1	0.0	10.0
Number of votes	(14)[a]	(3)	(10)

[a] Includes one Socialist vote.

The partisan and sectional patterns remained largely the same as in the McLemore resolution and Cooper amendment votes. German-American influence could be seen in the fact that four votes, the largest single bloc, came from Southern Wisconsin, and another from Chicago's South Side. Most other districts, however, were not heavily German. The strongest correlation was ideological. All three Democrats belonged to the Bryanite wing of the party, and eight of the ten Republicans can be identified as progressives. The presence of the Socialist, London, added to the leftist complexion of the vote.

The most important vote taken in these years came with the war resolution in April, 1917. It is described in Table 15.[13]

TABLE 15

Sectional Distribution of House Vote against War Resolution

	Percent of Total Vote	*Percent of Democratic Vote*	*Percent of Republican Vote*
Northeast	1.8[a]	0.0	0.0
South	22.2	55.5	5.7
Middle West	59.2	16.6	82.9
West	16.8	27.9	11.4
Number of votes	(54)	(18)	(35)

[a] Includes one Socialist vote.

Partisan, sectional, and ethnic patterns persisted from previous votes. Republicans supplied nearly two-thirds of the opposition. The Middle West was by far the strongest opposition section, furnishing about three-fifths of the votes. German concentrations were present in a number of districts. By a rough estimate, however, large German-American populations lived in no more than one-fifth of these districts. Scandinavian-Americans were strong in slightly fewer.

The ideological complexion of the antiwar vote is strikingly reformist. Nearly all eighteen Democrats can be identified as Bryanites, whereas twenty of the thirty-five Republicans seem to have been progressives. London's presence again reinforces the leftist cast of the vote. A comparison of this vote with that against passage of the naval appropriation bill shows both the same ideological bent and a degree of meshing with the antipreparedness group. The fourteen Representatives who opposed both measures were: Burnett (D-Ala.), Davis (R-Minn.), Connelly (D-Kans.), Dillon (R-S.Dak.), Haugen (R-Iowa), Helgesen (R-N.Dak.), Hilliard (D-Colo.), Kinkaid (R-Nebr.), Kitchin (D-N.C.), London (Socialist-N.Y.), Nelson

TABLE 16

Representatives Opposed to Three or More of Four Measures Involving Closer Contact with the World War

	Percent Opposed		*Percent Opposed*
Cary (*R-Wis.*)	100	Browne (*R-Wis.*)	75
Cooper (*R-Wis.*)	100	Church (*D-Calif.*)	75
Davis (*R-Minn.*)	100	Decker (*D-Mo.*)	75
Helgesen (*R-N.Dak.*)	100	Dillon (*R-S. Dak.*)	75
London (*Socialist-N.Y.*)	100	Esch (*R-Wis.*)	75
Nelson (*R-Wis.*)	100	Frear (*R-Wis.*)	75
Stafford (*R-Wis.*)	100	Fuller (*R-Ill.*)	75
Haugen (*R-Iowa*)	75	McLemore (*D-Tex.*)	75
Hayes (*R-Calif.*)	75	Meeker (*R-Mo.*)	75
Hensley (*D-Mo.*)	75	Powers (*R-Ky.*)	75
Hilliard (*D-Colo.*)	75	Reavis (*R-Nebr.*)	75
Hull (*R-Iowa*)	75	Roberts (*R-Nev.*)	75
Igoe (*D-Mo.*)	75	Shackleford (*D-Mo.*)	75
Johnson (*R-S. Dak.*)	75	Sherwood (*D-Ohio*)	75
Keating (*D-Colo.*)	75	Sloan (*R-Nebr.*)	75
King (*R-Ill.*)	75	Van Dyke (*D-Minn.*)	75
Kinkaid (*R-Nebr.*)	75	Wheeler (*R-Ill.*)	75
La Follette (*R-Wash.*)	75	Wilson (*R-Ill.*)	75[a]
Lindbergh (*R-Minn.*)	75[a]	Woods (*R-Iowa*)	75

[a] Not serving in House for all four votes.

(R-Wis.), Randall (D-Calif.), Van Dyke (D-Minn.), and Webb (D-N.C.).

The list is almost evenly divided between seven Bryanite Democrats and six progressive Republicans, with London once more adding to the leftward slant. Also, in two districts, one in Kansas and one in Minnesota, where the Representatives changed from the Sixty-fourth to the Sixty-fifth Congress, the successor to an opponent of the naval appropriation bill voted against the war resolution. The total overlap between the two votes was, therefore, a little less than one-third.

One other way to assess the components of anti-interventionist voting in the House is to "score" Representatives in the same way as Senators. Table 16 lists the thirty-eight Representatives who opposed overseas involvement on all or three of the four votes previously described.

This group may be taken as a fair sample of isolationist support in the House. Its partisan and sectional distribution is described in Table 17.

As in the individual votes, Republicans and Middle Westerners each accounted for about two-thirds of the opposition.

TABLE 17

Sectional Distribution of Representatives
Opposed to Three or More Measures

	Percent of Total	*Percent of Democrats*	*Percent of Republicans*
Northeast	2.6[a]	0.0	0.0
South	15.4	30.0	7.0
Middle West	65.6	40.0	81.9
West	15.4	30.0	11.9
Number	(38)[a]	(10)	(27)

[a] Includes one Socialist.

Ethnic influences were also similar. German communities were strong in about fifteen districts and Scandinavian communities in about ten. The clearest correlation, however, is ideological. All or almost all ten Democrats came from the Bryanite bloc, while twenty-one of the twenty-seven Republicans can be more or less reliably categorized as progressives. London adds still another leftist inclination. In all, approximately thirty-two of the total of thirty-eight—84 percent—belonged to the left side of the political spectrum.

These statistical descriptions of Congressional voting reinforce the view of isolationist support gained from other sources. The isolationist coalition rested upon an amalgam of reformist, partisan, sectional, and ethnic interests. The strongest element seems to have been liberalism or progressivism, which was in keeping with the greater frequency of idealistic views in isolationist utterances. Partisanship, however, significantly modified the reformist bent by deflecting many Democrats away from the inclinations that they originally displayed on the preparedness issue. Sectional and ethnic factors also seem to have modified somewhat the progressive and partisan bases of the isolationist coalition; these factors require further study on the local level. Generally speaking, the combination of factors revealed in Congressional voting during the First World War continued to characterize the support for the isolationist position over the following twenty-five years.

NOTES

1. The votes, described above, pp. 103, are from *Record,* 64th Cong., 1st sess., April 18, 1916, p. 6359; ibid., 17, 1916, p. 11192; ibid., July 21,

1916, p. 11379; ibid. July 21, 1916, p. 11384. The table agrees for the most part with Howard Allen's estimates, which are based upon a larger number of votes with less clear-cut issues posed. H. W. Allen, "Republican Reformers and Foreign Policy, 1913–1917," *Mid-America* 44 (October, 1962): 222–229.

2. For a kind of scorecard of Senatorial progressivism and conservatism during this period, see H. W. Allen, "Geography and Politics: Voting on Reform Issues in the United States Senate," *Journal of Southern History* 26 (May, 1961): 216–228. Some of Allen's assumptions and methods are open to question, especially regarding the role of partisanship in reform votes, but his tables do provide a convenient and provisionally acceptable indication of who progressives and conservatives in the Senate were.

3. The votes are on the Hitchcock amendment to prohibit munitions shipments, *Record,* 63rd Cong., 3rd sess., February 18, 1915, p. 4016; Gore resolution, ibid., 64th Cong., 1st sess., March 3, 1916, p. 3465; severance of relations with Germany, ibid., 64th Cong., 2nd sess., February 7, 1917, p. 2750; armed ships bill (drawn from those who did not sign the round robin) ibid., March 4, 1917, pp. 4988–4989, and other sources; see above, pp. 187, 210*n*38 and war resolution, ibid., 65th Cong., 1st sess., April 4, 1917, p. 261.

4. These estimates have been calculated from data in *Fourteenth Census of the United States . . . 1920: Population* (Washington: Government Printing Office, 1922), Vol. 3.

5. *Record,* 63rd Cong., 3rd sess., February 5, 1915, p. 3152. Sections used in this and succeeding tables are:

Northeast: Maine, New Hampshire, Vermont, Massachusetts, Rhode Island, Connecticut, New York, New Jersey, Pennsylvania.

South: Delaware, Maryland, West Virginia, Virginia, North Carolina, South Carolina, Georgia, Florida, Alabama, Mississippi, Tennessee, Kentucky, Missouri, Arkansas, Louisiana, Texas, Oklahoma.

Middle West: Ohio, Indiana, Michigan, Illinois, Wisconsin, Minnesota, Iowa, Kansas, Nebraska, South Dakota, North Dakota.

West: Montana, Wyoming, Colorado, New Mexico, Arizona, Utah, Nevada, Idaho, Washington, Oregon, California.

6. The votes are from *Record,* 64th Cong., 1st sess., March 23, 1916, p. 4729; ibid., June 2, 1916, p. 9189.

7. The vote is from ibid., August 15, 1916, p. 12700.

8. It is from ibid., March 7, 1916, p. 3720.

9. For a careful study of the Germans, with maps, see Hildegarde B. Johnson, "The Location of German Immigrants in the Middlewest," *Annals of the Association of American Geographers* 41 (March, 1951): 1–41.

10. One small piece of evidence might be this description of attitudes in the predominantly Scandinavian community in North Dakota in which the journalist Eric Sevareid lived as a boy at the time of the

First World War: "There were a good many Germans in town, but your parents never talked about them as *Germans,* never pointed them out and set them aside in your mind. . . . They were just the neighbors. You knew they came from Germany, but you did not move them into that side of your mind which contained the Germany of the devilish Kaiser, the spiked helmets, and the savage men who cut off the hands from Belgian children. The conception of Germans as a race, with racial (or, at least, national) characteristics of their own, was something that did not enter into my mind for many years." Eric Sevareid, *Not So Wild a Dream* (New York: Alfred A. Knopf, 1946), p. 10.

11. It is from *Record,* 64th Cong., 2nd sess., March 1, 1917, p. 4691.

12. Ibid., March 1, 1917, p. 4692.

13. Ibid., 65th Cong., 1st sess., April 6, 1917, p. 413.

Bibilographical Essay

A COMPLETE bibliography for this study is included in my doctoral dissertation of the same title, Columbia University, 1968 (available from University Microfilms, Ann Arbor, Michigan). Since several comprehensive discussions of primary and secondary sources for the World War era are readily available, it is more important to concentrate on two matters which no one has yet treated. One is a survey of the sources for the 1914–1917 period that illuminate the emergence of isolationism. The other is a critical review of previous interpretations of isolationism.

Sources for the Emergence of Isolationism, 1914–1917

Research in manuscript sources has usually been extensive rather than intensive. This reflects both a general thinness of materials and the value of many scattered materials. Manuscripts of isolationists are rarely as informative as one would wish. By far the best collections for the workings of anti-preparedness and anti-interventionist forces in Congress are the Claude Kitchin Papers, Southern Historical Collection, University of North Carolina, Chapel Hill, and the Warren Worth Bailey Papers, Princeton University Library. The Kitchin Papers have recently been made available on microfilm. Two relatively unused but helpful collections of Congressional isolationists are the E. Y. Webb Papers, Southern Historical Collection, and the John D. Works Papers, Bancroft Library, University of California, Berkeley. The Works Papers, Stanford University Library, contain little on his Senatorial career, except for his manuscript autobiography. The Henry Cabot Lodge Papers, Massachusetts Historical Society, include important correspondence with Roosevelt and information on alignments at the beginning of 1917.

Otherwise, the manuscripts of isolationists in Congress are disappointing. The collections in the State Historical Society of Wisconsin, including the papers of Henry Allen Cooper, John M. Nelson, and John J. Esch, are fragmentary. The papers of William E. Borah and George W. Norris, Library of Congress, yield relatively little of value in proportion to their tremendous bulk. Of the two, the Borah Papers are the more useful. The Hiram Johnson Papers, Bancroft Library, contain next to no comment on foreign policy until after intervention. Also fragmentary are the Charles Lindbergh and Moses Clapp Papers, Minnesota Historical Society; Meyer London Papers, Tamiment Institute, New York; and Robert N. Page Papers, Duke University Library. The Joseph Irwin France Scrapbooks, University of Maryland Library, contain only a handful of items from this period.

One collection of a central figure in the eventual isolationist line-up is still not open to scholars. These are the Robert

M. La Follette Papers, Library of Congress. Judging from excerpts and quotations in the biography of La Follette by his wife and daughter, these papers are crammed with significant material. Another collection of La Follette Papers, State Historical Society of Wisconsin, contains no important items for the World War period. Gleanings of reactions of La Follette and his followers can be extracted from the Herman Ekern, Nils Haugen, and Charles McCarthy Papers, State Historical Society of Wisconsin.

Manuscripts of isolationists outside Congress likewise vary in usefulness. The Albert J. Beveridge Papers, Library of Congress, furnish an excellent revelation of ultranationalist thinking. A hitherto untouched collection of surprising value is the Ellery Stowell Papers, Library of Congress. William Jennings Bryan's Papers in the same depository are thin but can be revealing especially when used in connection with his correspondence as Secretary of State, in the National Archives. Though not extensive, the Randolph Bourne Papers, Columbia University Library, do serve to illuminate his published writings. They also contain Bourne's unpublished paper, "Doubts about Enforcing Peace." The Oswald Garrison Villard Papers, Houghton Library, Harvard University, hold less material on isolationism in this period than one might expect. The Amos Pinchot Papers, Library of Congress, are another vast collection with a comparatively low yield of useful items. David Starr Jordan was a pacifist rather than an isolationist, but his papers in the Hoover Institution for the Study of War, Peace, and Revolution, Stanford, contain several letters of value for the study of isolationism.

Many collections of manuscripts of nonisolationists shed light either on isolationism or on the context of its emergence. The Woodrow Wilson Papers, Library of Congress, are invaluable not only for the development of the President's thought but also for information on nearly everything that happened between 1914 and 1917. The Wilson collection at Princeton also includes several significant items. The Ray Stannard Baker Papers, Library of Congress, contain extensive materials that Baker collected for his biography of Wilson. These papers are valuable, too, for Baker's own journalistic observations and his rather symptomatic idealistic thinking during the World War. The small Baker collection at Princeton contains a few useful pieces.

The papers of Wilson's two Presidential predecessors, also in the Library of Congress, provide additional material of great value. Theodore Roosevelt's correspondence illuminates crosscurrents of ultranationalist thinking, along with conflicts among Progressives over foreign policy. The William Howard Taft Papers are valuable both for the formation of the League to Enforce Peace and for the segment of Republican thinking that lay between Rooseveltian bellicosity and the various forms of Democratic and progressive idealism. Taft's correspondence with Gus J. Karger, Washington correspondent of the *Cincinnati Star-Times,* offers a fine exchange of political information and interpretation from the conservative viewpoint.

Three manuscript collections of nonisolationists in the Yale University Library provide important material on foreign policy debates. These are the Edward M. House Diary and Papers, Henry L. Stimson Diary and Papers, and William Kent Papers. Other useful collections in the Library of Congress are the papers of Josephus Daniels, Robert Lansing, Thomas J. Walsh, and William Allen White. There are also small collections of White Papers at Columbia and Stanford. Manuscripts of some value in widely scattered depositories include the Meyer Lissner Papers, Stanford; Louis Lochner, Morris Hillguit, and Raymond Robins Papers, State Historical Society of Wisconsin; Chester Rowell Papers, Bancroft Library; Socialist Party of America Papers, Duke; and Walter Hines Page Diary and Papers, Houghton Library.

Published sources also vary greatly in usefulness. The *Congressional Record,* Sixty-third, Sixty-fourth, and Sixty-fifth Congresses, is easily the most valuable of all sources, published or unpublished, for the emergence of the isolationist position. Besides the revelations of debates and votes, petitions to Congress and material inserted in the *Record* furnish information about opinion throughout the country. Other sources of nationwide opinion are the *New York Times* and *New York World* and the *Literary Digest,* which regularly polled editors on important questions. The historical reputation of the *Literary Digest* has suffered from its fiasco in attempting to poll public opinion in the 1936 election, but during the First World War the magazine conducted the most thorough and systematic surveys of newspaper opinion. These surveys provide an indispensable canvass of countrywide opinion. *Current Opinion* also collected newspaper reactions, and its surveys offer a convenient check on the findings of the *Literary Digest.*

As far as my research has gathered, virtually no metropolitan daily newspapers enunciated isolationist arguments during the period before intervention. Such papers as the *Milwaukee Journal, Omaha World-Herald, San Francisco Chronicle,* and *New York Evening Post* all expressed anti-preparedness, anti-interventionist convictions without using isolationist arguments. The *Chicago Tribune* followed an ultranationalist line, which tended toward but only occasionally reached an isolationist position. The one major journalistic exponent of isolationism, beginning in 1917, was William Randolph Hearst's chain of newspapers. Hearst's position was ultranationalist and anti-interventionist up to the last moment. His views were expounded in the premier organ of the chain, the *New York American*. For information about events generally and politics in particular, the *New York Times* and *New York World* are indispensable.

Among magazines, *The Commoner* offers the greatest exposure of isolationist arguments. It features Bryan's editorials, reprints most of his speeches, and contains articles by his supporters. *La Follette's Magazine* similarly records the evolving thought of its proprietor, both in his editorials and speeches and in Mrs. La Follette's column. The articles in *La Follette's* offer a clearinghouse for some more radical progressive thinking applied to foreign affairs. The *Outlook* and *Metropolitan* contain Roosevelt's commentaries. Other progressive magazines, especially the *New Republic, Nation, Public,* and *Survey,* disclose liberal opinion of different tendencies in their articles on diplomatic questions. Although not an isolationist journal, the *New Republic* is especially valuable for the observations of its sparkling trio of editors, Herbert Croly, Walter Lippmann, and Walter Weyl. A little-known but useful source is the mimeographed *League to Enforce Peace Weekly Bulletin,* which collected internationalist opinion and surveyed press views of the League's program. Shrewd comments about American politics and opinion can occasionally be found in two British magazines, the *Nation* and the *New Statesman*.

There are only two clearly isolationist books which were written during this period. One is the collection of Bryan's newspaper debates with Taft, published as *World Peace: A Written Debate between William Howard Taft and William*

Jennings Bryan (New York: George H. Doran Company, 1917), which also discloses Bryan's incipient desertion of isolationism. The other is Charles A. Lindbergh, *Why Your Country Is at War and What Happens to Your Country after a War, and Related Subjects* (Washington: National Capital Press, 1917). Lindbergh's book was published shortly after intervention and soon confiscated by Federal authorities. Useful books which take pacific and antipreparedness stands without becoming explicitly isolationist include Frederic C. Howe, *Why War* (New York: Charles Scribner's Sons, 1916); William I. Hull, *Preparedness: The American versus the Military Program* (New York: Fleming H. Revell Company, 1916); and Charles E. Jefferson, *Christianity and International Peace: Six Lectures at Grinnell College, Grinnell, Iowa, in February, 1915, on the George A. Gates Memorial Foundation* (New York: Thomas Y. Crowell Company, 1915). Three useful nonisolationist analyses of American foreign policy attitudes are Walter Lippmann, *The Stakes of Diplomacy* (New York: Henry Holt & Company, 1915; second edition, 1917); Roland G. Usher, *The Challenge of the Future* (Boston: Houghton Mifflin Company, 1916); and Walter Weyl, *American World Policies* (New York: Macmillan Company, 1917).

Although published collections of letters and speeches abound for the World War period, only three represent prominent isolationists. There are two collections of Borah's speeches: Horace Green, ed., *American Problems: A Collection of Speeches and Prophecies by William E. Borah* (New York: Duffield & Company, 1924) and *Bedrock: Views on National Problems* (Washington: National Home Library Foundation, 1936). The third collection is Constance Gardner, ed., *Some Letters of Augustus Peabody Gardner* (Boston: Houghton Mifflin Company, 1920). Useful for the same rea-

F. Mullen, *Western Democrat* (New York: Wilfred Funk, 1940) and Oscar W. Underwood, *Drifting Sands of Party Politics* (New York: Century Company, 1928). Three journalists' memoirs which furnish observations on politics surrounding foreign policy are J. Frederick Essary, *Covering Washington: Government Reflected in the Press, 1822–1926* (Boston: Houghton Mifflin Company, 1926); Arthur Wallace Dunn, *From Harrison to Harding* (two volumes, New York: G. P. Putnam's Sons, 1922); and David Lawrence, *The True Story of Woodrow Wilson* (New York: George H. Doran Company, 1924). *The Autobiography of William Allen White* (New York: Macmillan Company, 1946) offers insights into thinking in middle America and progressive circles. Patrician interventionist opinions are presented in Owen Wister, *Roosevelt: The Story of a Friendship* (New York: Macmillan Company, 1930) and Henry L. Stimson and McGeorge Bundy, *On Active Service in Peace and War* (two volumes, New York: Harper & Brothers, 1947). The many memoirs that emanated from Wilson's family and Administration provide varying amounts of information and sometimes conflicting opinions about the evolution of the President's thought and policies.

Since the massive historical literature about the First World War has received much discussion in a number of bibliographical essays, I may simply mention two books that have been especially useful to this study. Robert E. Osgood, *Ideals and Self-Interest in America's Foreign Relations: The Great Transformation of the Twentieth Century* (Chicago: University of Chicago Press, 1953) is a brilliant piece of pioneering work on intellectual influences behind twentieth-century American foreign policy. Although I have come to disagree with Osgood about isolationism and about several facets of Wilson's thought, his interpretations have greatly enriched my conception of what was involved in the development of foreign policy attitudes during the World War. Similarly, I have taken a less favorable view of Bryan than Lawrence W. Levine, *Defender of the Faith: William Jennings Bryan: The Last Decade, 1915–1925* (New York: Oxford University Press, 1965). Yet Levine's portrait has consistently enlarged my vision of the Great Commoner. James Holt's valuable study, *Congressional Insurgents and the Party System, 1909–1916* (Cambridge, Mass.: Harvard University Press, 1967) unfortunately did not come to my attention until after I finished writing this book.

Interpretations of Isolationism

Previous interpretations of American isolationism have followed two lines. The bulk of the historians, political scientists, and other investigators who have studied isolationism have treated it as a form of political behavior to be explained by characteristics of its following. They have tended to describe isolationism as the reflection of emotions and prejudices at its grass-roots level of support. The other line of interpretation follows a rhetorical approach. Two historians, Albert K. Weinberg and Manfred Jonas, have studied the utterances and ideas of isolationists as responses to diplomatic problems which the United States has faced. Interestingly, however, there has been little debate between proponents of these two lines of interpretation. Yet no one has viewed the two approaches as complementary, either.

The dominant, behavioral interpretation began with Ray Allen Billington, "The Origins of Middle Western Isolationism," *Political Science Quarterly* 60 (March, 1945): 44–

64. Billington defines isolationism as an attitude of resistance to foreign commitments that arose in the Middle West around the time of the First World War. Five characteristics of the region accounted for this isolationist attitude: the Republicanism of the majority of its people, which led them to oppose interventionism of Democratic Presidents; a minority Populist and free-silverite heritage of distrusting the East Coast and Great Britain as centers of plutocratic exploitation; the section's peculiar balance of agriculture and industry, which fostered illusions of self-sufficiency and encouraged indifference to the rest of the world; large numbers of immigrants from Germany, and, finally, pacifist tendencies among German- and Scandinavian-American Lutherans concentrated there. "These prejudices and attitudes, bolstered by a sense of security, which stemmed from the section's geographical position and economic self-sufficiency," concludes Billington, "help to explain middle western isolationism."

Various elaborations and emphases have subsequently been added to this view of isolationism as a form of Middle Western behavior. In his study of popular and literary images of the American West, *Virgin Land* (Cambridge, Mass.: Harvard University Press, 1950), Henry Nash Smith has argued that isolationism stemmed from the myths that were drawn from the geographical position of the region. Smith notes how the nineteenth-century vision of an agricultural Eden in the Middle West created "an introspective, narcissistic ideal" in which all evil was presumed to come from outside. "These inferences from the myth of the garden will be recognized as the core of what we call isolationism."

By contrast, Samuel Lubell has contended in *The Future of American Politics* (New York: Harper & Brothers, 1952) that the core of isolationism was not geographical but "ethnic and emotional." It consisted of the "existence of pro-German and anti-British ethnic prejudices" and the "exploiting of those prejudices by an opposition political party." But Lubell's interpretation still lays stress on the Middle West, because the necessary combination of prejudices and partisanship existed most strongly in that section. There, he holds, ethnic isolationists formed successive coalitions with dissident political elements, first with agrarian radicals and later with Republican anti-New Dealers.

Another work following a Middle Western behavioral approach is Ralph H. Smuckler, "The Region of Isolationism," *American Political Science Review* 47 (June, 1953): 386–401. By examining Congressional voting on foreign policy issues between 1933 and 1950, Smuckler has found that eleven of the twelve states with the highest isolationist records lay in a belt extending from Ohio to Idaho. Smuckler draws upon information about the Senators and Representatives and census data about their constituencies to investigate factors which may have influenced their votes. On the Congressional level, he has discovered a high correlation between isolationist behavior and Republican partisanship. On the local level, he has perceived a clear correlation between isolationist voting and the rurality of the areas. He has also found suggestive but spotty correlations with concentrations of German-Americans. In seeking the sources of isolationism, Smuckler concludes that "the soundest explanation would undoubtedly lie in the direction of a combination" of rural, ethnic, and partisan factors in the Middle West.

A different examination of Congressional voting has evoked a qualification and partial dissent from ethnic and sectional interpretations of isolationism. In "The Basis of Isolationist Behavior," *Public Opinion Quarterly* 24 (Winter, 1960): 645–

657, Leroy N. Rieselbach has studied voting on foreign policy issues from seventy-six Congressional districts during the periods 1939–1941 and 1949–1952. The districts selected were in all parts of the country and were high in either German- or Irish-American populations, so that both sectional and ethnic interpretations could be tested. Rieselbach has found that although Middle Western and ethnic districts showed some relationship to the incidence of isolationist voting, the correlations are neither strict nor convincing. He concludes that "the neglected complex we have termed Republican-conservatism" produces a much stronger correlation with isolationist voting. But Middle Western location and German-American population have played a part among such Republican votes, because the highest isolationist results have occurred where the sectional and partisan factors were combined with those ethnic concentrations.

One more Middle Western influence has been reasserted in Wayne S. Cole, *Senator Gerald P. Nye and American Foreign Policy* (Minneapolis: University of Minnesota Press, 1962). Besides ethnic feelings, partisanship, and insularity in the Middle West, Cole suggests that "important roots of isolationism may be traced to the needs, desires, and value systems of major segments of the American agricultural society." This interpretation presents a variation on the Populist-free silverite explanation. Thus, subsequent interpreters of isolationism as a form of Middle Western behavior have stressed all the factors which Billington first presented.

Several other studies which have approached isolationism from some angle besides its bases of support have also concluded that it has been primarily the embodiment of emotions and prejudices of Middle Western or ethnic adherents. In Selig Adler, *The Isolationist Impulse: Its Twentieth Century*

Reaction (New York: Abelard-Schuman, 1957), isolationism is described as a set of popular attitudes and prejudices brought into play in American politics in reaction to international challenges during this century. These attitudes, according to Adler, have been engendered principally by Middle Western conditions, particularly "the illusion of security" created by "the very vastness of the hinterland" and economic self-sufficiency, combined with anti-British ethnic feelings. The reaction, which occurred after 1914, has been against the threat of international complications to overthrow previously unchallenged American policies of noninvolvement in European affairs.

The two essays on isolationism in Alexander De Conde, ed., *Isolation and Security: Ideas and Interests in Twentieth-Century American Foreign Policy* (Durham, N. C.: Duke University Press, 1957) view it in much the same way. In "On Twentieth Century Isolationism," De Conde insists that isolationism has been a popular response to challenges to noninvolvement, based upon ethnic and cultural sentiments. Instead of embodying "a doctrine with a unique ideology" isolationism merely "reflected the ideas and attitudes of the differing groups espousing it." In "Isolation and Collective Security: The Uses and Limits of Two Theories of International Relations," Kenneth W. Thompson has agreed that ethnic sentiment "was more important than any set of international ideals" and that isolationism "lacked roots in an enduring theory. . . ."

The behavioral interpretation has been pushed furthest perhaps in Bernard Fensterwald, "The Anatomy of American 'Isolationism' and Expansionism," *Journal of Conflict Resolution* 2 (June–December, 1958): 111–139, 280–309. After summarizing earlier interpretations of isolationist behavior as the outgrowth of supporters' emotions and prejudices, Fensterwald employs several behavioral concepts in an effort to discover its psychological roots. Isolationism has been, in his view, a form of ethnocentrism—the phenomenon of a self-defined in-group stereotyping out-groups by projecting its fears and self-hatreds upon them. Isolationists cast the rest of the world in the role of the out-group, especially Europe, since to them it has appeared the most potentially harmful area. Such views have been taken by those groups most susceptible to traits of the authoritarian personality. In short, according to Fensterwald, isolationism has been a stereotype embodying the maladjustments and anxieties of its adherents—or, more simply, it has been an expression of xenophobia.

The rhetorical approach to isolationism has formed the minor line of interpretation. The two historians who have used this approach have attempted to defend isolationism in some measure. Manfred Jonas, *Isolationism in America, 1935–1941* (Ithaca, N. Y.: Cornell University Press, 1966) begins with a challenge to the dominant line of interpretation. Jonas initially rejects both the low valuation set on isolationist thought and the implication that isolationism has been some kind of mass disorder. Rather, he argues that isolationism "cannot be dismissed as simple obstruction based upon ignorance and folly" but was "the considered response to foreign and domestic developments of a large, responsible, and respectable segment of the American people." Jonas supports these contentions with evidence from books and articles expounding isolationist doctrines, which were produced in the late 1930s by a galaxy of the nation's intellectuals.

Surprisingly, however, Jonas fails to follow through with his contentions. Instead, he produces a portrait of isolationist thought which differs little from that in the dominant line of interpretation. A shaky "combination of unilateralism and *ad hoc* pacifism," he finds, comprised the basic ideas of the five major groups of isolationists—"foreign-oriented," "belligerent" [*sic*], "timid," "radical," and "conservative." This characterization appears to reduce isolationism to an intellectual hodgepodge, in which ideas served merely to rationalize deeper motives. Also, despite his frequent criticisms of the behavioral interpretations, Jonas adopts their perspective when he asserts that the "questionable validity" of policies expounded by isolationists indicated that they "must, therefore, have been largely immune to world events." At the heart of isolationism, he concludes, lay "basic emotions," particularly "an inordinate fear of war."

A more consistent application of the rhetorical approach came, oddly enough, in an essay which antedates the dominant line of interpretation. Albert K. Weinberg, in "The Historical Meaning of the American Doctrine of Isolation," *American Political Science Review* 24 (June, 1940): 539–574, applies Arthur O. Lovejoy's history-of-ideas analysis to identify eight well-developed policies within traditional isolation. First came Washington's "meager rule of avoiding permanent alliances" in the Farewell Address, soon followed by Jefferson's dictum of "entangling alliances with none" in his first inaugural. Thereafter, the principles of isolation were successively broadened in the nineteenth and early twentieth centuries to include nonintervention in the affairs of other nations, nonparticipation in European politics, avoidance of joint action in pursuing American goals, jealous regard for total sovereignty, independence of international political organizations and judicial bodies, and insulation against all conditions that might create foreign entanglements. Weinberg concludes that those policies expressed the political ideal of "maximum self-determination" in such ways that they constituted "an important, and certainly in some measure wise, contribution to the ideology of nationalism."

The strengths and weaknesses of these two lines of interpretation hardly require elaboration at the end of this book. Both approaches have analyzed parts of isolationism without recognizing that they were describing complementary facets of a political position. This failure to recognize the complementarity of these lines of interpretation apparently stems from the persistent failure to discard the polemical connotations of the term "isolationism." The behavioral approach has sprung from either an implicit or explicit acceptance of the charges that isolationist policies have been so foolish and ignorant that only prejudice, emotion, and self-interest can explain their acceptance and popularity. The different attempts by Jonas and Weinberg to defend isolationism likewise indicate a disinclination to use the term as a neutral descriptive category. The greatest need for further interpretation is the recognition that isolationism has been a political position with programmatic and ideological dimensions that must be considered along with, but not to the exclusion of, the bases of its popular following. That is the perspective which this book has adopted.

Index